NIETZSCHE'S *ON THE GENEALOGY OF MORALITY*

Nietzsche's *On the Genealogy of Morality* (1887) is a forceful, perplexing, important book, radical in its own time and profoundly influential ever since. This introductory textbook offers a comprehensive, close reading of the entire work, with a section-by-section analysis that also aims to show how the *Genealogy* holds together as an integrated whole. The *Genealogy* is helpfully situated within Nietzsche's wider philosophy, and occasional interludes examine supplementary topics that further enhance the reader's understanding of the text. Two chapters examine how the *Genealogy* relates to standard questions in moral and political philosophy. Written in a clear, accessible style, this book will appeal to students at every level coming to read the *Genealogy* for the first time, and a wider range of readers will also benefit from nuanced interpretations of controversial elements in Nietzsche's work.

LAWRENCE J. HATAB is Louis I. Jaffe Professor of Philosophy at Old Dominion University.

T0370917

CAMBRIDGE INTRODUCTIONS TO KEY
PHILOSOPHICAL TEXTS

This new series offers introductory textbooks on what are considered to
be the most important texts of Western philosophy. Each book guides the
reader through the main themes and arguments of the work in question,
while also paying attention to its historical context and its philosophical
legacy. No philosophical background knowledge is assumed, and the books
will be well suited to introductory university-level courses.

Titles published in the series:

DESCARTES'S *MEDITATIONS* by Catherine Wilson

WITTGENSTEIN'S *PHILOSOPHICAL INVESTIGATIONS* by David G. Stern

WITTGENSTEIN'S *TRACTATUS* by Alfred Nordmann

ARISTOTLE'S *NICOMACHEAN ETHICS* by Michael Pakaluk

SPINOZA'S *ETHICS* by Steven Nadler

KANT'S *CRITIQUE OF PURE REASON* by Jill Vance Buroker

HEIDEGGER'S *BEING AND TIME* by Paul Gorner

HEGEL'S *PHENOMENOLOGY OF SPIRIT* by Larry Krasnoff

KANT'S *GROUNDWORK OF THE METAPHYSICS OF MORALS* by
Sally Sedgwick

NIETZSCHE'S *ON THE GENEALOGY OF MORALITY* by Lawrence J. Hatab

NIETZSCHE'S *ON THE GENEALOGY OF MORALITY*

An Introduction

LAWRENCE J. HATAB

Old Dominion University

CAMBRIDGE
UNIVERSITY PRESS

CAMBRIDGE
UNIVERSITY PRESS

University Printing House, Cambridge CB2 8BS, United Kingdom

Cambridge University Press is part of the University of Cambridge.

It furthers the University's mission by disseminating knowledge in the pursuit of
education, learning and research at the highest international levels of excellence.

www.cambridge.org
Information on this title: www.cambridge.org/9780521697705

© Lawrence J. Hatab 2008

First published 2008

A catalogue record for this publication is available from the British Library

Library of Congress Cataloguing in Publication data
Hatab, Lawrence J., 1946–
Nietzsche's On the genealogy of morality : an introduction / Lawrence J. Hatab.
p. cm. – (Cambridge introductions to key philosophical texts)
Includes bibliographical references (p. 274) and index.
ISBN 978-0-521-87502-8
1. Nietzsche, Friedrich Wilhelm, 1844–1900. Zur Genealogie der Moral.   2. Ethics.
I. Title.   II. Series.
B3313.Z73H38   2008
170–dc22   2008021957

ISBN 978-0-521-87502-8 Hardback
ISBN 978-0-521-69770-5 Paperback

Contents

Acknowledgments		*page* vi
Abbreviations		vii
	Introduction	1
1	Nietzsche's thought and life	8
2	The preface	25
3	The first essay	37
4	The second essay	69
5	The third essay	113
6	Reflections on the *Genealogy*	172
7	The *Genealogy* and moral philosophy	204
8	The *Genealogy* and political philosophy	243
References		274
Index		279

Acknowledgments

I would like to thank Hilary Gaskin of Cambridge University Press for initiating this project and mentoring it along the way. Thanks also to the reviewers for many helpful suggestions. I am indebted to Old Dominion University for a leave in Fall 2007, which enabled me to complete the manuscript in a timely manner. Special thanks to Deborah Bond, whose mastery of our office allowed me space to do this work while being Chair of the department. Above all, I am grateful to my wife, Chelsy, who knows all too well how strange "we knowers" are. Finally, I want to dedicate this book to my students.

Abbreviations of Nietzsche's works

Cited numbers refer to text sections, except in the case of *KSA* where volume and page numbers are given. I have occasionally modified published translations.

A	*The Antichrist*, in *The Portable Nietzsche*, ed. and trans. Walter Kaufmann (New York: Viking Press, 1954).
BGE	*Beyond Good and Evil*, in *Basic Writings of Nietzsche*, ed. and trans. Walter Kaufmann (New York: Random House, 1966).
BT	*The Birth of Tragedy*, in *Basic Writings*.
CW	*The Case of Wagner*, in *Basic Writings*.
D	*Daybreak*, trans. R. J. Hollingdale (Cambridge: Cambridge University Press, 1982).
EH	*Ecce Homo*, in *Basic Writings*. The four main chapters will be indicated by roman numerals, with book titles in Chapter III abbreviated accordingly.
GM	*On the Genealogy of Morality*, ed. Keith Ansell-Pearson, trans. Carol Diethe (Cambridge: Cambridge University Press, 2007).
GS	*The Gay Science*, trans. Walter Kaufmann (New York: Random House, 1974).
HAH	*Human, All Too Human*, trans. R. J. Hollingdale (New York: Cambridge University Press, 1986).
KSA	*Sämtliche Werke: Kritische Studienausgabe*, ed. G. Colli and M. Montinari (Berlin: Walter de Gruyter, 1967).
TI	*Twilight of the Idols*, in *The Portable Nietzsche*. The chapters will be numbered in sequence by arabic numerals.

UDH   *On the Uses and Disadvantages of History for Life*, Part 2
       of *Untimely Meditations*
UM   *Untimely Meditations*, trans. R. J. Hollingdale
       (Cambridge: Cambridge University Press, 1983).
WP   *The Will to Power*, trans. Walter Kaufmann and R. J.
       Hollingdale (New York: Random House, 1967).
WS   *The Wanderer and His Shadow*, Part 2 of *Human, All Too
       Human*.
Z   *Thus Spoke Zarathustra*, in *The Portable Nietzsche*. The
       four parts will be indicated by roman numerals, the
       sections by arabic numerals according to Kaufmann's
       listing on pages 112–114.

Introduction

Friedrich Nietzsche's *On the Genealogy of Morality* is a forceful, perplexing, important book. It is widely recognized in philosophical treatments as a major text in Nietzsche's writings, and it has been the focus of much analysis in recent years. The *Genealogy* is taught and assigned in other disciplines as well, particularly in political philosophy and literary theory. One reason for the text's popularity, besides the power of its ideas, is that of all Nietzsche's writings after *The Birth of Tragedy*, it most resembles the form of a "treatise," with extended discussions of organized themes and something of a historical orientation. As distinct from Nietzsche's typical aphoristic or literary styles, the *Genealogy* offers some advantages for classroom investigations. Yet one can hardly call this book a typical academic treatise. Nietzsche calls it a "polemic" and it is loaded with hyperbole, ambiguity, misdirection, allusion, provocation, iconoclasm, invective, prognostication, experiment, and Nietzsche's own vigorous persona.

Since Nietzsche has become a respectable figure in the academy (and he is one of the few post-Kantian continental philosophers taken seriously in Analytic circles), it is hard to appreciate the radical nature of the *Genealogy* in its nineteenth-century setting. Some readings tend to domesticate Nietzsche by pressing the text into the standard logistics of professional philosophers and contemporary theoretical agendas. Other readings miss the intellectual power of the book by overplaying its radical character in the direction of unhinged celebrations of difference and creativity (which actually perpetuates another kind of domestication).

In its own historical moment, the *Genealogy* is something of a bombshell. It aims to diagnose esteemed moral traditions as forms of life-denial, in that what is valued as "good" in these systems stands opposed to actual conditions of natural life. Yet Nietzsche's text is not promoting an "immoral" or "amoral" posture on behalf of presumably value-free life forces. Rather, Nietzsche wants to explore new possibilities of life-affirming values by drawing from historical sources that were deemed "immoral" by traditional moral systems, but that can be redeemed as morally defensible life-values. Accordingly, the "polemical" character of the *Genealogy* implies a double-negative structure, a fight against life-denying values on behalf of life-affirming values.

Although Christian morality is a prominent target in the *Genealogy*, Nietzsche's critique pertains to much more than simply religion. Christianity was a world-forming force at every level of culture, and Nietzsche maintains that even so-called modern "secular" moralities have not escaped the formative influences of Christianity and its life-negating elements. Moreover, the polemic in the *Genealogy* is not limited to morality narrowly construed as ethics. According to Nietzsche, moralistic judgments against natural life have also marked the bulk of Western intellectual and cultural history, not only in religion and ethics, but also in philosophy, politics, psychology, science, and logic.

These preliminary remarks can be borne out by considering the *Genealogy* in relation to the book immediately preceding it in Nietzsche's published works: *Beyond Good and Evil*. Walter Kaufmann notes that the title page of the *Genealogy* is followed by these words: "A sequel to my last book, *Beyond Good and Evil*, which it is meant to supplement and clarify."[1] "To supplement" translates *Ergänzung*, which can also mean "completion." So it is particularly important to take *Beyond Good and Evil* into account when reading the *Genealogy*. In *Ecce Homo*, Nietzsche says that *Beyond Good and Evil* began his No-saying turn after the Yes-saying force of the *Gay Science* and *Zarathustra*, that it began his "great war" against established values (*EH* III, *BGE* 1). He further indicates that *Beyond Good and Evil* "is in all essentials a *critique of modernity*, not excluding the modern sciences, modern arts, and even modern politics, along with pointers to a contrary type that is as little modern as possible – a noble, Yes-saying type" (*EH* III, *BGE* 2). Thus the *Genealogy*, as a "completion" of this prior book, must also be read as a critique of the

---

[1] *Basic Writings of Nietzsche*, ed. and trans. Walter Kaufmann (New York: Random House, 1966), p. 439.

modern world and the full range of intellectual constructs bearing on modern life. Of course, questions of ethics and politics are at the core of the *Genealogy*, but it should be recognized that its critique of "morality" is also a gateway to larger questions of knowledge, truth, and meaning, the traditional approaches to which Nietzsche diagnoses as likewise harboring moralistic judgments against natural life. How should the *Genealogy* be approached as a philosophical text? Nietzsche rejects the notion that philosophy is an "impersonal" pursuit of knowledge; philosophy so conceived conceals a "personal confession," an "unconscious memoir," and so a philosopher's thought bears "decisive witness to *who he is*" (*BGE* 6). In considering a philosophical claim, one should ask: "What does such a claim tell us about the man who makes it?" (*BGE* 187). Philosophy can never be separated from existential interests, and so "disinterested knowledge" is a fiction (*BGE* 207; *GM* III, 12, 26). Perspectives of value are more fundamental than objectivity or certainty. There is no being-in-itself, only "grades of appearance measured by the strength of *interest* we show in an appearance" (*WP* 588). Philosophy so construed means that the standard of demonstrable knowledge should be exchanged for the more open concept of "interpretation" (*GS* 374). Interpretation is the "introduction of meaning (*Sinn-hineinlegen*)" and not "explanation" (*KSA* 12, p. 100).[2]

The logical limits of answers to the deepest intellectual questions are an obvious feature of the history of thought, given the endurance of unresolved critiques and counter-critiques in philosophy. Rather than give up on such questions or resort to mystical, transcendent, even relativistic solutions, Nietzsche focuses on philosophy as an embodied expression of psychological forces. Critical questions that follow such a focus would no longer turn on cognitive tests (How can you prove X?) but on psychological explorations and probes (Why is X *important* to you?). Accordingly, for Nietzsche, philosophy is always value-laden and cannot be reduced to descriptive, objective terms or to a project of logical demonstration; and he is consistent in recognizing this in the course of his own writing: "What have I to do with refutations!" (*GM* P, 4). He often enough indicates that

---

[2] For an important study, see Alan D. Schrift, *Nietzsche and the Question of Interpretation: Between Hermeneutics and Deconstruction* (New York: Routledge, 1990).

philosophy, including his own textual work, is a circulation of writing and reading that stems from, and taps into, personal forces and dispositions toward life. This does not mean that philosophy is nothing more than personal expression, even though the first person singular appears so often in Nietzsche's texts. For one thing, Nietzsche deploys the "we" as much as the "I," which suggests the importance of collective dimensions in culture. Moreover, Nietzsche explores a full range of philosophical questions about reality, the world, life, knowledge, and truth, with the aim of advancing compelling answers to these questions. Yet he insists that such advances cannot be understood adequately in a purely third-person fashion, *apart from* their meaning for human interests in the life-world.

The prevalence of the "I" and the "we" in Nietzsche's writings also implies a pervasive second-person perspective, that of "you" the reader. That is why we must engage Nietzsche's texts in their "addressive" function, because "reader response" is inseparable from the nature of a written text. Nietzsche's stylistic choices – hyperbole, provocation, allusions, metaphors, aphorisms, literary forms, and historical narratives not confined to demonstrable facts or theories – show that he presumed a reader's involvement in bringing sense to a text, even in exploring beyond or against a text. Nietzsche's books do not presume to advance "doctrines" as a one-way transmission of finished thoughts. Good readers must be active, not simply reactive; they must think for themselves (*EH* II, 8). Aphorisms, for example, cannot merely be read; they require an "art of interpretation" on the part of readers (*GM* P, 8). Nietzsche wants to be read "with doors left open" (*D* P, 5). This does not mean that Nietzsche's texts are nothing but an invitation for interpretation. Nietzsche's *own* voice and positions are central to his writings, and he takes many forceful stands on philosophical questions. Yet he did not write as, and did not want to be read as, a typical philosopher constructing arguments in pursuit of "objective truth." Whatever truth comes to mean in Nietzsche's philosophy, it cannot be a strictly objective or logical enterprise because truth must be *alive* in writers and readers.[3]

---

[3] An excellent study in this respect is David B. Allison, *Reading the New Nietzsche* (Lanham, MD: Rowman & Littlefield, 2001).

Nietzsche's vivid address to the cultural "we" and to "you" the reader is a baseline textual feature of the *Genealogy*, despite its surface resemblance to a treatise form. The book aims to stimulate an "introduction of meaning" between writer and reader which reaches further than the written text as such. Moreover, the question of meaning forged in the book presents deep challenges and dark provocations to traditional confidences and normal expectations about philosophy. Here is what Nietzsche says about the *Genealogy* in *Ecce Homo*:

Regarding expression, intention, and the art of surprise, the three inquiries which constitute this *Genealogy* are perhaps uncannier than anything else written so far... Every time a beginning that is *calculated* to mislead: cool, scientific, even ironic, deliberately foreground, deliberately holding off. Gradually more unrest; sporadic lightning; very disagreeable truths are heard rumbling in the distance – until eventually a *tempo feroce* is attained in which everything rushes ahead in a tremendous tension. In the end, in the midst of perfectly gruesome detonations, a *new* truth becomes visible every time among thick clouds. (*EH* III, GM)

As indicated earlier, some treatments of the *Genealogy*, while recognizing its unusual features, move to position the text in terms of current philosophical methods and agendas, or to situate it among previous thinkers and standard philosophical concepts. Other treatments take the book to be more wide open or enigmatic than any such placement. Much can be gained from all such approaches, but I have always been dissatisfied with them. Nietzsche was surely pursuing philosophical work of the highest order, and yet he specifically found fault with most philosophical methods as typically construed; and he challenged most traditional philosophical concepts as inadequate to the task of thinking. Nietzsche was a trained classicist, and so he knew quite well standard scholarly techniques and could have so deployed them in his writings. That he deliberately did otherwise shows that he *intended* his texts to display a disruptive *tension* with traditional academic work.

My own approach to the *Genealogy* can be summarized as follows: I try as far as possible to read the text on its own terms, in its own movements and counter-movements, with its own language and thought experiments. I try to avoid "translating" the text into this or that "theory" or this or that "-ism" or "-ology." I do this not out of some mere exegetical constraint of textual fidelity, but because

Nietzsche's text has its own kind of philosophical power that can be missed or suppressed when translated into familiar scholarly settings.[4]

In the Preface to the *Genealogy*, Nietzsche grants that some readers might find the book "incomprehensible and hard on the ears" (*GM* P, 8). He then suggests that the book will be clearer to those who "have first read my earlier works without sparing themselves some effort or trouble (*Mühe*)." Thus reading the *Genealogy* without much background in Nietzsche's thought can be a disadvantage. That is why my first chapter will provide an orientation in Nietzsche's philosophy that should provide some help. Succeeding chapters will take up the Preface and the three Essays of the *Genealogy*, moving through the numbered sections of the Essays in sequence. Yet my treatment cannot simply inhabit each section in its own textual space, because some flexibility is required in moving around the text for cross-referencing, and occasional excursions to some of Nietzsche's other books can be illuminating (this is particularly true with respect to *Beyond Good and Evil*, as has been noted). Also, in the course of my analysis, there will be occasional "Interludes" that engage supplemental topics or questions that should enhance comprehension of the material at hand. My hope is to provide readers of the *Genealogy* with as rich and nuanced an understanding of the book as possible. Yet the precautions about Nietzsche's writings sketched in this Introduction should always be kept in mind. As Nietzsche puts it (*GM* P, 8), his books "are indeed not easily accessible," and the *Genealogy* in particular requires "an art of interpretation," which is articulated as an "*art* of reading, a thing which today people have been so good at forgetting – and so it will be some time before my writings are 'readable' –, you almost have to be a cow for this one thing and certainly *not* a 'modern man': it is *rumination*." "Rumination" is a translation of *Wiederkäuen*, literally "chewing again," or "chewing over" a text in a slow, careful manner.

---

[4] For the purposes of my commentary, I will not overload the text with extensive discussions of the secondary literature, yet I will try to give readers enough guidance for recognizing and exploring a host of relevant scholarly treatments. Several sources will be drawn from the following collections: *Nietzsche's* On the Genealogy of Morals*: Critical Essays*, ed. Christa Davis Acampora (Lanham, MD: Rowman & Littlefield, 2006); *Nietzsche's Postmoralism: Essays on Nietzsche's Prelude to Philosophy's Future*, ed. Richard Schacht (Cambridge: Cambridge University Press, 2001); and *Nietzsche, Genealogy, Morality: Essays on Nietzsche's* On the Genealogy of Morals, ed. Richard Schacht (Berkeley: University of California Press, 1994).

As we will see, Nietzsche is notorious for castigating the "herd" and celebrating the "beast of prey." Yet it is interesting that, with respect to reading, he recommends a cow-like pace rather than, shall we say, "wolfing down" a text in big chunks, too quickly to savor every particle of thought. For Nietzsche, to read well is to "read slowly" (*D* P, 5). It is not simply a matter of speed here, but the kinds of analytical chunks that frame the text in familiar shapes, which are then swallowed whole. Moreover, we know that chewing food well is good for both our taste and our stomachs. Reading the *Genealogy* with rumination will not only reveal more complex and subtle flavors, it will also decrease the chances of indigestion.

CHAPTER I

Nietzsche's thought and life

What follows is not an overview of all or most of the main elements of Nietzsche's thought but a sketch of those elements that I think will have particular relevance in engaging the *Genealogy*.[1]

FROM METAPHYSICS TO NATURALISM

We can best gain entry to Nietzsche's philosophy by beginning with his critique of metaphysics. According to Nietzsche, "the fundamental faith of the metaphysicians is *the faith in opposite values*" (*BGE* 2). The Western religious and philosophical tradition has operated by dividing reality into a set of binary opposites, such as constancy and change, eternity and time, reason and passion, good and evil, truth and appearance – opposites that can be organized around the concepts of being and becoming. The motivation behind such divisional thinking is as follows: Becoming names the negative and unstable conditions of existence that undermine our interest in grasping, controlling, and preserving life (because of the pervasive force of uncertainty, variability, destruction, and death). Being, as *opposite* to becoming, permits the governance or exclusion of negative conditions and the attainment of various forms of stability untainted by their fluid contraries.

Nietzsche wants to challenge the priority of being in the tradition, so much so that he is often read as simply reversing this scheme by extolling sheer becoming and all its correlates. This is not the case, even though Nietzsche will often celebrate negative terms rhetorically

---

[1] Much of this chapter is drawn from Chapter 1 of my *Nietzsche's Life Sentence: Coming to Terms with Eternal Recurrence* (New York: Routledge, 2005).

to unsettle convictions and open up space for new meanings. In fact, Nietzsche exchanges oppositional exclusion for a sense of *crossing*, where the differing conditions in question are not exclusive of each other, but rather reciprocally related.[2] Nietzsche suggests that "what constitutes the value of these good and revered things is precisely that they are insidiously related, tied to, and involved with these wicked, seemingly opposite things" (*BGE* 2). Rather than fixed contraries, Nietzsche prefers "differences of degree" and "transitions" (*WS* 67). Even the idea of sheer becoming cannot be maintained, according to Nietzsche. Discernment of such becoming can only arise once an imaginary counter-world of being is placed against it (*KSA* 9, pp. 503–504). As we will see shortly, Nietzsche rejects the strict delineation of opposite conditions, but not the oppositional *force* between these conditions. He grants that circumstances of struggle breed in opponents a tendency to "imagine" the other side as an "antithesis," for the purpose of exaggerated self-esteem and the courage to fight the "good cause" against deviancy (*WP* 348). Yet this tendency breeds the danger of oppositional exclusion and its implicit denial of becoming's "medial" structure, a structure based on an *inclusive* tension with opposing forces in any particular position. A theme that will recur again and again in this study is that Nietzsche will exchange binary clarity for a sense of *ambiguity*, because a proper understanding of any philosophical topic will have to reflect an irresolvable mix of tensions: "Above all, one should not want to divest existence of its *rich ambiguity*" (*GS* 373).

In restoring legitimacy to conditions of becoming, Nietzsche advances what I call an *existential naturalism*. The finite, unstable dynamic of earthly existence – and its meaningfulness – becomes the measure of thought, to counter various attempts in philosophy and religion to "reform" lived experience by way of a rational, spiritual, or moral "transcendence" that purports to rectify an originally flawed condition (*GS* 109; *TI* 3, 16). In turning to "the basic text of *homo natura*" (*BGE* 230), Nietzsche is not restricting his philosophy to what we would call scientific naturalism, which in many ways locates itself on the "being" side of the ledger. For

---

[2] I borrow the term "crossing" from John Sallis' *Crossings: Nietzsche and the Space of Tragedy* (Chicago: University of Chicago Press, 1991).

Nietzsche, nature is more unstable and disruptive than science would allow; it includes forces, instincts, passions, and powers that are not reducible to objective, scientific categories. Stressing a darker sense of "nature red in tooth and claw," Nietzsche claims that "the terrible (*schreckliche*) basic text of nature must again be recognized" (*BGE* 230). Nietzsche's naturalism is consonant with scientific naturalism in rejecting "supernatural" beliefs, but the source of these beliefs, for Nietzsche, stems not from a lack or refusal of scientific thinking, but from an aversion to overwhelming and disintegrating forces in nature that science too suppresses and wants to overcome. Indeed, Nietzsche identifies nature with chaos, as indicated in his alteration of Spinoza's famous equation: *"chaos sive natura"* (*KSA* 9, p. 519).[3] At the same time, Nietzsche also rejects a romantic naturalism, which spurns science or reason and calls for a return to an original condition of innocence and harmony with nature (*GS* 370). Naturalism, for Nietzsche, amounts to a kind of philosophical methodology, in that natural forces of becoming will be deployed to redescribe and account for all aspects of life, including cultural formations, even the emergence of seemingly anti-natural constructions of "being." The focus for this deployment can be located in Nietzsche's concept of will to power, to be discussed shortly. First, however, we must locate the historical focus for Nietzsche's naturalistic turn, namely the death of God.

THE DEATH OF GOD

Nietzsche advances the death of God through the figure of a madman (*GS* 125), whose audience is not religious believers, but nonbelievers who are chastised for not facing the consequences of God's demise. Since God is the ultimate symbol of transcendence and foundations, his death is to be praised, but its impact reaches far beyond religion. In the modern world God is no longer the mandated centerpiece of intellectual and cultural life. But historically the notion of God had been the warrant for all sorts of cultural constructs in moral,

---

[3] See Babette Babich, "A Note on *Chaos Sive Natura*: On Theogony, Genesis, and Playing Stars," *New Nietzsche Studies* 5, 3/4 and 6, 1/2 (Winter 2003/Spring 2004), 48–70. For an insightful treatment of Nietzsche's naturalism, see Christoph Cox, *Nietzsche: Naturalism and Interpretation* (Berkeley: University of California Press, 1999).

political, philosophical, even scientific domains – so the death of God is different from atheism, since divinity had been "living" as a powerful productive force. From Plato through to the Enlightenment, a divine mind had been the ultimate reference point for origins and truth. With the eclipse of God, any and all inferences from theological grounds must come undone as well (*TI* 9, 5). The death of God therefore announces the demise of substantive truth, or at least that "the will to truth becomes conscious of itself as a *problem*" (*GM* III, 27). Even though divinity is no longer an intellectual prerequisite, we still have confidence in the "shadows" of God (*GS* 108), in supposedly secular truths that have nonetheless lost their pedigree and intellectual warrant. This matter is especially significant with respect to modern moral and political constructs.

The consequences of God's death are enormous because of the specter of nihilism, the loss of meaning and intelligibility. The secular sophistication of the modern world has unwittingly "unchained this earth from its sun," so that we are "straying as through an infinite nothing" (*GS* 125). The course of Western thought has led it to turn away from its historical origins, but the unsuspected result has been that "the highest values devalue themselves" (*WP* 2). So we are faced with a stark choice: either we collapse into nihilism or we rethink the world in naturalistic terms freed from the reverence for being-constructs. "Either abolish your reverences or – *yourselves*! The latter would be nihilism; but would not the former also be – nihilism? – This is *our* question mark" (*GS* 346).

For Nietzsche, the threat of nihilism – the denial of any truth, meaning, or value in the world – is in fact parasitic on the Western tradition, which has judged conditions of becoming in life to be deficient and has "nullified" these conditions in favor of rational, spiritual, or moral corrections. If, in the wake of the death of God, the loss of these corrections is experienced as nihilistic, it is because the traditional models are still presumed to be the only measures of truth, meaning, and value – and thus the world seems empty without them (*WP* 12A). For Nietzsche, philosophers can embrace the death of God with gratitude and excitement, not despair, because of the opening of new horizons for thought (*GS* 343). Various motifs in Nietzsche's texts can be read as counter-nihilistic attempts to rethink truth, meaning, and value in naturalistic terms, in a manner consistent with conditions of becoming. A central motif in this regard is will to power.

WILL TO POWER

"The world viewed from inside . . . would be 'will to power' and nothing else" (*BGE* 36). A world of becoming, for Nietzsche, cannot simply be understood as a world of change. Movements are always *related* to other movements and the relational structure is not expressive simply of differences, but also resistances and tensional conflicts (*WP* 568). "Will to power" names in dynamic terms the idea that any affirmation is also a negation, that any condition or assertion of meaning must overcome some "Other," some obstacle or counterforce.[4] In this regard, Nietzsche proclaims something quite important that will figure in our investigation: "will to power can manifest itself *only* against resistances; therefore it *seeks* that which resists it" (*WP* 656; my emphasis). A similar formation is declared in *Ecce Homo* in reference to a warlike nature: "It needs objects of resistance; hence it *looks for* what resists" (*EH* I, 7; emphasis in text). We must notice the following implication: Since power can *only* involve resistance, then one's power to overcome is essentially related to a counter-power; if resistance were eliminated, if one's counter-power were destroyed or even neutralized by sheer domination, one's power would evaporate, it would no longer *be* power. Power is *overcoming* something, not annihilating it: "there is no annihilation in the sphere of spirit" (*WP* 588). Power is more a "potency" than a full actuality because it retains its tensional relation with its Other. Accordingly, Nietzsche's phrase *Wille zur Macht* could be translated as "will *toward* power," which would indicate something other than a full "possession."

Will to power, therefore, cannot be understood in terms of individual states alone, even successful states, because it names a tensional force-field, *within which* individual states shape themselves by seeking to overcome other sites of power. Power cannot be construed

---

[4] See John Richardson, "Nietzsche's Power Ontology," in *Nietzsche*, eds. John Richardson and Brian Leiter (Oxford: Oxford University Press, 2001), pp. 150–185, which does well in showing how will to power is a comprehensive concept, rather than limited in scope, as some scholars maintain.

as "instrumental" for any resultant state, whether it be knowledge, pleasure, purpose, even survival, since such conditions are epiphenomena of power, of a drive to overcome something (*GM* II, 12, 18). For this reason, Nietzsche depicts life as "that which must always overcome itself" (*Z* II, 12). This accounts for Nietzsche's objections to measuring life by "happiness," because the structure of will to power shows that *dissatisfaction* and *displeasure* are intrinsic to movements of overcoming (*WP* 696, 704), and so conditions of sheer satisfaction and completion would dry up the energies of life.

According to Nietzsche, any doctrine that would reject will to power in his sense would undermine the conditions of its own historical emergence as a contention with conflicting forces. All scientific, religious, moral, and intellectual developments began as elements of dissatisfaction and impulses to overcome something, whether it be ignorance, worldliness, brutality, confusion, or competing cultural models. Even pacifism – understood as an impulse to overcome human violence and an exalted way of life taken as an advance over our brutish nature – can thus be understood as an instance of will to power.

AGONISTICS

A prefiguration of will to power and Nietzsche's naturalism can be found in an early text, *Homer's Contest* (*KSA* I, pp. 783–792).[5] Arguing against the idea that "culture" is something antithetical to brutal forces of "nature," Nietzsche spotlights the pervasiveness in ancient Greece of the *agōn*, or contest for excellence, which operated in all cultural pursuits (in athletics, the arts, oratory, politics, and philosophy). The *agōn* can be seen as a ritualized expression of a world-view expressed in so much of Greek myth, poetry, and philosophy: the world as an arena for the struggle of opposing (but related) forces. Agonistic relations are depicted in Hesiod's *Theogony*, Homer's *Iliad*, Greek tragedy, and philosophers such as Anaximander and Heraclitus.[6] In *Homer's Contest*, Nietzsche argues that the *agōn*

---

[5] A translation is contained in the Cambridge University Press *Genealogy* edition, pp. 174–181.
[6] See my discussion in *Myth and Philosophy: A Contest of Truths* (Chicago: Open Court, 1990), Chs. 2–6.

emerged as a *cultivation* of more brutal natural drives in not striving for the annihilation of the Other, but arranging contests that would test skill and performance in a competition. Accordingly, agonistic strife produced excellence, not obliteration, since talent unfolded in a struggle with competitors. In this way, the Greeks did not succumb to a false ideal of sheer harmony, and so they insured a proliferation of excellence by preventing stagnation and uniform control. The *agōn* expressed the general resistance of the Greeks to "unified domination" (*Alleinherrschaft*) and the danger of unchallenged or unchallengeable power – hence the practice of ostracizing someone too powerful, someone who would ruin the reciprocal structure of agonistic competition.

The Greek *agōn* is a historical source for what Nietzsche later generalized into the reciprocal structure of will to power. And it is important to recognize that such a structure undermines the idea that power could or should run unchecked, either in the sense of sheer domination or chaotic indeterminacy. Will to power implies a certain "measure" of oppositional limits, even though such a measure could not imply an overarching order or a stable principle of balance. Nevertheless there *is* a capacity for measure in agonistic power relations. Nietzsche tells us (*KSA* 8, p. 79) that Greek institutions were healthy in not separating culture from nature in the manner of a good–evil scheme. Yet they overcame sheer natural energies of destruction by selectively ordering them in their practices, cults, and festival days. The Greek "freedom of mind" (*Freisinnigkeit*) was a "measured release" of natural forces, not their negation. Accordingly, Nietzsche's concept of agonistic will to power should be construed not as a measureless threat to culture but as a naturalistic redescription of cultural measures. The reciprocal structure of agonistic relations means that competing life forces productively delimit each other and thus generate dynamic formations rather than sheer form or sheer indeterminacy.[7]

---

[7] For important discussions of this idea, see two articles in the *Journal of Nietzsche Studies* 24 (Fall 2002): Paul van Tongeren, "Nietzsche's Greek Measure," 5–24, and H. W. Siemens, "Agonal Communities of Taste: Law and Community in Nietzsche's Philosophy of Transvaluation," 83–112. See also Christa Davis Acampora, "Of Dangerous Games and Dastardly Deeds: A Typology of Nietzsche's Contests," *International Studies in Philosophy* 34/3 (Fall 2002), 135–151.

PSYCHOLOGY AND PERSPECTIVISM IN PHILOSOPHY

A central feature of Nietzsche's naturalism is that his diagnosis of the philosophical tradition goes beyond a conceptual critique of beliefs and theories: "the path to fundamental problems" is to be found in psychology (*BGE* 23), which is not to be confused with a mere "science of the mind." Nietzsche maintains that the origins of problematic constructs of "being" are not based merely in mistaken beliefs but in psychological weakness in the face of a finite world, an *aversion* to the negative conditions of life, which he describes as "decadence, a symptom of the *decline of life*" (*TI* 3, 6). Thus a certain kind of psychological strength is needed to affirm life and rethink it in ways that are more appropriate to its natural conditions of becoming. What follows is that Nietzschean psychology does not suggest a universal human nature, but a delineation of *types* along the lines of weakness and strength – hence Nietzsche's notorious objections to human equality[8] and his promotion of a hierarchical arrangement of types: "My philosophy aims at an ordering of rank" (*WP* 287).

In general terms Nietzsche maintains that no form of thought is "value-free." Elements of desire and interest are always operating in human thinking – what we think about has to *matter* to us. Even principles of "disinterest" or "objectivity" serve certain values. When we are asked not to act out of personal interests, the principle itself is animated by values and interests: "The 'disinterested' action is an *exceedingly* interesting and interested action" (*BGE* 220).

With Nietzsche's insistence that philosophy cannot be separated from personal interests and meaning-formation, his turn to psychology means that knowledge cannot be based in an absolute, fixed, objective standard, but in a pluralized perspectivism: "There is *only* a perspective seeing, only a perspective 'knowing'" (*GM* III, 12). There are many possible takes on the world, and none could count as exclusively correct. A plurality of perspectives exhibits not only different, but also differing interpretations, so that even the coexistence of conflicting positions can no longer be ruled out of play. Nietzsche expresses his outlook as follows: "Profound aversion to resting once

[8] See my discussion in *A Nietzschean Defense of Democracy: An Experiment in Postmodern Politics* (Chicago: Open Court, 1995), Ch. 2.

and for all in any one total view of the world. Enchantment (*Zauber*) of the opposing point of view" (*WP* 470). This matter is relevant to the charge that Nietzsche's writing exhibits contradictory positions across different texts (even within texts). Assuming, however, that Nietzsche knew what he was doing, we can say that such incidents portray his warning against oppositional thinking by deliberately disturbing a fixed position through the insertion of a counter-position. Moreover, his hyperbolic attacks can be seen as a rhetorical strategy to unsettle thinking and reveal possibilities otherwise concealed by commonplace assumptions.

One other methodological implication of Nietzsche's naturalism is worth mentioning. I call it a *presumption of immanence*. We can only think in terms of how we are *already* existing in the midst of forces not of our choosing and not imaginable as stemming from, or implying, some "other" realm beyond the lived world. Such forces are "native" to our lives, we are "born" into them, and it should be noted that this sense of nativity is a non-scientific connotation of "nature" in both the Latin *natura* and the Greek *phusis*. Nativistic immanence mandates that we accept as *given* all forces that we can honestly recognize at work in our lives, from instinct to reason, from war to peace, from nature to culture, and so on (see *BGE* 36). This includes the abiding *contest* between such forces, which undermines traditional projects of "eliminative" opposition (which can arise in any sphere, from religion to science). For Nietzsche, all evident native forces play a role in cultural life, and a failure to embrace the whole package betrays weakness and the seeds of life-denial.

THE MEANING OF LIFE

In a certain sense Nietzsche's philosophy, in all its elements, is focused on the question of the meaning of life – not in the sense of finding a decisive answer to "Why are we here?" but rather the *problem* of finding meaning in a world that ultimately blocks our natural interest in happiness, preservation, knowledge, and purpose. To be precise, the question is not "What is the meaning of life?" but "Can there be meaning in life?" So the question that preoccupies Nietzsche's investigations runs: Is life as we have it meaningful, worthwhile, affirmable *on its own terms?* No culture, no form of thought has ever denied (how could it?) that our "first world," immediate existence, is constituted by negative constraints – change, suffering, loss, and death – that limit all positive possibilities in life. In the end one must confess that life as we first have it is tragic, measured against our highest aspirations.

Nietzsche's diagnosis of the Western tradition is that, in one form or another, the answer to this question of meaning in natural life has been: No. "Concerning life, the wisest men of all ages have judged alike: *it is no good*" (*TI* 2, 1). Whether in scientific, rationalistic, religious, or moralistic terms, initial conditions of existence have been judged to be deficient, confused, fallen, alien, or base, and thus in need of correction or transcendence altogether. Nietzsche judges all such judgments as implicitly nihilistic, and sees as his task the aim for an affirmative revaluation of a necessarily tragic existence: "I want to learn more and more to see as beautiful what is necessary in things; then I shall be one of those who make things beautiful. *Amor fati*: let that be my love henceforth . . . And all in all and on the whole some day I wish only to be a Yes-sayer" (*GS* 276).

It is important to establish that life-affirmation – in response to the *question* of meaning in life and the danger of nihilism after the death of God – is the core issue in Nietzsche's thought; it lies behind and animates all of his supposed "doctrines," such as will to power, perspectivism, and especially eternal recurrence.[9] Accordingly, Nietzsche's texts cannot be reduced to doctrines or positions that call for assessment as philosophical "propositions," measured by conceptual, empirical, or logical criteria.[10] Nietzsche's philosophical work always bears on the existential *task* of coming to terms with the meaning and value of life, in one way or another. In the wake of the death of God, the problem of meaning turns on the choice between a looming nihilism or a revaluation of life. Nietzsche's own philosophy aims to join two notions that had previously been held apart: *becoming* and *the value of existence*, which he claims to have brought

---

9 See Bernard Reginster, "Nihilism and the Affirmation of Life," *International Studies in Philosophy* 34/3 (2002), 55–68. On eternal recurrence, see my *Nietzsche's Life Sentence.*

10 See Ivan Soll, "Attitudes Toward Life: Nietzsche's Existentialist Project," *International Studies in Philosophy* 34/3 (Fall 2002), 69–81. Reading Nietzsche is more like being "propositioned" by a seducer. He even says that philosophy is more seduction than argument (*D* 330).

together "in a *decisive* way" (*WP* 1058). His guiding concern, contrary
to the tradition, is to find meaning and value *in* becoming.

Nietzsche's interest in tragedy is exposed in his first published work,
The Birth of Tragedy. This book planted the seeds for every issue
that Nietzsche subsequently undertook, especially the critique of
morality. Nietzsche calls *The Birth of Tragedy* "my first revaluation
of all values," and the "soil" for his later teachings (*TI* 10, 5). The
text sets up the historical character of Nietzsche's engagement with
the Western tradition, in the way in which he calls for a retrieval of
something within Greek culture that has been lost or suppressed.[11]

In *The Birth of Tragedy* Nietzsche focuses on the Greek deities
Apollo and Dionysus in order to understand the meaning of tragic
drama. Tragedy, for Nietzsche, was far more than a literary form; it
reflected and consummated an early Greek world-view that was more
faithful to the finite conditions of life than subsequent developments
in philosophy, especially in Socrates and Plato. Early Greek myth and
religion were quite different from religions that promote transcendence of earthly existence in favor of eternal conditions and salvation
from suffering. Greek mythopoetic works and various cults expressed
a religious outlook that sacralized all the conditions of concrete life,
celebrating all its forces, both benign and terrible, constructive and
destructive.[12] Early Greek religion was (1) pluralistic, in not being
organized around, or reduced to, a single form or deity, (2) agonistic, in that its sacred stories exhibit a tension between opposing
forces, and (3) fatalistic, in that mortality and loss are indigenous
to human existence, not to be repaired, reformed, or transcended.
Human beings must always confront a negative fate that limits their
power and ultimately brings death. Nietzsche understands tragedy
as the culmination of this early Greek world-view, and the figures of
Apollo and Dionysus can be understood as paradigmatic of the dual-
ities and tensions of Greek religious experience, displayed together

---

[11] In addition to Sallis' book *Crossings*, an excellent source is M. S. Silk and J. P. Stern, *Nietzsche
on Tragedy* (Cambridge: Cambridge University Press, 1981).

[12] See my extensive discussion in *Myth and Philosophy*, Ch. 2. See also Walter Burkert, *Greek
Religion*, trans. John Raffan (Cambridge, MA: Harvard University Press, 1985).

on the same stage in tragic drama. With the narrative portrayal of a noble hero experiencing an inevitable downfall, tragedy expresses the unfolding of a meaningful but finite life limited by a negative fate.[13]

Dionysus was a deity of earth forces and his mythos expressed the natural cycle of birth, death, and rebirth: in various versions the god suffers a cruel death and dismemberment, but is restored to life again. The god's devotees would experience both wild erotic feasts and dark rites of animal sacrifice, in order to experience a cathartic communion with forces of life and death. In this way Dionysian worship promoted ecstatic self-transcendence, where the boundaries between self and nature are dissolved. To lose oneself in the amorphous surgings and shatterings of the life cycle is to gain a kind of peace and union with what is ordinarily "other" to the self.

Apollo was an Olympian god representing light, beauty, measure, prophecy, poetry, and plastic arts. For Nietzsche, Apollo expresses the "principle of individuation" (*BT* 1), meant to counteract the dissolving flux of Dionysus by setting boundaries of form, the measured shaping of individual entities and selves. But because of the primal power of Dionysus that animates tragedy, the forming power of Apollo is only temporary and it must yield to the negative force of Dionysian flux. In abstract terms, the confluence of Apollo and Dionysus represents a finite flux of forming and deforming that never rests or aims for a finished state or preserved condition.

Although the Dionysian has a certain primacy in Nietzsche's interpretation of tragedy (in that forms must always yield to formlessness), nevertheless the Apollonian is of equal importance; tragedy is not a purely Dionysian phenomenon. As a sophisticated art form, the Apollonian forces of poetry and plastic imagery are essential to the meaning and significance of tragedy. Tragic drama, with its Apollonian artistic constructions, transforms amorphous Dionysian experience into an articulated cultural world. In *BT* 21, Nietzsche calls tragedy a mediating mixture of the Dionysian and the Apollonian: tragedy presents a negative limit, but "without denial of individual existence." Pure Dionysian experience would preclude the awareness and comprehension of cultural production, and so the formative and educative

---

[13] See my *Myth and Philosophy*, Ch. 5.

capacity of mythical symbols "would remain totally ineffective and unnoticed." With the force of sensuous imagery, intelligible ideas, and sympathetic emotions, the Apollonian prevents a collapse into the "orgiastic self-annihilation" of sheer Dionysian abandon. The Dionysian, by itself, entails the *danger* of nihilism and pessimism, voiced by the "Wisdom of Silenus": It is best "not to be born, not to *be*, to be *nothing*. But the second best for you is – to die soon" (*BT* 3). It is the *pain* of individuated states (intrinsically subject to dissolution) that prompts an interest in dissolution as a *deliverance* from pain. Thus, the force of Apollonian individuation is a deliverance not from pain but from the danger of life-denial (*BT* 7). Nietzsche sees the artistic Apollonian elements in tragedy as essential to the life-affirming spirit of the Greeks. Apollonian art shaped a world of meaning in which the Greeks could dwell, and through which they could bear the terrible truth of Dionysian deformation, thus avoiding the danger of self-abnegation.

Tragic myth preceded the advent of philosophy in the Greek world. In *The Birth of Tragedy*, philosophy is embodied by Socrates, the third important voice in that text. Socrates sought logical consistency, precise definition, and conceptual universals secured in the conscious mind. With such powers of rational thought, humans could overcome confusion, mystery, and limits, and thus come to "know" the true nature of things. Now meaning is no longer placed in mythical images associated with a negative force, but in universal, fixed ideas that ground knowledge and supersede the life-world. Such a transformation is clinched in Plato's designation of eternal Forms as the ground of "being" that transcends negative conditions of "becoming." Plato's seemingly transcendent aims brought him to critique tragic art precisely because of the characteristics that Nietzsche considered life-affirming. In Books II, III, and X of the *Republic*, Plato attacks tragic poetry because it falsely portrays the divine as unstable, dark, immoral, and unjust; and the sensuous pleasures of artistic works prompt the passions and seduce us to the attractions of bodily life, which block the higher possibilities of intellectual and spiritual transcendence. Although the *Republic* is a complex text susceptible to a wide array of readings, it is plausible to say that the entire dialogue is a confrontation with the Greek tragic tradition, a notion that will be developed in Chapter 6.

Nietzsche's retrieval of the tragic is a fundamental challenge to traditional conceptions of morality that began with Plato. The burden of tragedy is that what is good or valuable is not preserved at the heart of reality, but rather limited and checked by counter-forces that cannot be eradicated or explained away (the most telling example is the fate and downfall of Oedipus). Ever since Plato, the Western tradition has typically aimed to avoid or overcome moral tragedy in various ways: by a secured governance of the good's counter-forces, by the prospect of a deliverance from finite life, by utopian hopes for historical transformation, or at the very least by a secured moral "theory" that can provide intellectual resolve despite limits on the good. Inspired by the Greeks, Nietzsche calls for a renewed orientation that can find meaning and value in tragic conditions. That is why Nietzsche's critique of morality is not a critique of values per se, but of certain kinds of value that have diminished or superseded the value of a finite world of becoming.

The reason I have given some emphasis to Nietzsche's early work on tragedy is that he himself called it a precursor to his re-evaluation of Western values, and I believe that the tragic and the possibility of tragic values hover in the background of the *Genealogy*. Recalling that Dionysus was the god of *both* life and death, I note that when Nietzsche, in *Ecce Homo*, called the *Genealogy* "uncanny" (*unheimlich*) and threatening, he adds this remark: "Dionysus, as is known, is also the god of darkness" (*EH* III, GM). The "also" points to the double movement of tragic life, in that the *value* of life cannot be separated from the *limits* of life. We will have much more to say about the tragic in coming discussions.

A SKETCH OF NIETZSCHE'S LIFE[14]

Friedrich Nietzsche was born on October 15, 1844, in Röcken, Germany. His younger sister, Elisabeth, was born in 1846. A younger brother, Ludwig Joseph, died in 1850 at the age of two. Their father was a village Lutheran pastor and Nietzsche was very attached to

[14] For reliable and insightful biographies, see Rüdiger Safranski, *Nietzsche: A Philosophical Biography*, trans. Shelley Frisch (New York: Norton, 2002), R. J. Hollingdale, *Nietzsche: The Man and His Philosophy*, 2nd edn (Cambridge: Cambridge University Press, 1999), and Ronald Hayman, *Nietzsche: A Critical Life* (Oxford: Oxford University Press, 1980).

him. He died in 1849, and Nietzsche was deeply affected by the loss. In 1850 the family moved to Naumberg, where Nietzsche lived with his mother, sister, and two aunts. Friedrich was a well-behaved, studious boy, and he displayed a certain charisma and air of authority among other students. The family expected him to become a pastor.

In 1858 Nietzsche was accepted at the prestigious Pforta boarding school. There he exhibited a strong drive for knowledge, writing, and his individual development. He was something of a nerd who showed little taste for the ordinary interests of his fellow students. At Pforta he nurtured a keen interest in classical studies. In 1864 Nietzsche enrolled at the University of Bonn to study theological and classical philology. He mostly kept to himself, occupying his energies with studying, writing, and playing the piano. He began to drift from Christian belief and was profoundly affected when he read Schopenhauer's philosophy. Displeased with the atmosphere at Bonn, in 1866 he transferred to the University of Leipzig, where his favorite teacher, Friedrich Ritschl, had taken a professorship.

In October 1867 Nietzsche began his one-year military service in the Naumberg artillery. He was discharged after a serious accident while riding a horse, from which he endured months of painful recovery and convalescence. In November 1868 he met the composer Richard Wagner and was elated at becoming an acquaintance of such a great artist. In May 1869 he was invited to the Wagner home in Tribschen, and he came to spend Christmas and New Years there as well. Thus was established his important friendship with Wagner and his wife Cosima.

In February 1869 Nietzsche was appointed to a teaching post at the University of Basel. This was unusual because he had not yet completed his graduate work. His teacher Ritschl was instrumental in procuring the appointment, owing to his belief in Nietzsche's superior talent and potential. At Basel Nietzsche lectured on Greek poetry, drama, and philosophy, and he developed a strong interest in Greek tragedy, in part inspired by Schopenhauer's pessimistic philosophy. In August 1870, after the outbreak of the Franco-Prussian War, Nietzsche began military service as a medic, attending to the wounded and the dead on the battlefield. He became stricken with dysentery and diphtheria, and was released to return to Basel.

In January 1872, *The Birth of Tragedy* was published. Happily for Nietzsche, Wagner was enthusiastic about the book, particularly because of its celebration of Wagner's music as a rebirth of the tragic spirit. Yet the unusual, adventurous character of the text was not well received by the philological community. At this time Nietzsche was suffering from much illness and eye disease, and he worried that he would suffer an early death like his father. In the Fall of 1876 he took a leave of absence from Basel. Then he met and developed a friendship with the moral philosopher Paul Rée. Nietzsche remained ill and suffered debilitating headaches from his eye troubles.

In 1878 Nietzsche published *Human, All Too Human*, an iconoclastic book that broke with his earlier idealism and call for cultural renewal, a shift that alienated Wagner and other friends. Despite unrelieved sickness and suffering, his work on philosophy and morality inspired him and provoked elevated feelings. Nevertheless, his illness forced him to resign his post at Basel, which provided him with a pension. In 1881 *Daybreak* was published, and in August of that year the idea of eternal recurrence came to him, a life-affirming thought that would animate much of his subsequent thinking and writing.

In 1882 *The Gay Science* was published. Nietzsche's eyesight became so bad that he had to procure a typewriter, a new device at the time. That year Paul Rée met Lou Salomé in Rome. Lou was a charming young Russian woman who was studying philosophy and history, and Rée persuaded Nietzsche to join them in Rome. Nietzsche became captivated by Salomé and was so impressed by her mind and passion that he came to see her as a soul mate, even a potential intellectual heir. He proposed marriage to her twice, but was turned down. Rée, Nietzsche, and Salomé traveled together, but a competition between the two men for Lou's affection dampened their friendship. Nietzsche's sister Elisabeth was quite antagonistic toward Salomé, as was Nietzsche toward his sister in return.[15]

In 1883 Nietzsche began work on *Thus Spoke Zarathustra*, which would gather together his philosophical and artistic energies at the time into an inspired and inspiring narrative about coming to terms with earthly life. In February of that year, Wagner died, which affected

---

[15] For a study of Lou Salomé, see Rudolph Binion, *Frau Lou: Nietzsche's Wayward Disciple* (Princeton: Princeton University Press, 1974).

Nietzsche deeply despite his falling out with the composer and his change of heart about cultural renewal through Wagner's music. Nietzsche was experiencing a growing distance from the world, from his mother and sister on a personal level, and from his own time on an intellectual level. His vision for humanity to be liberated from tradition accentuated his sense of alienation. In 1884 he broke with Elisabeth over her association with anti-Semitism. In 1885 she married a prominent anti-Semite, Bernard Förster, and in 1886 the couple moved to Paraguay to establish a German colony, which eventually failed.

In 1886 *Beyond Good and Evil* was published. Nietzsche's illness and sufferings continued to be a burden, and friends noticed in him an unsettling visionary hyperbole. In 1887 *On the Genealogy of Morality* was published, continuing his vigorous critique of the Western moral and philosophical tradition. Nietzsche retained a growing sense of alienation and solitude. He was working on his major work, *The Will to Power*, but in 1888 he decided to divide the material for this text into two separate books, which were published as *Twilight of the Idols* and *The Antichrist*. In 1889 he began work on his philosophical autobiography, *Ecce Homo*. His health and mood started to improve, yet his behavior and writing began to appear erratic.

On January 3, 1889, Nietzsche was taking a walk in Turin, Italy. Upon seeing a carriage driver beating a horse, Nietzsche threw his arms around the animal and collapsed into unconsciousness. After he wrote a number of disturbing letters to friends, one of them, Franz Overbeck, went to Turin and brought Nietzsche back to Basel. Nietzsche had fallen into irrevocable madness and he spent a year in a psychiatric clinic. In 1890 his mother brought him to Naumberg, and, after her death in 1897, Elisabeth took him to Weimar to care for him. Nietzsche died in Weimar on August 25, 1900.[16]

---

[16] The tragedy of Nietzsche's breakdown was made worse by Elisabeth's influence after his death. She took over the management of Nietzsche's works and encouraged the image of her brother as a mad genius who sacrificed sanity for the depth of his philosophy. She was unscrupulous in many ways and nurtured the mistaken picture of Nietzsche as a German nationalist, racist, and militarist, which fed the later Nazi appropriation of Nietzsche's thought. For a treatment of Elisabeth and her effects, see H. F. Peters, *Zarathustra's Sister: The Case of Elisabeth and Friedrich Nietzsche* (New York: Markus Wiener, 1985). For a thorough account of Nietzsche's reception after his death, see Steven E. Ascheim, *The Nietzsche Legacy in Germany, 1890–1990* (Berkeley: University of California Press, 1992).

CHAPTER 2

The preface

SECTION I

The first line of the Preface is strange and disconcerting: "We are unknown (*unbekannt*) to ourselves, we knowers (*Erkennenden*), even to ourselves, and with good reason." What a way to begin a philosophical work! This line and section are not announcing the familiar need to pursue self-knowledge or knowledge of the mind in the face of initial ignorance. Rather, we are told that there is something concealed in the pursuit of knowledge itself, and inevitably so.

We remain strange to ourselves out of necessity, we do not understand ourselves, we *must* confusedly mistake who we are, the motto "everyone is furthest (*Fernste*) from himself" applies to us forever (*in alle Ewigkeit*), – we are not "knowers" when it comes to ourselves.

In addition to challenging the general idea that self-awareness provides reliable self-knowledge, Nietzsche's claim addresses high-order pursuits of knowledge (*Erkenntnis*), including philosophy. There is something within knowers that will *always* be unfamiliar to them ("unfamiliar" being another meaning of *unbekannt*). What are we to make of this claim, and why does it come at the very start of the *Genealogy*?[1] Two questions about this section seem pressing: (1) What is necessarily self-concealed within the pursuit of knowledge? And (2) Who are the "we" in question?

With regard to the first question, what is the unknown or unfamiliar "self" concealed to knowledge seekers? Nietzsche mentions "the

[1] See Ken Gemes, "'We Remain of Necessity Strangers to Ourselves': The Key Message of Nietzsche's *Genealogy*," in Acampora, ed., *Nietzsche's* On the Genealogy of Morals, pp. 191–208.

rest of life" and life "experiences," and then asks: "Who of us ever has enough seriousness for them? Or enough time?" Is the unfamiliar "self" the living self that reflection passes by in order to bring home its intellectual "treasure" to the "hives of our knowledge"? Indeed, Nietzsche points to a posture of knowers that is "absent-minded" and "sunken-in-thought," which could explain why thinkers must necessarily mistake "who they are" (note the "who" rather than a "what"). Is this a personal reference to thinkers who sacrifice their living selves for their knowing selves? Is a living self a different kind of entity that can be known in a different way? Or is there something within life that cannot be captured as an "entity"?[2] Is there something dark and forbidding hidden within a *living* thinker, even something self-consuming? I will let these questions stand for now, but I think that our coming tour of the text will show that each question elicits something of an affirmative answer.

With regard to the second question, who does the "we" designate, and does Nietzsche include himself in this group? Is the "we" simply a rhetorical device that Nietzsche deploys while implicitly exempting himself, so that the target is simply knowledge and knowers "so far"? I think not, because in the next section of the Preface Nietzsche repeats the phrase "we knowers" in the setting of some autobiographical remarks. The question remains: Does Nietzsche implicate himself in what seems to be a challenge to the very posture of philosophical knowledge? Yes and no. This question can also be held in some suspense for now, but I want to stress how important this first section of the book is, because I believe it forecasts some remarkably vexing passages in the last sections of the *Genealogy's* third Essay.

At this stage in the reading, however, let me offer some hints about the implications of this section. Nietzsche will offer that there is something self-alienating, even self-undermining, in the history of Western morality and philosophy. While Nietzsche presents himself as a new kind of philosopher, I do not believe that he utterly exempts his own thinking from this problem. Philosophy, for Nietzsche, is not only an examination of strange questions; philosophy *as such* is a strange phenomenon. Any philosophy, as a pursuit of knowledge and truth, will necessarily involve a productive alienation from "the

---

[2] Actually Nietzsche is not examining "selfhood" in a formal sense because his language simply gives the reflexive address of *selbst* and *uns*.

rest of life," owing to philosophy's *reflective* posture and productions as such. Nietzsche therefore must include himself among "we knowers." Yet Nietzsche can distinguish his own work by uncovering this dynamic and advancing an alternative philosophy of natural life over against anti-life philosophies. Yet the posture of any philosophy, even Nietzsche's, dwells within and runs up against life forces that outstrip reflection. I believe that Nietzsche recognizes an intrinsic dilemma in philosophy, and particularly in his own life-philosophy, in that he must recognize and adopt a self-limiting element in philosophizing "about" life, because life is not an abstraction but a *living* force that beats even in the heart of a philosopher. In sum, "we knowers unknown to ourselves" can suggest both a critique of philosophy's traditional alienation from natural life as well as the admission that even a philosophy *of* natural life is always exceeded *by* life. It must be added that this self-limiting character of philosophy is caught up in Nietzsche's unorthodox styles of writing; and it cannot be an accident that the *Genealogy* – which most resembles a typical treatise – opens with intimations of its own limits by declaring the self-concealing character of knowledge.

SECTION 2

Nietzsche tells us that his polemic about "the descent (*Herkunft*) of our moral prejudices" in the *Genealogy* is not a new project because it was first sketched in 1876–1877 in *Human, All Too Human*; and his thoughts on the matter go back even further than that.[3] Then Nietzsche says in strong terms that such thoughts "did not arise in me individually, randomly, or sporadically but from a common root, from a *fundamental will* to knowledge deep inside me..." So alongside the *problem* of knowledge-seeking announced in Section 1, here Nietzsche openly declares his own will to knowledge driving his philosophy. Note that he distinguishes this drive from anything

---

[3] In Section 3, referring again to his early development on the question of morality, Nietzsche designates the "origin" (*Ursprung*) as his focus. *Herkunft* could also be translated as "origin," but "descent" captures the important sense in which moral origins have been born, handed down, and sustained in our culture. Both words complement each other and do not indicate any "original" condition that defines morality in any substantive way, but rather the intrinsically *historical* character of morality. I do not think there is any technical difference between *Herkunft* and *Ursprung* in Nietzsche's usage; in Section 4 he seems to use the two terms interchangeably.

merely subjective or individual; indeed, it "took control" of him in a commanding way. Continuing, he says:

And this is the only thing proper for a philosopher. We have no right to stand out *individually*: we must not either make mistakes or hit on the truth individually. Instead, our thoughts . . . grow from us with the same necessity as fruits born on the tree.

Philosophy, for Nietzsche, is clearly not simply an individual perspective, but a compulsion toward world-disclosive knowledge, even though he has warned about the vital limits that bear on philosophical knowledge.

SECTION 3

Nietzsche's "curiosity and suspicion" about the origin (*Ursprung*) of good and evil expressed themselves early in his life. As a young boy he wrestled with the origin of evil from a theological perspective, and concluded that God had to be "the *father* of evil." In time Nietzsche came "to separate theological and moral prejudice" and "no longer searched for the origin of evil *beyond* the world." In a more naturalistic manner his question became: "under what conditions did man invent the value judgments good and evil?" But right away he adds a question that goes beyond a mere historical or anthropological consideration of these values: "*and what value do they themselves have?*" He elaborates: "Have they up to now obstructed or promoted human flourishing?" Do they reflect "the degeneration of life" or "the fullness, strength, and will of life"? In the course of pursuing these questions through varied historical and psychological studies, he came to refine his interrogations and conjectures further, until he had his "own territory," his "own soil" for examining morality. In the next sections of the Preface Nietzsche sketches some of the ways in which his own soil nourished and produced the distinctive character of the *Genealogy*.

SECTION 4

Nietzsche says that a motivation to work out his hypotheses concerning the origin of morality came from his reading a friend's book: Paul

Rée's *The Origin of Moral Sensations*, published in 1877. He associates Rée's work with a "perverse" kind of genealogy, which he calls the "English kind," and which will be critiqued in the first Essay. In earlier works he was working critically with various passages from Rée's book in order to shape his own alternative genealogical approach. He points to specific sections from *Human, All Too Human, The Wanderer and His Shadow*, and *Daybreak* that prefigured key themes of the *Genealogy*.[4] As he highlights his disputes with Rée's work, Nietzsche alerts us to the atypical manner of his critical posture, which is not a matter of refuting errors: "What have I to do with refutation!" Rather, as a "positive spirit," he aims "to replace the unlikely (*Unwahrscheinlichen*) with the more likely and in some circumstances to replace one error with another." This remark has important significance for how we read Nietzsche's genealogical investigations, and at this point it might be useful to offer some preparatory discussion of how he understood "genealogy."[5]

Nietzsche deploys quasi-historical, genealogical discussions to subvert the confidence of traditional belief systems (not to refute them). Genealogy shows that revered doctrines are not fixed or eternal: they have a history and emerged as a contest with existing counter-forces; indeed, they could not avoid being caught up in the conditions they were opposing. Such analysis reveals the complexity of cultural beliefs and undermines the presumed stability and purity of long-standing measures of thought. Genealogy, then, is a kind of history different from those that presume discrete beginnings, substantive grounds in "original" conditions, or simple lines of development.

Some writers think that Nietzsche's genealogy implies a nostalgia for a more noble original condition.[6] But Nietzsche does not advocate a return to the past: In *The Gay Science*, when extolling "we children of the future," who are "homeless" in the present and dismissive of hardened "realities," he adds: "We 'conserve' nothing; neither do we

---

[4] Taking up these earlier treatments will be helpful in the course of our analysis, when appropriate. Happily, the Cambridge University Press translation of the *Genealogy* includes all the sections noted by Nietzsche in its "Supplementary Material."

[5] A very helpful essay is Raymond Guess, "Nietzsche and Genealogy," in Richardson and Leiter, eds., *Nietzsche*, pp. 322–340. For a discussion of critical responses to genealogy, see S. Kemal, "Some Problems of Genealogy," *Nietzsche Studien* 19 (1990), 30–42.

[6] See Jürgen Habermas, *The Philosophical Discourse of Modernity*, trans. Frederick G. Lawrence (Cambridge, MA: MIT Press, 1987), pp. 125–126.

want to return to any past conditions" (*GS* 377). Genealogy is a strategy for critique in the face of hardened convictions (*GM* P, 6) and a preparation for something new (*GM* II, 24). Attention to the complexities of historical emergence destabilizes foundationalist models and transcendent warrants; and the agonistic crossings intrinsic to this history tear at the clear boundaries of conceptual categories. In this way, genealogy does not simply look back at history for explanations of the past and the present; it aims to be disruptive and preparatory for new ventures. Finally, although Nietzsche is working with actual historical forces and periods, he is certainly not pretending to offer standard historical work. As we will see, Nietzsche is deliberately selective and he arranges narratives more for their rhetorical force – to provoke us to think about larger philosophical questions evoked by broad historical considerations.

SECTION 5

The beginning of this section is quite significant. Continuing an account of his development toward the *Genealogy*, Nietzsche says: "I was preoccupied with something much more important than the nature of hypotheses, mine or anybody else's, on the origin of morality..." The historical treatment was instrumental "only for one purpose," and in fact Nietzsche calls such a treatment "one means among many" toward that purpose. The core of Nietzsche's concern was not simply a genealogy of morality but the "question of the *value* of morality." There is no objective, value-free agenda at the heart of Nietzsche's analysis, and his question about the value of moral values goes much further than an account of how morality itself is valuable for human existence. For Nietzsche, the estimation of morality has a decidedly polemical edge, which is evident when he couches this question in terms of his need "to confront my great teacher Schopenhauer."

Schopenhauer was a pessimist who unashamedly answered No to the question of meaning in life, and yet he forged a robust ethics out of this pessimism by recasting morality as a denial of our natural tendencies rather than a positive cultivation of a moral nature. Nietzsche summarizes Schopenhauer's ethics as a "morality of pity (*Mitleid*)," which includes a valorization of selflessness, self-denial, and self-sacrifice. Why does Nietzsche single out Schopenhauer in this regard? Some background remarks are in order.

INTERLUDE: SCHOPENHAUER, PESSIMISM, AND NIHILISM

Schopenhauer was an important early influence on Nietzsche's philosophy, and Nietzsche greatly admired him, particularly for his intellectual honesty. Schopenhauer's pessimism rejected all forms of optimism, all forms of worldly and otherworldly redemption from finite existence, as philosophically unjustified. For Schopenhauer, the ultimate nature of reality is Will, an aimless, amorphous force that eludes human knowledge and consumes all its manifestations. In life, suffering and lack are the bottom line. Wisdom, for Schopenhauer, entailed recognizing the ultimate pointlessness of existence and practicing resignation, in a way similar to religious ascetic traditions, but without otherworldly hopes. Schopenhauer's pessimism advocated a life of self-denial and looked to the prospect of annihilation as the only authentic form of "salvation."

Nietzsche came to see Schopenhauer's philosophy as the secret code to the entire Western tradition. First of all, Schopenhauer shared the West's chronophobic assessment of life. Even though he dismissed optimistic projects, his proposal of life-denial showed that he agreed with the tradition's criteria of value, but simply disagreed that such criteria could be realized in any positive form. In other words, pessimism implies that life *should* support human existential and intellectual aspirations but *cannot* support them. Why else turn away from life? At the same time, Nietzsche recognized Schopenhauer's philosophical rigor in deconstructing Western optimism. Schopenhauer was right when he based reality in an aimless force that limits all human prospects. Nietzsche then concluded that Schopenhauer's pessimism was the hidden truth of Western thought, that all the rectification projects in the name of truth, knowledge, salvation, justice, and so on were in fact esoteric, concealed forms of pessimistic life-denial. Schopenhauer, then, exemplified the Western tradition without all the false ornamentation. For Nietzsche, every "positive" prospect of resolving temporal finitude was at bottom a form of life-negation.

Nietzsche and Schopenhauer were philosophical brethren in that the core of their thinking was an acute, unflinching concentration on one question: Is existence worth it? Schopenhauer's honest answer was No. Nietzsche's answer was Yes, and he accused Western thought of both evading this stark question and concealing a repressed No, a hidden nihilism. This brings us again to the question of nihilism in Nietzsche's thought. There is some ambiguity (especially in the notebooks) as to whether Nietzsche is promoting or rejecting nihilism, defined as "the radical repudiation of value, meaning, and desirability" in life (*WP* 1.1). To clarify, I think we can say that Nietzsche welcomes nihilism as a denial of *traditional* constructs (e.g., in the death of God), but only as a transition to revaluation, which would overcome the deep danger of nihilism.[7]

As we will see, nihilism is a consequence of the tradition's own self-deconstruction. Accordingly, Nietzsche declares that nihilism shows itself as the heretofore *covert* essence of the tradition, an annulment of finite becoming stemming from weakness in the face of life. Yet in keeping with tradition, *overt* nihilism becomes its own kind of binary dogma, a peculiar form of certainty that simply reverses traditional doctrines while covertly retaining their confidence in achieving a fixed position. Nihilism is a "belief in unbelief" (*GS* 347). In a time of cultural upheaval and uncertainty, nihilism amounts to a preference for the certainty of nothingness over conditions of uncertainty (*BGE* 10). No matter how courageous it might appear, nihilism is still a sign of weakness and despair (*BGE* 10).

For Nietzsche, the "positive" postures of the tradition are in fact creative ornaments for nothingness (*GM* III, 17, 25; *TI* 3, 6). The denial of traditional beliefs (without revaluation) is simply *honest* nihilism. This is why Nietzsche admired Schopenhauer so much. His unflinching pessimism was the secret code for deciphering the motives of Western philosophy and religion. Nihilism is more realistic and beneficial in dismantling the past; it rightly recognizes that we have no right to posit a divine, moral, or rational ground in existence. But its conclusion is the "absolute untenability of existence" (*WP* 3). Accordingly, it turns out that traditional optimism was a disguised nihilism and that nihilism is simply a disenchanted or failed optimism. For Nietzsche, nihilism admits radical becoming as the only reality but cannot endure it; without the categories of purpose,

[7] See Richard Schacht, "Nietzsche and Nihilism," in *Nietzsche: A Collection of Critical Essays*, ed. Robert Solomon (Garden City, NY: Anchor Books, 1973), pp. 58–82.

unity, truth, and being, the world now "looks valueless" (*WP* 12A). A nihilist is someone who believes that the world as it *ought* to be does not exist and that the world as it *is* ought not to be (*WP* 585A). Nihilism can be beneficial, but only as a transitional stage, the overcoming of tradition that permits a new advance (*WP* 7, 111–112). Devaluing the tradition is "no longer any reason for devaluing the universe" (*WP* 12B). There is an urgent need for new values, wherein the world can be seen as "far more valuable than we used to believe" (*WP* 32). What is required is a form of thinking that is liberated from both the tradition and its nihilistic core (whether covert or overt). Those capable of such thinking will accomplish a "redemption" of the life-world:

a redemption from the curse that the hitherto reigning ideal has laid upon it. This man of the future, who will redeem us not only from the hitherto reigning ideal but also that which was bound to grow out of it, the great nausea, the will to nothingness, nihilism; . . . this Antichrist and antinihilist, who has overcome both God and nothingness – *he must come one day*. (*GM* II, 24)

Against this background discussion, Nietzsche's remarks about Schopenhauer in Section 5 can stand out more sharply. A morality of pity and self-denial can seem wholly worthy as a call to turn away from our selfish interests toward the suffering of others. *Mitleid* could be better translated as "compassion," literally a suffering-with others, an experience of their pain as one's own, which would prompt an interest in relieving pain or refraining from causing pain, to the same extent as one would value these modes when directed toward oneself by others. Yet Nietzsche recounts his growing suspicion (*Argwohn*) of this Schopenhauerian ethic as a "*great* danger to mankind, its most sublime temptation and seduction – temptation to what? To nothingness?" It is important to recognize that Nietzsche attributes this danger to an "over-valuation" of pity rather than the phenomenon of pity as such. The problem of pity is its latent aversion to a life of suffering, which can give birth to nihilism.[8] In any case, the danger

---

[8] See Michael Ure, "The Irony of Pity: Nietzsche Contra Schopenhauer and Rousseau," *Journal of Nietzsche Studies* 31 (Autumn 2006), 68–91. A good critical discussion is Martha C. Nussbaum, "Pity and Mercy: Nietzsche's Stoicism," in Schacht, ed., *Nietzsche, Genealogy, Morality*, pp. 139–167.

of mankind "turning its will *against* life" surely cannot be a revelation about Schopenhauer's philosophy, since that is precisely his
manner of recasting morality. Rather, Nietzsche describes this pessimistic disposition of pity "casting around ever wider to catch even
philosophers and make them ill, as the most uncanny (*unheimlich*)
symptom of our European culture . . ." Once again, Schopenhauer's
pessimism is important to Nietzsche as a diagnosis and recasting of
Western developments that have *not* been understood as pessimistic
or nihilistic, and this self-deceiving understanding is a primary target
of Nietzsche's genealogical critique.

SECTION 6

When the *value* of a morality of pity is understood as a *problem*, a "vast
new panorama opens up," which brings on vertigo (*Schwindel*), mistrust, suspicion, and fear, an ambivalent condition in which "belief
in morality, every kind of morality, wavers." A "new demand" presses
upon us:

> We need a *critique* of moral values, *the value of these values should itself, for
> once, be put into question* – and so we need to know about the conditions and
> circumstances under which the values grew up, developed, and changed.

Nietzsche tells us that the *value* of these values has heretofore been
taken as given, "as beyond all questioning." No one has even doubted
that the so-called "good man" advances human life, as opposed to
the "evil man." Then Nietzsche asks:

> What if the opposite were true? What if a regressive trait lurked in "the
> good man," likewise a danger, a seduction, a poison, a narcotic, so that the
> present *lived at the expense of the future?*

What if morality were to blame if the human species never achieved
its "highest potential power and splendor?" What if morality itself
was "the danger of dangers?" With these words Nietzsche poses the
disturbing and forceful prospects of his genealogical critique. What if
our most cherished moral norms were actually bad for us? We should
keep in mind that this section, despite its ominous tone, expresses
degrees of ambiguity in its mixed descriptions, and we should also
notice that its disturbing prospects are all put in the form of *questions*.

SECTION 7

This section closes Nietzsche's account of his development up to the *Genealogy*. He searched for scholarly colleagues who could examine morality with "new eyes," who could portray morality "as it actually (*wirklich*) existed and was actually lived." He adds that he is still looking for such colleagues today. Paul Rée is mentioned again and Nietzsche says he wanted to focus Rée's "sharp eye" in a better direction, toward "an actual *history of morality*." He wanted to warn Rée against "English" genealogy, which he calls "hypothesis-mongering into the *blue*." In German, *Fahrt ins Blaue* means something like a mystery tour, but I think Nietzsche wants to highlight blue as a sharp color, because he goes on to say: "It is quite clear which color is a hundred times more important for a genealogist than blue: namely *grey*." The color reference seems to pinpoint the complexity, contingency, and murkiness of morality's history, because when Nietzsche depicts genealogical "grey" as reflecting what has "actually existed," what can be documented and "actually confirmed," he summarizes this vista as "the whole, long, hard to decipher hieroglyphic script of man's moral past."

It was this grey orientation, Nietzsche says, that Rée lacked. He goes on to portray Rée's approach as a kind of scholarly bemusement and indolence, even when confronting the Darwinian juxtaposition of our beastly lineage and modern gentility. Nietzsche detects there a hint of "pessimism and fatigue," as though it were not worth taking this problem of morality "so seriously." Nietzsche, on the other hand, thinks "there is nothing which more *rewards* being taken seriously" than the problems of morality. Interestingly, Nietzsche offers an example of such reward as the possibility of being allowed to take these moral problems "*cheerfully*" (*heiter*), in the manner of his "joyful science" (*fröhliche Wissenschaft*). The reward of joy and cheerfulness can come after a long and courageous "subterranean seriousness." In this regard, Nietzsche finishes with some surprising remarks that hearken back to *The Birth of Tragedy*:

The day we can say with conviction: "Forwards! Even our old morality belongs in *comedy*!" we shall have discovered a new twist and possibility for the Dionysian drama of the "fate of the soul."

There is expressed here, I think, an important link between tragedy and morality in Nietzsche's vision, which we will consider further in due course.

SECTION 8

We have already considered the importance of this section for understanding Nietzsche's approach to reading and interpretation. There is, however, a remark about the Third Essay that we will postpone treating until we get to that part of the text.

CHAPTER 3

The first essay: "Good and Evil," "Good and Bad"

The truth of the first essay is the psychology of Christianity:
the birth of Christianity out of the spirit of *ressentiment*, *not*, as
is believed, out of the "spirit" – a countermovement by its very
nature, the great revolt against the rule of *noble* values.

(*EH* III, GM)

A NEW HISTORY OF MORALITY (SECTIONS 1–3)

Nietzsche begins by retrieving his discussion of English psychologists
in the Preface. He praises some of their qualities, especially their suspicious stance toward Christianity, Platonism, and moral idealism, as
well as their courage in confronting undesirable truths about morality (1). Yet Nietzsche sets the stage for his own genealogical approach
by claiming that these historians of morality are lacking in "*historical spirit*" (2). How so? For them, the origin of the term "good" is
found in the *usefulness* of unegoistic acts, in the praise given by the
beneficiaries of such acts. In time, however, this mundane instrumental origin was "forgotten" and selfless acts came to be deemed
as intrinsically good. While Nietzsche can appreciate the "deflation-
ary" effect of this treatment, he charges the English historians with
missing another history that undermines their assumption that moral
goodness is equivalent to the value of selfless acts and their benefits.
They have not questioned the very value of this concept of morality
in the context of its history.[1]

In Section 2 Nietzsche initiates his alternative history of moral
concepts. The "actual origin" of goodness should be located *prior* to

---

[1] Regarding the work of Paul Rée, Nietzsche's earlier investigations were actually closer to Rée's
position (see *WS* 40). See Robin Small, ed., *Paul Rée: Basic Writings* (Urbana: University of
Illinois Press, 2003), pp. xi–liii.

the emergence of selfless values; indeed such values were historical reactions *against* this earlier measure of goodness. Here Nietzsche advances the notion that moral estimations were originally the province of aristocratic status. What was first deemed "good" in human culture was neither selfless acts nor their usefulness, but rather a noble "*pathos of distance*" from low and common types in society. In noble morality, goodness was experienced in the settings of success, power, and rule over inferiors, and not in the "calculation of prudence or reckoning of usefulness" (2). So the origin of moral values is to be found in aristocratic, hierarchical concepts of "good and bad," which denoted gradations of superiority and inferiority, nobility and commonness. The notion that morality is founded on selfless actions only arose upon the "*decline* of aristocratic value-judgments," whereupon the very antithesis between egoistic and unegoistic actions came gradually to redefine moral values. Nietzsche will attribute this redefinition of morality to the rise of "slave morality" and its rebellion against "master morality."[2] But here Nietzsche designates the reversal as a function of the "herd instinct," a wider term than any historical association with slavery or subjugation. In any case, Nietzsche claims that the visibility of aristocratic moral origins has been covered up by the predominance of herd values, and that even contemporary European thought has sustained the prejudice of equating morality with selflessness and disinterest.

THE LANGUAGE OF MORALITY (SECTIONS 4–5)

In Section 2 Nietzsche had mentioned "words" and "names" as a source of moral understanding and proliferation. In Section 4 he follows through with this important part of his genealogical investigation, namely an etymological analysis of moral words in earlier cultures and languages. As opposed to other historical treatments that falsely presume more current meanings of moral terms, Nietzsche insists that ancient words be our first historical "data," and here he

---

[2] In my discussions I will deploy the master–slave distinction even though in *GM* Nietzsche uses the term "noble morality" rather than the term "master morality" that was used in *BGE*. The master–slave distinction has become a term of art in treatments of Nietzsche, and I do not see any significant difference between "master" and "noble." Nietzsche does mention the term "master" on occasion in *GM* (e.g., Section 5), and in the Epilogue to *CW* "master" and "noble" morality seem to be interchangeable terms.

finds confirmation for his alternative thesis. The earliest forms of moral language available to us show that "good" and "bad" indeed denoted hierarchical associations of superiority and inferiority. He cites the example of the German word *schlecht* (bad) that originally carried connotations of plain and simple, as contrasted with noble qualities. Other etymologies will bear out this distinction as well, and Nietzsche calls this linguistic approach "an *essential* insight into moral genealogy" (4).

In Section 5 Nietzsche turns to Greek and Latin for further confirmation of his etymological tactic, which shows "that in these words and roots that denote 'good,' we can often detect the main nuance which made the noble feel they were men of higher rank." Beyond typical associations with physical power and wealth, goodness also named certain character traits such as truthfulness and genuineness (in the Greek word *esthlos*), which was counterposed to the deceitfulness of common people. The Greek word for "good" was *agathos*, which originally meant well-born, wealthy, brave, and capable. Nietzsche notes that, even with the decline of the Greek aristocracy, *agathos* retained a sense of "spiritual *noblesse*" evident in the continued use of the word *kakos* (bad) to mean weak, ugly, cowardly, worthless. The force of Nietzsche's etymological analysis brings us to realize that the earliest recorded senses of "morality" displayed selective grades of performative, social, and psychological *rank*, forms of stratification and power that in many ways are morally questionable, if not immoral, by modern measures. Nietzsche now begins to address the question of how, and under what conditions, an original aristocratic moral sense came to be supplanted by contrary norms.

THE PRIEST (SECTIONS 6–9)[3]

The figure of the priest plays an important role in Nietzsche's genealogy. Unfortunately, Nietzsche is not very helpful in aiding the reader's

[3] This begins Nietzsche's deployment of figure-types to animate his genealogical analysis. See Aaron Ridley, *Nietzsche's Conscience: Six Character Studies from the "Genealogy"* (Ithaca, NY: Cornell University Press, 1998), for an excellent treatment of central figures operating in the text (slave, priest, philosopher, artist, scientist, noble). Each examination is a nuanced attempt to sort out the complexities within and between the different figures. On occasion I think that important ambiguities are traded for neater resolutions that accord more with modern philosophical methods and expectations about rationality and morality.

comprehension. The discussion is ambiguous and unfocused because of the following set of relationships: The priest will provide the creative power that shapes slave morality in its reversal of master morality; yet the priest type is introduced in its first form as part of the noble class. Despite the difficulties posed by this dual appearance of the priest and the question of its possible historical instances, I think we can gain some traction by following some general features of Nietzsche's account. He seems to be spotlighting the fact that early aristocratic cultures were not confined to master types and their outward powers. Religion was comparably important for these cultures in dealing with spiritual forces and meanings for nobles and commoners alike. Priests functioned as mediators between human life and spiritual dimensions by conducting religious rituals and exhibiting prophetic, visionary, and divining powers. So there were two main spheres in the ruling class, which Nietzsche designates by the warrior–priest distinction. The priest at this point does not seem to be equivalent to the coming figure in Judeo-Christian morality, but it does seem to function as a precursor to that figure, and there are evident overlaps that bear scrutiny.

Nietzsche is addressing the difference between martial rule (warriors) and religious authority (priests), but his primary focus is the psychology of these basic types with regard to the following questions: Why do some people gravitate toward action and others toward spiritual affairs? What effects follow from this cultural differentiation of types? For Nietzsche, the warrior seems to embody healthy instincts and actions when measured by the primal conditions of natural life. By comparison the priest seems to represent a less natural vitality by withdrawing from action toward the more hidden recesses of spiritual domains. From the standpoint of natural life, Nietzsche calls the priest a "dangerous" development for life that nevertheless released important new cultural powers. Let us see how this is so.

In Section 6 Nietzsche identifies the priest as a precarious and unhealthy turn from the vitality of action, as a "brooding" and "emotionally explosive" contrast with warrior types, as even the forerunner of nihilism. And yet, the priest introduces something new and highly significant for human culture, and does so despite, or even because of, this "cleft" between human types – between a strong physical life of action and a weaker life that must find its meaning apart from external accomplishment. Initially, says Nietzsche, the priest presided over crude differentiations of "purity" and "impurity" having to do with things like hygiene and diet. In time such religious designations became "internalized" in symbolic ways, having to do with dispositions, values, and ways of life. It is here, Nietzsche tells us, that the differentiation between the warrior and the priest, between vital action and withdrawn states, began to be "sharpened." And for all the departures from natural vitality, the priest opened up cultural spaces that could elevate humanity over its more animal elements and beyond the crude martial powers of the warrior class. Nietzsche here articulates an ambiguity that continues to mark his genealogical approach: It was through the vitality-threatening danger of the priest that "man first became an *interesting animal*," and that "the human soul became *deep* in a higher sense" (6).

In Section 7 Nietzsche provides the transition from the aristocratic warrior–priest *distinction* toward the *oppositional* framework of master morality and slave morality that emerged in Judaism and Christianity, with their respective moralities of "justice" and "love" in opposition to overt forms of worldly power. The posture of religious priests in noble society provided the precedent conditions for the tactics of slave morality. The priest was outwardly powerless compared to the warrior. The internalized trajectory of priestly dispositions opened up new forms of power that inverted the status of warriors by "revaluing" martial values, by cultivating "spiritual" dimensions deemed to be superior to, and lacking in, a life of physical power (the term Nietzsche uses is *Geist*, which can mean both "spirit" and "intelligence"). Even though priestly values were based in weakness and revenge against the warrior class, the turn away from crude action was a remarkable benefit: "the history of mankind would be far too stupid a thing if it had not had the intelligence (*Geist*) of the powerless injected into it" (7). Nietzsche then says that the *greatest* example of this intelligence was the priestly culture of Judaism, which crystallized the spiritual inversion of values prepared by aristocratic priests. The Jewish experience of exile and slavery produced "an act of the most spiritual (*gestigsten*) revenge" against the aristocratic conception of goodness (nobility, power, wealth, beauty, happiness), now deeming it wicked and damnable, and then redefining goodness according to the conditions of the powerless, those who are weak and who suffer at the hands of the wicked. Thus began what Nietzsche calls "the slave revolt in morality," which, he adds, became *victorious* and remained so for two thousand years.

Section 8 sketches the emergence of Christianity as a consequence of Jewish revenge against worldly power, a creative hatred that changed the world. Jesus introduced a "new love" that preached a renunciation of force, to such an extreme point that God's rectifying wrath against wickedness (in the Old Testament) gave way to non-resistance ("love your enemies," "turn the other cheek"). But Nietzsche claims that this apparent denial of revenge was the most subtle and powerful consummation of Jewish revenge. The paradox of "God on the cross" – the self-sacrifice of Jesus to a cruel death as the promise of salvation for the weak – was the most seductive form of overturning noble values, precisely because it crystallized the power and glory intrinsic to a *willing* self-renunciation of worldly power. In the course of European history, Nietzsche tells us, Christian values succeeded in replacing noble values by elevating the values of the powerless, the weak, and the common to the highest status (9).

MASTER AND SLAVE MORALITY (SECTIONS 10–12)

At this point in my analysis I include a broader view of the sections at hand by incorporating some material and issues from other texts (especially *Beyond Good and Evil*) in my attempt to lay out the significance of the master–slave distinction.[4]

We have noted that Nietzsche's genealogical treatment of moral ideals aims to disturb the pretense of moral purity and the presumption of moral foundations by suggesting a different look at the historical context out of which certain moral values arose. Ideals such as neighbor-love, peacefulness, and humility were not derived from some transcendent source, but from the interests and needs of particular types of human beings, weaker peoples suffering at the hands of stronger types. Hierarchical domination was the ruling condition

---

[4] For an insightful examination of the master–slave relation and a critical response, see Robert C. Solomon, "One Hundred Years of *Ressentiment*: Nietzsche's *Genealogy of Morals*," in Schacht, ed., *Nietzsche, Genealogy, Morality*, pp. 95–126.

of early human societies (*BGE* 257). What has been exclusively called "morality" was originally only a particular kind of morality, one quite different from another kind of morality that reflected the interests of stronger types: "There are *master morality* and *slave morality*... The moral discrimination of values has originated either among a ruling group whose consciousness of its difference from the ruled group was accompanied by delight – or among the ruled, the slaves and dependents of every degree" (*BGE* 260). Note the added phrase "and dependents of every degree," which tells us that "slavery" should be read as rhetorical shorthand for various kinds of submission.

In Sections 10–11 of the *Genealogy*, master and slave morality are distinguished by Nietzsche according to two sets of estimation: good and bad in master morality, and good and evil in slave morality. Master types discover what is good out of their own condition of strength; they experience pleasure and exaltation in their victories and their distance from the powerless. Characteristics such as courage, conquest, aggression, and command that produce the feelings of power are deemed "good," while traits of weaker types such as cowardice, passivity, humility, and dependence are deemed "bad." What is important for Nietzsche here is that good and bad are not absolutes. What is good is good only for the master; what is bad in the slave arouses embarrassment and contempt in the master, but not condemnation or denial. In fact the existence of the slave is essential for maintaining the master's sense of distance, rank, and thus "goodness." The condition of the slave is not esteemed but at the same time it is not annulled, since it provides the master with psychological (and material) benefits. In sum, what is good for the master is something active, immediate, and spontaneous, arising directly out of the master's accomplishment; what is bad is a *secondary* judgment in contrast to an antecedent experience of self-worth.

In relation to master morality, slave morality is constituted by a number of reversals. What the master calls "bad" is deemed good by the slave, and what is good for the master is called "evil" by the slave. The difference between "bad" and "evil" is important for Nietzsche. What is evil is absolutely negative and must be annulled if the good is to endure (here is a moral example of the "metaphysical faith" in binary opposites). Nietzsche traces this different kind of judgment to the existential situation of the slave: The *immediate* condition of the slave is one of powerlessness and subservience; the master is a threat to the very existence and well-being of the slave; in effect the slave lacks agency and so the initial evaluation is a negative one: the "evil" of the master is in the foreground, while what is "good," the features of the slave's submission, is a reactive, secondary judgment. Moreover, because of its immediate powerlessness, the slave's power for revenge cannot be actualized except in an *imaginary* realm of divine punishment (*GM* I, 10).

According to slave morality, anything that opposes, destroys, or conquers is evil and should be eliminated from human relations. In master morality, however, strife, opposition, and danger are essential to the feelings of power and accomplishment that spawn a sense of goodness (one thinks of the warrior ideals in Homer's *Iliad*). Harmlessness and security, which are good for the slave, are an embarrassment and encumbrance for the master (*GM* I, 11). Slave morality reverses master morality and recommends humility, selflessness, and kindness as the measure for *all* human beings, but only out of a condition of weakness and as a strategy for self-protection and self-enhancement. Slave morality seeks the simultaneous exaltation of the weak and incapacitation of the strong; but in doing so, slave types find enhancement not through their own agency but through the debilitation of others.

Slave morality is Nietzsche's redescription of Judeo-Christian ideals, as we have noted. The stories and exemplars embodying this moral outlook have promoted the ideal of supplanting worldly power with "justice" and "love." In the context of cultural history, however, Nietzsche sees in this ideal a disguised form of power, in that it is meant to protect and preserve a certain type of life; even more, the images depicting divine punishment of the wicked suggest to Nietzsche that the slave type has simply *deferred* its own interest in conquest (*GM* I, 15). Both master and slave moralities, therefore, are expressions of will to power. A current distinction in the literature draws from Nietzsche's differentiation of *aktive* and *reaktive* attitudes (*GM* II, 11) and stipulates that the master expresses active will to power, while the slave expresses reactive will to power. The slave has no genuine agency and therefore can compensate only by reacting to an external threat and attempting to annul it. For Nietzsche, slave morality is not immediately an affirmation of a good, but a denial of something dangerous and fearful, and he grounds this evaluation-by-negation in the psychological category of resentment.[5]

> The slave revolt in morality begins when *ressentiment* itself turns creative and gives birth to values: the *ressentiment* of those beings who, denied the proper response of action, compensate for it only with an imaginary revenge. Whereas all noble morality grows out of a triumphant Yes-saying to itself, slave morality from the outset says No to what is "outside," what is "different," what is "not itself"; and *this* No is its creative deed. This reversal of the value-positing eye – this *necessary* orientation to the outside instead of back onto itself – is a basic feature of *ressentiment*: in order to come about, slave morality always first needs an opposing, external world; it needs, physiologically speaking, external stimuli in order to act at all – its action is fundamentally reaction. (*GM* I, 10)

For Nietzsche, it should be said, the difference between active and reactive will to power, between affirmation and resentment, is a fundamental issue that bears on *all* intellectual and cultural topics. The general question is the ability or inability to affirm a finite world of limits, losses, conflicts, and dangers (see *Z* II, 20 and *TI* 2, 1). His analysis of the social arena targets the concrete soil out of which grew a host of intellectual movements. Nietzsche is trying to subvert long-standing social values that are animated by notions of universality, equality, harmony, comfort, protection, and the like – seemingly positive notions that Nietzsche insists are connivances of negative attitudes: fear of danger and difference, hatred of suffering, resentment and revenge against excellence, superiority, and domination. With literal slavery disappearing,[6] Nietzsche tends to designate this condition of weakness and its voluntary perpetuation of the slave attitude as the herd instinct, which is continually seeking to exercise its own mode of power by enforcing conformity and comfort; in so doing it protects the self-esteem of ordinary humans by neutralizing differences and denigrating excellence. It is in this light that we can better understand Nietzsche's blistering attacks on democratic egalitarianism.

It must be stipulated that Nietzsche's genealogical analysis is not meant to reject or even regret the slave/herd mentality, as much as

---

[5] Nietzsche uses the French term *ressentiment*, probably because German lacks an effective equivalent. See Kaufmann's discussion in *Basic Writings*, pp. 441–446.

[6] Nietzsche suggests in *HAH* I, 101 that slavery is no longer just.

to redescribe the environment of moral values in naturalistic terms. In doing so Nietzsche aims to disarm the high-minded pretense of egalitarian thinking by contextualizing it and showing it to be no less interested in power and control than is aristocraticism (*BGE* 51; *GM* I, 15). Moreover, for Nietzsche, slave morality is no less *creative* than master morality; it is the *motive* behind creative forming that differentiates master and slave (*GM* I, 10).

A careful reading of Nietzsche's texts does not support the thesis that his genealogy is exclusively a defense of crude physical power or overt social control. Throughout the writings, the meaning of weakness, strength, and power is polymorphous and far from clear. For instance, Nietzsche calls the values he criticizes necessary for life. Morality has been essential for human development in its contest with nature and natural drives (*WP* 403), and for this it deserves gratitude (*WP* 404). The exceptional individual is not the only object of honor for Nietzsche; the conditions of the ruled are equally important for the species (*GS* 55). The "weakness" of the herd mentality turns out to be a practical advantage, since it has prevailed over the strong: "The weak prevail over the strong again and again, for they are the great majority – and they are also more intelligent" (*TI* 9, 14). Indeed, the higher types of creative individuals that Nietzsche favors are more vulnerable and perish more easily, because of their complexity, in contrast to the simplified order of herd conditions (*BGE* 62).

In addition to recognizing the preserving strength of herd factors, Nietzsche can also shift perspective and talk about creativity as a form of "degeneracy" as measured against social norms (which adds a complicating element to Nietzsche's critical charge of degeneracy leveled against modern social forces). In *HAH* 224 (a section titled *Ennoblement through degeneration*), Nietzsche discusses the preserving "strength" of social custom counterposed against "morally weaker individuals" who cannot or will not fit in with social norms and capacities. Yet such individuals, precisely because they do not fit in, can discover new pathways and effect "spiritual progress." Nietzsche is playing on the fact that the *possibility* of innovation stems from misfits, who from the perspective of social cohesion *must* be perceived as weak or degenerate. So Nietzsche can analyze weakness and strength from various perspectives and show their shifting virtues and tensions. In this passage Nietzsche highlights the intrinsic tension of necessary forces in human life that promote both stability and novelty. The cohesion of "strong communities" faces the danger of a "gradually increasing inherited stupidity such as haunts all stability like its shadow." Individuals who are weak by social standards *may* bring forth new horizons, but it is also true that "countless numbers of this type perish on account of their weakness without producing any very visible effect." Yet when such types can discover something new, their "social degeneracy" corrects for the stupidity of "social strength."

Degenerate natures are of the highest significance wherever progress is to be effected. Every progress of the whole has to be preceded by a partial weakening. The strongest natures *preserve* the type, the weaker help it to *evolve*... The more sickly man, for example, will if he belongs to a war-like and restless race perhaps have more inducement to stay by himself and thereby acquire more repose and wisdom... To this extent the celebrated struggle for existence does not seem to me to be the only theory by which the progress or strengthening of a man or a race can be explained. Two things, rather, must come together: first the augmentation of the stabilizing force through the union of minds in belief and communal feeling; then the possibility of the attainment of higher goals through the occurrence of degenerate natures, and, as a consequence of them, partial weakenings and injurings of the stabilizing force; it is precisely the weaker nature, as the tenderer and more refined, that makes any progress possible at all.

Material such as this must be kept in mind when considering Nietzsche's complicated and ambiguous analysis of weakness and strength. In the *Genealogy* sections under discussion, the perspective on weakness and strength shifts to the debilitating capacity of social norms in slave morality measured against the natural strength and vitality of master morality. In sum it can be said that "weakness" can exhibit productive strength, but it matters whether this strength is understood from the perspective of social regulation or social transgression. Regulation is a cohesive strength, for which transgression is a weakness. Yet transgression (whether in master morality or innovative movement) is a life-advancing strength, for which cohesion is a weakness. The text sections at hand exhibit much of this perspectival ambiguity, which must be recognized if the course of Nietzsche's text is to be fathomed well.

In Section 11 Nietzsche introduces the notorious figure of "the blond beast of prey," which has been cited as evidence of Nietzsche's preference for brutality and force. But his discussion far from supports such a crude result. The slave's conversion of masterly "goodness" into "evil" is situated by Nietzsche in an expanded discussion of early cultural settings, particularly the stress between violent noble energies and noble society's *own* restraints of custom and social norms. Nietzsche indicates that nobles are able to release violent impulses *outside* their social territory, beyond the bonds of restraint, in the "wilderness" of foreign spheres. Here they can vent their "freedom" and engage in all sorts of violent acts; moreover, their exploits will be celebrated by poets as glorious achievements. Nietzsche mentions a host of noble cultures – a prime example being the Homeric world – to illustrate this dynamic, and he even cites Pericles' praise for Athenian daring and delight in dangerous, violent, victorious deeds.

Such cultural dynamics were certainly characteristic of early noble societies, and Nietzsche is happy to evoke them. But I must say that Section 11 is not at all clear in the course of its analysis. It is surely possible that the "blond beast" is Nietzsche's own rhetorical choice for embodying the virtues of noble vitality. But I think that it is at least as likely that this figure is the rhetorical choice for slave morality's *reinterpretation* of noble values. The discussion is launched out of the slave's inversion of noble goodness into evil, whereupon Nietzsche says that the slave now saw in any opponent "nothing but *evil enemies.*" It is right here that the discussion ensues of nobles as "caged beasts" outside the bonds of society. The two possible readings of the blond beast here need not be mutually exclusive, but I am trying to make sense of the full section by calling for some caution. The slave's charge of evil against the master would be *reinforced* by the image of the extra-social "beast," which would not likely be the nobility's own image for its exploits. In addition, the trajectory of Nietzsche's discussion is directed against a certain theory of culture, which assumes that "the *meaning of all culture*" is the taming of the human "animal," of the "beast of prey" looming in human nature. But Nietzsche clearly rejects this theory as the *full story* of culture. In fact he calls slavish "domestication" a cultural *decline*, a vindictive repression of human vitality. So the "blond beast" figure may be the construction of the slave-account of culture, which assumes that the masters are nothing but caged animals (as evidenced by their extra-social exploits), that their "cultural" posture as rulers is an inflection of this beastly core, and that consequently true civilization demands the overcoming of this aristocratic posture. I cannot say that I have complete confidence in my interpretation here, but I can simply ask the reader to follow the entire section carefully to see if it bears any fruit.[7]

There is another reason for being cautious about Nietzsche's supposed admiration for the blond beast. Near the end of the section he says: "We may be well justified in retaining our fear of the blond beast at the center of every noble race and remain on our guard." Nevertheless, it is the polarized picture of culture as the domesticated *antithesis* of animal nature that elicits Nietzsche's ire. He goes on to say that mixed with *admiration* for domesticating forces there should also be *fear* of the cultural consequences that have produced a docile, mediocre humanity presumed to be the highest achievement and meaning of history. There should be fear that there is no longer anything to fear of mankind. Nietzsche closes the section by encouraging the right to feel this fear, to feel a distance from the presumed human ideal of domestication, and he connects this critical distance with "still being capable of living" and with "saying Yes to life."

In Section 12 Nietzsche interjects a "last hope" he has concerning the dire effects of a pacifying, dulling, devitalizing culture inherited from slave morality. With domestication has come the "greatest danger" that nihilism will prevail, that the life-affirming and life-promoting effects of daring creative transgression and the heroic disdain for security will fade as mankind becomes more and more "improved," becomes "better-natured, more clever, more comfortable, more mediocre, more indifferent." The safer we become, the less we can experience the fearful challenges of life that actually give birth to and animate values. Nietzsche expresses his hope against nihilism with a surprising invocation:

But from time to time grant me – assuming that there are divine benefactresses beyond good and evil – a glimpse, grant me just one glimpse of

---

[7] For an insightful analysis, see Daniel W. Conway, "How We Became What We Are: Tracking the 'Beasts of Prey,'" in Acampora, ed., *Nietzsche's* On the Genealogy of Morals, pp. 305–320.

something perfect, finally successful, happy, powerful, triumphant, which still leaves something to fear! . . . Right here is where the destiny of Europe lies – in losing our fear of man we have also lost our love for him, our hope in him, and even our will to be man.

INTERLUDE:

BEFORE GOOD AND EVIL: HEROIC VALUES IN HOMER

Our analysis has shown that Nietzsche's push to move beyond good and evil is not a call to overcome morality, but only a certain kind of morality: the good–evil binary in slave morality and its displacement of the good–bad distinction in master morality. In Nietzsche's quasi-historical study of these two moral spheres, on occasion he draws on early Greek heroic values as an embodiment of master morality. At this point it might be helpful to explore in more detail some early Greek forms of valuation, in order to flesh out further Nietzsche's comparative treatment and what it could imply for Nietzsche's own philosophy. To this end I will offer a sketch of the heroic ideal in Homer's poetry. And I want to add something that is more implicit than explicit in the *Genealogy*: Master values may turn on successful achievement and victory over opponents, but as such they also coexist with the possibility of failure and defeat.[8] Indeed I want to argue that there is much to connect heroic life in Homer with a tragic world-view. Heroic/tragic elements in Greek poetry can be articulated as a kind of ethical sense that was specifically targeted by subsequent moral impulses, and that culminated in the good–evil scheme identified by Nietzsche as the source of Western nihilism.

With the notion of "tragic values" I follow the Nietzschean idea that the "value" of life can only be affirmed by coming to terms with its negative elements of death, loss, resistance, and failure; otherwise life as we have it becomes "nihilated" in the wake of otherworldly scripts or worldly projects of rectification. Tragic valuation, therefore, holds that whatever is good or worthy in life is necessarily checked by finite limits – and more, that *as* good or worthy it is necessarily informed by these limits, such that without these limits it would not *be* good or worthy.

---

[8] There is an indication of such a notion in *GM* I, 11, where Nietzsche talks of the "daring" of noble exploits in the face of uncertainty, improbability, and danger.

By considering a tragic element in Homer, I actually take a cue from Plato, who in the *Republic* calls Homer a tragic poet (598e, 605d). From the formal standpoint of poetic genres, this seems odd, but I believe that Plato was advancing the material point that both epic and tragic poetry present a view of *life* that ultimately limits human aspirations and that stands in the way of a moral reformation guided by the order of reason. As long as we read Plato's critique of poetry not as an epistemological judgment, but as a moral-cultural project of reform, we get a clearer sense of what is at stake in Plato's texts; and we also notice that Plato's account of the Greek poetic tradition as a tragic world-view is indeed accurate. And we note that Nietzsche identifies "Plato *versus* Homer" as a classic instance of life-denying force in Western thought (*GM* III, 25). The question at hand is whether a tragic world must be renounced as the antithesis of a moral life.

My claim is that Homeric poetry gives vivid expression of heroic values and their tragic character, and it can easily seem difficult to locate in Homer much of a sense of morality in our sense of the term. Yet this is precisely the virtue of Nietzsche's genealogical reflections on the history of morality. We can begin by considering the term "moral," not in terms of familiar principles of "right and wrong," but first in terms of valuing in a broad sense, of articulating what is worthy and unworthy, better or worse in human affairs, particularly what is worthy of praise and blame, which opens up the social element necessary for valuation.

In Homer, the praiseworthy is in most respects different from later moral outlooks, even to the point of being blameworthy in these systems. Rather than egalitarian, Homeric values are aristocratic; rather than a call for harmony and peace, they celebrate competition, strife, and power; and rather than a turn to an inward, reflective self, they embody the outward field of action, circumstance, worldly achievement, and social recognition. Moreover, within this field of values is an intrinsic fatalism that is manifested in two forms: (1) the divine management of heroic life – in the course of events generally, and even to the point of psychological intervention in heroic behavior; and (2) the pervasive force of death and ruination that ultimately cannot be mastered by mortals, or even by the gods themselves. Homeric fatalism gives us a first look at what "tragic valuation" might mean: (1) what is worthy cannot be attributed to full self-sufficiency; and (2) what is worthy is intrinsically caught up in limits and loss.

Early Greek myth and religion did not exhibit any transcendent realm beyond earthly life, but rather the sacred manifestations of all the forces and meanings in the lived world. The divine realm was divided into Olympian "sky" deities, marked by beauty and intelligence, and Chthonic "earth" deities of the underworld, marked by violence and brutish passion. Human beings live on the earth's surface, in between these two realms and subject to their competing powers. In religious practices, both realms were honored in rituals, at times conjointly. Moreover, Olympian gods often had Chthonic counterparts.[9] So these divine spheres were not separated from each other; their interpenetration was a part of Greek religious experience. Human life, therefore, dwelled in the ambiguity of sacred tensions: passion and moderation, natural drives and culture, malevolence and benevolence, death and life.

The most crucial feature in epic poetry is the horizon of death that limits human existence; humans are typically called "mortals," those who know that death is their ultimate fate (*Odyssey* 13.59–60), as opposed to the immortal gods. Death is the departure of the *psuchē*, or "life force," out of the living body.[10] There is a place for the departed *psuchē* in Hades, but this can hardly count as an afterlife in any meaningful sense. As depicted in Book 11 of the *Odyssey*, the realm of Hades is a shadow-world with none of the features of a living existence, a kind of ghostly, sleep-like condition that held no attraction at all for humans: Achilles tells Odysseus that he would rather be a poor laborer on earth than king of all the dead (485ff.); even the gods find Hades loathsome (*Iliad* 20.64–65). The dead cannot be said to have any kind of personal life: Hesiod calls the dead in Hades *nōnumnoi*, nameless and unknown (*Works and Days* 154); Homer says they are without intelligence or perception (*Odyssey* 11.475–476); death is at times associated with "forgetting" life (*Iliad* 16.776). The only sign of life for the dead is when they appear to the living, and

---

[9] See Burkert, *Greek Religion*, pp. 199–203.
[10] See David B. Claus, *Toward the Soul: An Inquiry into the Meaning of* Psuchē *Before Plato* (New Haven: Yale University Press, 1981).

then only as a phantom (*eidōlon*) that has no real substance (*Iliad* 23.99ff.; *Odyssey* 11.204ff.).

What are we to make of Hades, a "place" that is really "no place" when compared with life? The departed *psuchē* in Homer is not a "soul" apart from a body, but a visual *image* of a hero, indeed an image reflecting the specific circumstances and moment of a hero's death (*Odyssey* 11.40–41); and it is an image that cannot be "grasped," as illustrated by the *psuchē* of Odysseus' mother that flits away like a shadow when he tries to embrace her (11.206). I think it is useful to adopt a phenomenological approach to these renditions and the way they function in the poetic narrative. With Hades and the phantom *psuchē*, we can say that the absence of death is given a vivid *presence*, a life-*lacking* presence that is more than nothingness and less than life, a counter-*image* to life that in fact is more striking and more telling than an abstract nothingness or absence. In other words, the *meaning* of death as the absence or lack of living features is "placed" on the other side of life.[11] At the same time, the *value* of life is sharply enhanced against this repellant counter-image.[12] This is especially true in the context of Homeric poetry, where the normally stark divide between earth and Hades is bridged when a living hero encounters Hades and the phantom dead. Following Redfield, it seems right to say that the significance of Hades has more to do with the *living* than a straightforward description of a place called Hades.[13] In this way, the counter-image of Hades helps to shape some of the central themes in the life-narratives of Homeric poetry, the most significant of which is the heroic ideal.

The *Iliad* is built around the figure of Achilles, who faces an existential dilemma: He knows he is fated to die young in battle; if he left the war he would live a long life, but without the fame and glory attaching to death in battle. The heroic ideal can be organized around the following tensions: (1) Humans are essentially mortal and subject to fate (*Iliad* 6.488–489). (2) Although the hero's ultimate

---

[11] See Jean-Pierre Vernant, "*Psuchē*: Simulacrum of the Body or Image of the Divine?" in *Mortals and Immortals*, ed. Froma Zeitlin (Princeton: Princeton University Press, 1991).

[12] An excellent study on such themes is Jasper Griffen, *Homer on Life and Death* (Oxford: Oxford University Press, 1980).

[13] J. M. Redfield, *Nature and Culture in the* Iliad (Chicago: University of Chicago Press, 1975), pp. 177ff.

fate is death, he can achieve the worldly compensation of honor and the quasi-immortality of glory and fame. The heroes are often called god-like and god-favored, and they are honored by others as protectors and defenders (see *Iliad* 22.392ff. and 430ff.). (3) Honor, glory, and fame can only be achieved by risking one's life and facing death or defeat. (4) The courage to face death and risk life isolates and alienates the hero from normal life, but it also elevates him above the rest of humanity.

It is clear that heroic values are incongruous with what is *normally* most desirable in human life; and the importance of such normal values is vividly portrayed in the epics through the voices of female family members and children; and the appeal of these values to the heroes themselves is displayed in their emotional and often poignant conversations with family members.[14] Indeed, the course of both Homeric epics is animated by the value of the home: The *Iliad* begins with the breakup of a household and the *Odyssey* ends with the restoration of a household. And in both epics, particularly in the *Odyssey*, heroes experience the alienation from home life as part of their noble exploits. Homeric heroes, therefore, are not reckless thrill-seekers who spurn normal values. They encounter the dilemma of *conflicting* values: the benefits and importance of heroic achievement measured against the comforts, pleasures, and significance of home life; and all of this in the midst of mortality and fate.

Homeric poetry presents a much more nuanced account of heroism than simply the idea that heroes achieve their excellence and stature "despite" an indigenous mortality and fate. We can notice in the text a reciprocal relation between mortality and heroic values. The heroic ideal (and its larger importance for the community) can be seen as *informed* by mortality. The clearest example of this is found in Book 12 of the *Iliad*. After praising the virtue of fighting for one's country, Hektor asks a hesitant warrior: "Why are you so afraid of war and hostility?" (244). For us this can seem a strange question, but the heroic rationale is presented a short time later (310ff.), when Sarpedon says something to Glaukos right before they go into battle. His speech amounts to encouragement in the face of the heroic dilemma: Why, he asks, are they honored above other men and looked upon as gods?

---

[14] See Griffen, *Homer on Life and Death*, Ch. 4.

Why do they have wealth, land, status, and all their privileges at home? Because the people honor and admire their courage in defense of country. So if they want to preserve their status, it is necessary (*chrē*) for them to fight. But what about death? Sarpedon poses a hypothetical scenario: If they were ageless and immortal, they would not have to strive for glory, which is the source of their station. The meaning seems clear: If there were no death or danger, there would be no *need* for valor and its rewards. If a hero values aristocratic privilege, he must also value the possibility of death. Mortality and noble values, therefore, are structured together with reciprocal force. Accordingly, Sarpedon returns from his hypothetical back to mortal reality and closes his speech with these remarkable words: "But now, seeing that countless fates of death close around us – fates that no man can escape or avoid – let us go forward and gain glory for ourselves, or give it to others" (326–328).

Here we find exemplified the starkest sense in which human life dwells "between" Olympian and Chthonic forces, between the death-less gods and lifeless Hades. Both realms together give humans the attraction–repulsion dynamic that constitutes a *mortal* life, its virtues and limits.[15] The apportioned sphere of mortal existence "between" immortal life and Hades is delineated in the following way: (1) The *aversion* of both humans and deities to the realm of the dead high-lights the beauty and value of life – a vivid instance of this disclosive structure is given in Book 3 of the *Iliad* (428ff.); (2) The *exclusion* of humans from Olympian immortality assures the maintenance of this disclosive structure by forbidding mortals an escape from death. Although the heroes are praised for being god-*like*, they are always warned against over-stepping their limits. When Apollo is challenged by a warrior, he says: "Take care and fall back; do not think you can match the spirit of the gods, because never the same are the race of immortal gods and humans who walk the earth" (*Iliad* 5.434ff.). We should note that Apollo's famous maxim, "Know thyself," was not a call for self-discovery, but a reminder of one's limits, that one is not a god.[16]

Heraclitus tells us that justice (*dikē*) is strife, that the way of things and their meaning are structured by conflicting tensions, that "peace"

[15] Ibid., p. 162.   [16] Burkert, *Greek Religion*, p. 148.

would actually amount to nothingness or meaninglessness.[17] We can call this a formal account of the material narratives of conflict and its cultural significance in Greek poetry. Hesiod's *Theogony* presents an organization of this world-view by telling the story of "how the gods and the earth first came into being" (108) and the nature of their relationships. The early generation of Strife (*Eris*) in the *Theogony* is significant for understanding the specific narratives in epic poetry. The course and structure of the world-order in the *Theogony*, in fact, unfolds by way of violent battles between the progeny of Earth, which can be organized around the Chthonic–Olympian division. Olympian Zeus is ultimately victorious, yet the result is not the destruction of Chthonic forces but a threefold apportionment of power: Zeus (Olympus), Poseidon (Sea), and Hades (Underworld). Each god will have his own domain of power, which will be respected by the others. Divine strife is retained in Homer, but in a new manner. The original battles of the gods (as depicted in Hesiod) are in the past and have been resolved by the apportionment of divine powers. But an essential feature of Homeric poetry is the apparent need the gods have for witnessing and enjoying the spectacles of heroic conflict.[18] Indeed, the gods instigate most of the conditions and terms that prompt the mortal struggles they love to watch. Such elements in Homer have often been the source of consternation for readers of this picture of divinity, which seems to suggest that human life is just a plaything for the pleasure of the gods. Yet I think we should begin with a principle of charity that assumes serious intent and cultural value in epic narratives, at the very least in order to understand why Homer remained such a lasting source of education and exemplification. We should appreciate the rich portrayal of human action and divine observation as a serious and complex world-view that turns on the alluring, yet tragic character of earthly existence.

The overall narrative of gods and mortals in Homeric poetry suggests that the experience and witnessing of heroic conflict are the primary source of meaning for both humanity and divinity. The gods do not suffer from mortal limits; they are ageless and deathless,

[17] Fragment 80, G. S. Kirk, J. E. Raven, and M. Schofield, *The Presocratic Philosophers*, 2nd edn (Cambridge: Cambridge University Press, 1983), p. 193.
[18] See Griffen, *Homer on Life and Death*, Ch. 6.

they do everything with ease and generally live a life "without cares or sorrow" (*Iliad* 24.526). With their brutal struggles behind them, they nevertheless still need to witness and engage in the drama of human affairs. Like a theater audience, they find great pleasure and excitement at the sight of human exploits, without having to suffer their real consequences. They experience both joy and sorrow over the fluctuations of human fortune, even to the point of laughing and weeping. Yet unlike a theater audience, the gods also leave their abode to intervene in and influence events in the human drama. It is evident, then, that the tragic structure of meaning-amidst-limits is at the heart of epic poetry, because even the gods in their non-tragic condition seem to need the vicarious experience of mortal limits and conflict; and the gods sustain their own conflicted patterns in their engagement with human events.

We should surely concede that the epic world-view (as something more than mere "literature") presents an ambiguous array of human and divine values, which at the very least makes understandable the later complaints and criticisms of many Greek writers. Aside from the supposed "immoral" behavior of the gods – the target of Xenophanes and Plato, among others – the conflict *among* the gods in their engagement with mortal exploits presents unresolvable burdens on human "piety." That is to say, honoring or obeying "the gods" in a pluralized, conflicted sacred arena means that one and the same course of action can find both favor and disfavor among different gods – this is precisely why Socrates in the *Euthyphro* (7bff.) rejected the definition of piety as doing what is loved by the gods. Homeric heroes confront the *double* strife of their human contests that are also caught up in divine contests. Book 13 of the *Iliad* offers a clear model of this situation: The brothers Zeus and Poseidon are of "divided purpose" (*amphis phroneonte*) in their respective support for the Trojans and the Achaeans, and accordingly they are "fashioning grievous woes for mortal warriors," who are thus caught in an unbreakable "knot" of strife and war (345ff.).

What follows from the conflicted pluralism of early Greek religion is a kind of ethical ambiguity that might frustrate us, but that should be taken on its own terms as a lasting motif in Greek poetry: Heroic values give grandeur to mortal life, but in an environment constituted by strife between mortals, between deities, and between mortals and deities. Homeric "piety," therefore, cannot mean mere subservience or acquiescence to the gods or fate. The *global* network of multiple sacred forces shows that *resistance* to the gods and fate is not an irreligious disposition but an intrinsic consequence of this network when it comes to the *local* circumstance of a hero's particular actions or allegiance to a divine sponsor. Obedience or subjugation to one particular god entails resistance to another. Heroic achievement, then, cannot help but be an ambiguous virtue within the overall sacred order. Human life is both fated and free; it is neither autonomous nor slavish. The inaptness of any such binary code is another telling mark of the "tragic" that must be addressed when trying to assess Greek poetry and its depiction of life.

Given the competitive environment of the Homeric world, it is no surprise that the predominant value is power, especially for the gods but also for the heroic ideal of achievement in the midst of contention. In such a setting the many traits that might seem immoral for later moralities – pride, aggression, rank, and powerful emotions – should be taken (following Nietzsche) as a different kind of morality. Moreover, the epic self lacks a distinct sense of interiority because the primary standard of value is *performance* in an external field of action. Such a standard helps us understand the near-obsessive concern for honor (*timē*) in the manner of praise and reward. Honor too must be externalized, thus the fixation on tangible prizes and the spoils of victory. Excellence can only be measured by public signs of recognition. The wrath and withdrawal of Achilles may indeed be excessive, but they were brought on by Agamemnon's seizure of Briseis, Achilles' captured concubine; and this was surely an offense to heroic honor. Without an "internal" sense of worth, it would do no good to ask Achilles to "swallow" his pride, because his sense of worth is thoroughly informed by public measures and markers.

Another feature of heroic behavior that runs afoul of later moral assumptions is the absence of autonomy or a strict sense of responsibility. In addition to divine management and instigation in the course of events, the gods will often intervene in and alter the motives, emotions, and capacities of the heroes themselves.[19] Agamemnon even

---

[19] For example, see *Iliad* 5.185, 13.59–60, and 17.210–212.

describes his seizure of Briseis as the result of a divine seizure: "I am not responsible," he says, because Zeus and the fates "cast upon my heart fierce delusion (*atē*) that day, when in my arrogance I took from Achilles his prize. But what could I do? It is god that brings all things to completion" (19.86ff.). Yet the heroes do not seem to rebel against such intercessions as diminishments of their worth or to bemoan ruinous consequences as "unfair" or wretched enslavement to cruel deities. Once again, the Homeric self seems to be a confluence of fate and freedom, of noble achievement in the midst of forces larger than its own efforts.

The figure of Odysseus in the *Odyssey* is a remarkable expression of early Greek values.[20] He embodies the heroic tension of glory and alienation from home in the most acute manner. After the war he embarks on the long journey back to Ithaca and Penelope, a journey packed with danger, death, challenges, and the typical mix of assistance and hindrance from the gods. One of the continuing descriptions of Odysseus is a man who endures great suffering. Yet the word for endurance, *tlēnai*, can also mean resolve and daring. Odysseus exhibits great courage, resourcefulness, and intelligence in the face of his troubles on the way home.

Odysseus is called *polutropos*, a man of "many ways," which can also mean "many turns," to capture the shifting personas and behaviors he displays in the varying contexts of his journey. He is also called the man of many "wiles" (*kerdea*) and "tricks" (*doloi*), and his ventures are permeated with a host of deceptions in speech and performance. The term summing up such traits is *mētis*, or cunning, which to us can seem morally questionable. Yet *mētis* contains much ambiguity because it can also mean wisdom, skill, craft, and planning. In any case, Odysseus' capacity for *mētis* is not put into question morally in the poem because it is a skill required of Odysseus in his many circumstances of challenge and danger. Without *mētis* he would not have succeeded in his quest for return. To the dismay of many later critics, *mētis* is even affirmed as a divine virtue. After Athena recounts Odysseus' renown for cunning, crafty counsel, and artful stories, she

---

[20] For reflections on Nietzsche and Odysseus, see Daniel W. Conway, "Odysseus Bound?" in *Why Nietzsche Still? Reflections on Drama, Culture, and Politics*, ed. Alan D. Schrift (Berkeley: University of California Press, 2000), pp. 28–44.

notes that they are both well versed in this manner, and she says, "I among all the gods am famed for cunning (*mēti*) and wiles (*kerdesin*)" (*Odyssey* 13.291ff.). Concealing truth, therefore, is affirmed as a virtue, but not as an absolute value; rather, it is a capacious virtue for success in certain contexts of practice in the face of obstacles and threats.

The most important feature of the Odysseus figure has to do with what I think is the dramatic core of the poem: the affirmation of mortality in the course of homecoming. We have noted how heroic values are informed by death and alienation from normal values. Odysseus' arduous journey is obviously a condition of alienation, but it aims for a restoration of the values of home life that heroes also hold dear. Yet since Odysseus survives his ordeal and is restored to his homeland, shouldn't we take his story as something other than tragic when compared with Achilles?

If the question is posed in terms of mortality the answer is clearly No. In Book 5 Odysseus is being held captive by the beautiful goddess Calypso, and is longing to return to Penelope and Ithaca. Calypso surprises him by saying she will release him for his journey home (he is not told that she was commanded to do so by Zeus). Calypso, however, has enticed him to stay by offering to make him "immortal and ageless all his days" (5.136). She enhances the offer by foretelling how much suffering he will have to endure on the way back, and by reminding him how much more beautiful and glorious she is than his mortal wife. Odysseus nevertheless turns down Calypso's offer, while conceding that she is finer in form than Penelope. Despite the vital benefits and pleasures of this proposal, he still longs to return to Ithaca. As for the pains and perils of his journey, he says: "I will endure it, having in my breast a heart that endures suffering. For before now I have toiled and suffered much amid the waves and in war; let this trouble be added to those" (5.221–224).

This is a stunning moment in the poem. With the condition of mortality and limits in the Homeric world, Odysseus is offered release, so that Sarpedon's hypothetical immortality is now a real prospect. Yet Odysseus refuses and thus *chooses* to trade an ageless and deathless existence for his mortal life with Penelope, along with the sufferings that will accompany his return to that life. And it should be noted that Odysseus makes this choice *after* he had witnessed the grim reality of Hades. This episode in the text is remarkable in being the utmost possible affirmation of mortality, because it is a deliberate refusal of immortality. And my claim for the importance of this episode in the poem can be borne out by the text, because it is highlighted right at the start of the narrative in Book 1. The gods are surveying the situation of Odysseus' story and the Calypso scene is cited first (11ff.). The captivity of the hero is marked by his suffering at being kept from home. Calypso is trying to beguile him into forgetting Ithaca, but Odysseus, "in his yearning even just to see the smoke rising from his own land, longs to die (*thaneein himeiretai*)" (1.57–59). We might read this simply as despair, in the sense that he just wants to be put out of his misery. But in context I think it is more plausible to read this as a powerful forecast of the meaning and import of his coming choice: In yearning to return home he must also yearn for mortality. Homecoming in the poem is far more than simply a return to home life; it is also a recollection and reclamation of mortal finitude.

In sum, Achilles and Odysseus both embody from different angles the tragic structure of significance and value. Both encounter the coincidence of death and meaning in their lives. If we keep in mind that normal values of home and hearth are part of the epic world, then Achilles and Odysseus can be understood in their tragic dimension, in terms of what they must sacrifice for meaning. Both live for the heroic ideal, but Achilles is the one who perishes and pays the ever-looming price for heroic action: he sacrifices normal life for glory and fame. Odysseus does not pay this price in the war, but he sacrifices immortality for the heroic return to normal life. The two epics together can be said to celebrate the value of heroic deeds *and* normal life in one sweeping narrative; and both spheres of value are affirmed in the face of death and fate, indeed these spheres are *informed* by the force of mortality and limits.

I hope that this interlude has provided a richer historical perspective for understanding Nietzsche's genealogy of morality. Indeed we will take up the theme of the tragic in Greek thought again in a later discussion, to keep in play my belief that the notion of tragic values is an essential factor in whatever moral sense of the world can be attributed to Nietzsche, and that various forms of resistance to the tragic are a common feature in the moral and intellectual traditions challenged by Nietzsche.[21]

After his expression of hope for new possibilities, in Section 13 Nietzsche returns to the historical discussion of master and slave conceptions of goodness. To illustrate the difference he presents an image of birds of prey victimizing lambs. In such a natural setting it is no surprise that the lamb resents the bird of prey, but this is no reason to blame the bird for carrying off the lamb. Nietzsche says that actually there should be no objection to the lamb judging the bird as evil, except that the bird would see things differently. The bird will simply view the lamb-ideal with derision and bear no grudge against it – indeed the bird loves (to eat) the lamb.

At this point Nietzsche engages a fundamental position that occurs again and again in his writings: a critique of free agency (this part of the text will be quite important for interpreting the opening sections of the Second Essay). From a natural standpoint the power of the bird cannot be blameworthy because it cannot help but express itself. The resentful judgment of the lamb presumes that the bird could refrain from its violent actions. Here Nietzsche is targeting a long-standing assumption in Western moral philosophy and ethical sensibilities: that moral blame must presuppose the possibility to act otherwise and thus the freedom to choose whether or not to act in a certain way. Yet Nietzsche claims that the force of the bird's action is its very nature; it could not act otherwise. He notes "the seduction of language" that tempts us to distinguish an agent from its deeds by way of the grammatical difference between nouns and verbs (The eagle killed the lamb). Nietzsche believes that the very notion of agency is a fiction born from such linguistic constructions. For Nietzsche, activity itself is primal; it is not "caused" by an "agent." But moral judgment relies on just such a fiction of agency.

... popular morality separates strength from the manifestations of strength, as though there were an indifferent substratum behind the strong person

[21] Bernard Williams offers extensive discussion of Greek values counterposed to modern moral assumptions in *Shame and Necessity* (Berkeley: University of California Press, 1993).

which had the *freedom* to manifest strength or not. But there is no such substratum; there is no "being" behind the deed, its effect and what becomes of it; "the doer" is invented as an afterthought – the doing is everything.

Nietzsche tells us that emotions of revenge *require* a belief in free agency, since otherwise moral blame and responsibility would be futile exercises. For those driven by moral revenge, nothing is defended more vigorously "than that *the strong are free* to be weak, and the birds of prey are free to be lambs – in this way they gain the right to make the birds of prey *responsible* for being birds of prey." It is only the weak lamb that requires concepts of freedom and responsibility in order to rectify its powerlessness and suffering. Now the strong are deemed "free" to renounce their power, and weakness (not exhibiting power) is converted into an "accomplishment," something chosen, desired, and thus something virtuous and praiseworthy. Nietzsche says that the concept of a "subject" – which is "free" to choose its course (of exercising or not exercising power) – has been crucial for the self-preservation and self-affirmation of the downtrodden, in that it has given natural weakness its meaning, its simultaneous judgment of the strong and valorization of the lowly. Yet here Nietzsche does not utterly disparage the value and importance of free moral agency; indeed he says that it "has been, until now, the best doctrine on earth." Until now . . .

Section 14 catalogues how various incapacities of the weak are converted by slave morality into admirable virtues that are an "accomplishment" as something chosen. Impotence now becomes a primary measure of "goodness," timidity is now the virtue of "humility," submission to the strong is now "obedience," cowardice is now "patience," and an incapacity for actual revenge is now "forgiveness" and loving one's enemies. Such values represent, for Nietzsche, a kind of alchemy that makes a virtue out of necessity. With external subordination to the master, slave morality fashions an "internal" sphere that judges master values as inferior to slave virtues, and this internalized sphere is even promoted as a recipe for happiness.

But how can such a revised measure of virtue and happiness gain traction and attraction in worldly circumstances of deprivation? Here the images of a promised life of bliss after death provide incentive and motivation. But such rewards come only in the future in another life, and so the slave type can only "in the meantime" present *earthly* life as a preparation for bliss and as a *continuation* of servile characteristics now converted into estimable virtues. In the context of Christian morality, Nietzsche says that the slave's life on earth can only be one of "faith" (in salvation), "hope" (for its rewards), and "love" (expressed toward all the abusive conditions of earthly life).

In Section 15 Nietzsche turns a merciless look at the twofold character of the Last Judgment in Christian morality: eternal rewards for the righteous and eternal punishments for the wicked. Here Nietzsche is highlighting his contention that slave morality is not only the rectification and elevation of weak values, but also a deferred expression of a desire for power *over* the master (which cannot be actualized in natural conditions). But Nietzsche's analysis reaches further than simply the understandable notion that "our abusers will get their just deserts some day." He plumbs the psychology of resentment that has a current *need* for experiencing the satisfaction and delight that turning the tables on the master would provide.

As evidence for his psychological diagnosis, Nietzsche offers two documents from the Christian theological tradition. First he cites Aquinas, who says that the bliss of paradise is *enhanced* by the *enjoyment* of witnessing the torments of the damned (one wonders why simply *knowing* of these torments would not suffice for bliss, why *seeing* the torments is required). Then Nietzsche cites the remarkable passage from Tertullian, which goes one better than Aquinas with a detailed picture of such a spectacle. In one respect the passage is a full condemnation of the pagan world, but it does this by out-bidding the *attractions* of that world with greater enhancements in the world to come. The context of Tertullian's message is his advice to early Christians not to attend cruel pagan spectacles, which will tempt them toward worldly vices. His reasons turn on the comparative worth of Christian motifs: martyrs rather than athletes, the blood of Christ rather than bloodlust. But then Tertullian touts the alternative "spectacles" awaiting believers after the "old world" has been consumed by fire and God's judgment has been meted out. He forecasts: Think of the marvelous sights available then! We will be able to gaze with wonder, exultation, and laughter at scenes of worldly and anti-Christian figures wailing in their eternal torture in hellfire. Not surprisingly, political rulers who had persecuted Christians are described in their reversed fortune. But even philosophers (uh-oh) who had argued against Christianity and spiritual realities are burned in torment. Yet more surprising is the list of cultural types who are likewise doomed: poets and tragic actors scream out upon their judgment, not by a tribunal in an arts competition, but by "the unexpected Christ." Even mime actors are tortured (well, maybe this is not so surprising). Athletes, too, are on fire. Such is the range of pagan activities brought to justice at the end of the world. Tertullian also describes an *"insatiable* gaze" cast upon the sufferings of those who abused Christ on earth. He then asks his audience: What benefactor on earth could provide anything comparable to "seeing and *exulting in such things?"* Even at present, he says, we can have access to such things through faith and "the imagining spirit." The passage closes with a wrap-up of its advisory purpose when Tertullian claims that the spectacles of the Last Judgment are "more pleasing" than any pagan circus or race-track.

Nietzsche is happy to quote this amazing passage because it confirms his psychological account of resentment in slave morality. One wonders if Nietzsche is being fair by exploiting the passage as a central element in Christian morality. Yet the texts from Aquinas and Tertullian are there to be engaged. Perhaps they were simply props offered to common believers, but even so Nietzsche is entitled to open up the question of why such dispositions may have arisen at all. His hyperbolic approach may provoke us to examine human psychology and moral motivation by asking: What is our disposition toward moral offense and what is the source of this disposition? Such questions pervade the *Genealogy* and are not restricted to Christianity. Christian morality does represent the clearest (and most successful) example of a moral psychology that Nietzsche wants to expose for criticism. And we can be prompted to wonder about the implications of Tertullian's exhortation. Why would he talk of an "insatiable gaze" upon torments that go on for eternity? Would it be unsatisfying to have these torments end at a point and have the wicked simply put out of existence (torture *plus* capital punishment)? Or what would be lacking if the salvation scheme simply rewarded the virtuous with a blissful existence and mandated nothingness for the wicked? Why is retribution necessary and why need it take on a form of total (and eternal) victory? Part of Nietzsche's answer is that a worldly lack of overt power not only redirects power to the inward imagination (confirmed by Tertullian's "imagining spirit"), but the lack of any worldly satisfaction and its effects also prompts an escalation of power beyond its natural (agonistic) structure of overcoming something toward the unnatural vision of a total disarmament and degradation of opponents.

In any case, Nietzsche's interest in the retributive vision of Christianity does not really concern its specific content, which from his standpoint is sheer fiction. What matters to Nietzsche is how such a fiction is symptomatic of a certain form of *life* that came to contest and succeed master morality, how a "supernatural" vision had natural *effects* in promoting the self-overcoming of more natural expressions of power. In particular, the link between slave morality and a morally responsible free will was a prime example of a powerful effect on life that changed human history. One way to put this point is as follows: We could imagine a version of slave morality that simply counseled passive subjugation to the master with only the prospect of future salvation as the focus of interest. But for Nietzsche it is unsurprising that this was not the case, because his naturalism dictates that immanent life-effects are the only "real" issue, and the history of slave morality bears this out in the sense that salvation was not enough. The doctrine of free will and responsibility showed that slave morality was not satisfied simply with otherworldly rectification; it wanted to *convert* master morality to the slave perspective, so that the strong would *willingly* renounce their worldly forms of power and way of life.

THE CONTINUING CONFLICT OF MASTER AND SLAVE VALUES (SECTIONS 16–17)

In Section 16 Nietzsche brings the First Essay to conclusion. The opposition between good–bad and good–evil has been a "terrible battle" on earth for thousands of years. Nietzsche's shorthand "symbol" for this oppositional history is "Judea against Rome." Rome, he says, saw the Judaic-Christian religion as something contrary to nature and as a hatred against the rest of mankind. And he singles out the Apocalypse of John as the most telling indication of the

Judaic-Christian estimation of the pagan world: The Second Coming of Christ will produce a sweeping conflagration that obliterates the wicked in a decidedly martial display of divine force and retribution. Nietzsche identifies the eventual conversion of pagan Rome to Christianity (and the Holy Roman Empire of subsequent history) as conclusive evidence of the victory of Judaic-Christian morality over noble morality. Although slave morality has been dominant in European history, Nietzsche points to instances of noble morality that had emerged nevertheless: in Rome, the Renaissance, and with figures such as Napoleon. In addition to identifying the key forces of slave morality in Judaism and Christianity, he also names continuations of moral resentment in the Reformation and the French Revolution.

It is important to recognize that in this section Nietzsche reiterates an ambiguity in the master–slave opposition. Beyond the historical examples of noble morality he had mentioned, he says something that we should note is put in the present tense: Despite the victory of slave morality and its enduring power over master morality,

There is still no lack of places where the battle remains undecided. One might even say that meanwhile it has been raised ever higher and because of this it has become ever more profound and more spiritual (*geistiger*): so that there is today perhaps no more decisive mark of the "*higher nature,*" the spiritual nature, than to be divided in this sense and actually be another battleground for these opposites.

This is a very significant passage that can be compared with a remark in *Beyond Good and Evil* 260. There Nietzsche introduced the opposition between master and slave morality. But before he even begins to describe the two standpoints, he interjects:

I add immediately that in all higher and mixed cultures attempts to mediate between the two moralities also appear, yet more often a confusion and mutual misunderstanding of the two, indeed on occasion their severe, difficult coexistence (*Nebeneinander*) – even in the same person, within a single soul.

Such remarks are crucial provisos for coming to understand the meaning and scope of Nietzsche's genealogy. The conflict between master and slave morality is not exclusively a matter of two discrete cultural camps. The conflict can be *mediated* within a culture and even within a single self. The reason why this is important has already been intimated when we noted that the original sphere of master morality was rather crude and that the slave mentality allowed for more refined and deeper cultural possibilities. In other words, the reason why Nietzsche does not reject the importance of slave morality goes beyond its value for sustaining weaker types. The slave mentality opened up creative pathways that were an advance beyond the limited sphere of the original masters. Moreover, Nietzsche believes that such creative pathways can intersect with noble dispositions to generate an advance beyond *both* the original master *and* slave morality by "mediating" their opposition. We will have much more to say about this in coming discussions.

The brief concluding Section 17 offers more intimations that Nietzsche's genealogy is not simply a historical account of slave morality's displacement of master morality. He asks if the conflict between these ideals has come to an end or if there are still possibilities of its being furthered after the ascension of slave morality. He asks if one should not desire and even promote the furtherance of this conflict. He then closes with an indication of his own posture on the question of morality, his own interest in retrieving in some way elements of noble morality as a correction for the dominance of slave morality. He addresses his readers on this matter with the following assumption:

that it has been sufficiently clear for some time what I *want*, what I actually want with that dangerous slogan which is written on the spine of my last book, *Beyond Good and Evil*. . . at least this does *not* mean "Beyond Good and Bad." –

Nietzsche not only grants historical importance to the good–bad distinction in noble morality, he also considers this distinction to be a workable alternative to the good–evil distinction for his own thinking on morality, his own recommendations for a moral sense that can overcome traditional versions of slave morality. We will have more to say on how we might understand Nietzsche's own sense of ethics in due course.

CHAPTER 4

The second essay: "Guilt," "Bad Conscience," and related matters

> The second essay offers the psychology of the *conscience* – which is not, as people may believe, "the voice of God in man": it is the instinct of cruelty that turns back after it can no longer discharge itself externally. Cruelty is here exposed for the first time as one of the most ancient and basic substrata of culture that simply cannot be imagined away.
>
> (*EH* III, GM)

FORGETTING, MEMORY, AND PROMISING (SECTIONS 1–2)

The Second Essay builds on the psychology of slave morality while also pointing beyond its early forms toward its later progeny in modern culture and the crisis of this inheritance for human life that represents the ultimate target of Nietzsche's genealogy. Section 1 begins with a claim that gathers Nietzsche's historical treatment into a specific focus on "promising," which marks the course of morality's conflict with more natural drives: "To breed an animal with the prerogative to *promise* – is that not precisely the paradoxical task that nature has set herself with regard to humankind?" In fact Nietzsche calls this process *the* "real problem of humankind." As we will see, the capacity to make promises functions as a central phenomenon in moral and political life, and it also serves to regulate time and becoming in important new ways. In any case, Nietzsche indicates that the task of producing a promising animal "has been solved to a large degree," which means that the human world has indeed come to be shaped by the measure of promising. Yet, continuing his genealogical tactic of disturbing the complacency of established beliefs, Nietzsche situates promising in the midst of its natural "opposing force, *forgetfulness.*" Forgetfulness, he tells us, is not simply some passive inertia that loses awareness of an event; it is "an active ability to inhibit" conscious memory, an ability that is "positive in the strictest sense" and "a form of *robust* health." Why? An excess of conscious memory would confine us to a fixation on the past and thus retard open activity toward the future. Nietzsche claims that the *benefit* of active forgetfulness is that it makes room for "the new" and for the "more noble functions" of ruling, foreseeing, and predetermining. Moreover, he says that "there could be no happiness, no cheerfulness, no hope, no pride, no *present* without forgetfulness."

Active forgetting, as I read it, is not so much the absence or the loss of memory as the *letting go* of the past so that life can move on, so to speak. I believe that the notion of active forgetting plays a fundamental role in Nietzsche's genealogical critique of slave morality. I will have more to say about this in due course, but for now I want to suggest that active forgetting opens up an alternative to slavish resentment because it is the letting go of *moral offense*. This would not mean literally forgetting that one was harmed, nor would it require forgiveness; rather, it is an active passing beyond the psychological *effect* of being harmed, the offense taken at the injury, and the retention of offense in the memory.

Some support for my reading can be found in Section 10 of the First Essay, and I would like to digress somewhat to explore the ramifications of that text. Near the end of the section, Nietzsche is discussing the noble characteristic of straightforward speech and spontaneous displays of action, attributes that were typically contrasted with the base "deceptiveness" of slave types. Nietzsche notices something that may not be as pejorative as the noble assessment of weaker types when he says: "A race of such men of *ressentiment* will inevitably end up *more clever* (*klüger*) than any noble race, and will respect cleverness to a quite different degree as well." Nietzsche describes noble activity as being governed by "*unconscious* instincts," which cannot mean simply automatic behavior, but rather *unreflective* behavior owing to the self-manifesting success of noble power. The slave type, because of its subjugation and the continuing blockage of its interests, finds some small advantage in warding off abuse through dissemblance, through insincere deference, concealed intentions, or fabricated defenses of alleged misdeeds. The point is that such capacities emerge within certain contexts that render them less a character flaw (as nobles would have it) and more an appropriate tactic in circumstances of diminished power and impeded agency. Proof of this can be found in the celebrated virtue of Odysseus' cunning and deceptiveness. In the setting of his precarious journey, unmoored from the advantages and controls of his rule in Ithaca, Odysseus was able to succeed because of various concealments in the face of continuing danger. In any case, there is established in this section a certain counter-tension between instinctive spontaneity and reflection, which is a lasting theme in Nietzsche's writings. But my present purposes are served by what is said next in the section.

Nietzsche maintains that the lack of reflective cleverness in noble types accounts for their daring in the midst of danger and their typical "sudden fits" of emotion, such as anger, love, and revenge. Because of the nonreflective immediacy of their emotions, Nietzsche says that when a noble person does experience something like resentment, "it is consumed and exhausted in an immediate reaction, and therefore it does not *poison*." Homeric heroes certainly displayed such emotional bearings. Embedded in their active circumstances without much of an inwardness that might pause before reacting, the warriors are given to immediate and forceful expressions of rage, rejoicing, lamentation, and weeping. Yet because such emotions are not "internalized," they do not persist beyond their circumstantial origin and expression; they quickly subside after their public ventilation.[1] In Homeric psychology, rage is not internalized into a lingering "hatred," grief does not become "despair," fear does not become "anxiety."

Nietzsche goes on to say that a noble person – because of the immediacy of emotion and the external resources of power and accomplishment – does not get trapped in persisting negative dispositions; a noble individual is "unable to take his enemies, his misfortunes, even his *misdeeds* seriously for long." There is here an "abundance of power" that can "make one forget." Nietzsche specifically distinguishes such forgetting from forgiveness, and this suggests the kind of active moral forgetting that I have highlighted as an essential ingredient of Nietzsche's genealogy.

---

[1] A common construction in Homer has a hero moving on "after having taken his fill of lamentation" (see, for example, *Iliad* 24.513). In fact this usage stems from the word *terpō*, which connotes the pleasure of satisfying an appetite.

The end of the section draws a final implication of noble dispositions, and it amounts to an agonistic conception of noble conflict
that is contrasted with what could be called the "antagonistic" format
of good and evil in slave morality. We recall that the concepts of good
and bad in master morality had a relational, inclusive structure. Yet
here Nietzsche is going beyond the superiority–inferiority relation of
master and slave to entertain the relational (agonistic) structure of
values *within* the noble sphere itself and *between* noble competitors.
Nietzsche declares:

How much respect a noble man has for his enemies! – and a respect of that
sort is a bridge to love . . . For he wants his enemy for himself, as a mark of
distinction, indeed he can bear no other enemy than one in whom there is
nothing to be despised and *very much* to honor!

Once again Homeric poetry offers exemplifications of Nietzsche's
position. There seems to be an agonistic structure of worth in the *Iliad*
that is not reducible to any particular agent or side of the conflict. It is
evident that both the Greeks and the Trojans are displayed in a worthy
light; and both sides are favored by (different) deities. There are many
instances of admiration and respect between mortal combatants in
the midst of vicious fighting. In Book 7, as Ajax prepares to do battle
with Hektor, the following prayer is voiced:

Father Zeus, most great and glorious, watching over us from Ida, grant Ajax
victory and glorious renown; but if you love Hektor too and care for him,
grant to both of them equal might and glory. (202–205)

After their brutal and exhausting fight, Hektor proposes to Ajax that
they stop their battle and agree to a postponement, so that they can
"fight again until the divinity chooses between us" (291–292). Then
they exchange gifts! The effect of this moment, Hektor says, is that
both the Greeks and the Trojans will be able to say: "The two of them
truly fought in the rivalry of heart-devouring strife, but thereafter they
made an agreement and parted in friendship" (301–302).

Nietzsche finds enormous importance and value in this kind of
competitive respect because it combines a contentious will to power
with the *honoring* of opponents as co-constituents of achievement

and worth. In another text he develops this idea with specific reference to the Homeric sense that "the Trojan and the Greek are both good" (*HAH* 45). Nietzsche closes the section with a pointed contrast between agonistic respect and the construction of the "evil" enemy in slave morality, the enemy that is not to be "contested" but liquidated. Nietzsche even takes some devilish pleasure in nominating agonistic respect as the only possible sense in which "loving one's enemies" could be achievable on earth.

This has been a lengthy digression, but I think it can be helpful for comprehending the scope and reach of "forgetting" in Nietzsche's analysis of moral psychology. Returning to the question of promising in Section 1 of the Second Essay, we should ask: What does it mean to make a promise? If I promise to do something I am intending to insure a future act with a present prediction, and in that future I must bind my action by the memory of my now past promise. A sincere promise, therefore, gathers time into a secure shape and can do so only by working against the uncertainty of the future and the drift of the past into the absence of forgetting. This is why Nietzsche stresses the dynamic of memory and forgetting in his discussion of promise-making. Memory is the "counter-capacity" to active forgetting that must be bred into humans if promising is to be possible. But because forgetting is such a natural (and healthy) force, this kind of memory cannot be simply a passive retention; it must be *actively* cultivated. As Nietzsche puts it, a promise "is an active *desire* not to let go, a desire to keep on desiring what has been once desired, a genuine *memory of the will*." Consequently there is an intrinsic conflict between promising and forgetting because the power of memory required for promising is an *active* desire to work against *active* forgetting. If a future act of the will is to be bound by a present promise, a "world of strange new things" has to emerge "in between" the present, the future, and the past so that this "long chain of the will" cannot be broken. Promising implies a "control over the future" and it presupposes a host of new capacities to regulate time. Mankind must *learn* to distinguish between accident and design and to think causally, which means:

to view the future as the present and anticipate it, to grasp with certainty the difference between ends and means to those ends, in all, to be able to calculate, predict – and before he can do this, man himself must first have become *predictable, regular, necessary,* even in his own self-image, so that as someone making a promise he is answerable for his own *future!*

In Section 2 Nietzsche identifies this development of promise-making as "the long history of the origin of *responsibility,*" which aims to establish the individual self as the source of action and the locus of accountability for action. Since moral responsibility of this sort is so familiar to us, Nietzsche persists in forcing us to consider the vast course of historical practices that was required as a "precondition and preparation" for the emergence of responsibility, a notion which therefore is not a timeless characteristic of human nature but something that came forth in history. Because promising was at odds with the natural power of forgetting, it had to struggle for its place in human life. So before the responsibility of the promising individual could fully take shape, there had to ensue "the more immediate task of first *making* man to a certain degree necessary, uniform, a peer among peers, regular, and consequently predictable." It is here that Nietzsche cites the "morality of custom," the original and longest-running manner in which human beings were given their norms. He refers to an earlier text (*Daybreak* I, 9) as a source for his thinking on this matter: The morality of custom is essentially a culture of *tradition,* where the individual self must be subjugated to the community's values, which are inherited by and instilled within the individual by the force of convention and conformity. Because such a conventional system had to work against individuated traits and the natural power of forgetting, such early societies had to enforce their norms with visible and cruel forms of public punishment. Such displays created a powerful "register" in consciousness that would prompt the capacity of memory to retain the force of communal norms.

Let us get our bearings here. The opening sections of the Second Essay are trying to establish a genealogy of moral responsibility, which shows that what we take for granted is not a timeless property but a historical emergence that had to battle countervailing forces for its place in history. Moreover, Nietzsche is presuming a *naturalistic* genealogy, which means that something like moral responsibility cannot be based in some transcendent source different from finite life, some "pure" origin that in fact would presuppose the existence of the moral norm (say, in the mind of God) before it comes to pass in life. For Nietzsche, the origins of moral responsibility can only be located in actual historical practices, and it is evident that early human cultures did in fact engage in cruel forms of punishment to enforce their norms. So the structure of Nietzsche's genealogical strategy runs as follows: The modern sense of moral responsibility developed out of the capacity of memory and promising to overcome active forgetting and to render people predictable. This development required a long history of "breeding" that capacity in people, and such a breeding process, in a strictly natural setting, required cruel interventions and violence to overcome competing natural forces. Nietzsche will elaborate on this natural history of punishment in Section 3, but here he simply summarizes the notion that modern conceptions of moral responsibility would not have been possible apart from the *help* of earlier, even "prehistoric," forms of life, despite their apparent "hardness and tyranny." Today we might easily look back on such times as barbaric, but Nietzsche's claim is that our own sense of human (and presumably more humane) responsibility entails a structure of predictable, accountable promise-making (built from memory's regulation of time and forgetting), and that this structure owes its possibility to previous forms of communal force and violence, because "with the help of the morality of custom and the social straitjacket, man was *made* actually predictable."

THE SOVEREIGN INDIVIDUAL (SECTIONS 2–3)

In Section 2, right after sketching the process of mankind being made predictable, Nietzsche adds the following:

If we place ourselves, however, at the end of this terrible process where the tree actually bears fruit, where society and its morality of custom finally reveal what they were simply *the means to*: we then find the *sovereign individual* as the ripest fruit on its tree.

Most commentators have assumed that the sovereign individual expresses in some way Nietzsche's ideal of a self-creating individual in contrast to the herd, but I am not convinced.[2] The "sovereign individual" (*souveraine Individuum*) is a term that appears nowhere else in Nietzsche's published writings, only here in the context of Nietzsche's treatment of promising and responsibility. In my reading, the sovereign individual names the modern ideal of individual rational autonomy, which is something that Nietzsche critiques as a vestige of slave morality. The sovereign individual is the result of the "long history" of making people calculable and uniform for the sake of promising and moral responsibility.

In the passage above there is an ambiguity about the "end of this process." Those who take the sovereign individual to be an anticipation of Nietzsche's own "men of the future" read the end as ahead of the present. But it is more plausible to read the end as the modern consummation of premodern sources; a "ripe fruit" is more likely something that has been actualized, and in Section 3 it is called a "late fruit." If "placing ourselves at the end" were to forecast a coming possibility, the more likely language would be something like "if we look to the end," and "bears fruit" would be "will bear fruit." Moreover, in Section 3 Nietzsche clearly states that this process culminates in the power of *reason* to control the affects. The sovereign individual is called "an autonomous, supra-moral individual," because "autonomous" and "moral" are "mutually exclusive" (*GM* II, 2). This can surely sound like a Nietzschean liberation from morality, but the German term for "supra-moral" is *übersittlich*, and the sovereign individual has been liberated from *der Sittlichkeit der Sitte*, the morality of custom. It seems that *übersittlich* is more in

---

[2] Commentators have tended to read the sovereign individual as the model for the creative type and/or as having applications to liberal politics. See the following: Mark Warren, *Nietzsche and Political Thought* (Cambridge, MA: MIT Press, 1988); David Owen, "Equality, Democracy, and Self-Respect: Reflections on Nietzsche's Agonal Perfectionism," *Journal of Nietzsche Studies* 24 (Fall 2002), 113–131; Keith Ansell-Pearson, "Nietzsche: A Radical Challenge to Political Theory?" *Radical Philosophy* 54 (Spring 1990), 10–18; Bonnie Honig, *Political Theory and the Displacement of Politics* (Ithaca, NY: Cornell University Press, 1993), pp. 47–49; and Richard White, *Nietzsche and the Problem of Sovereignty* (Urbana: University of Illinois Press, 1997). For a time I think I was alone in questioning these interpretations (*A Nietzschean Defense of Democracy*, pp. 36–39). But there is now a little movement in my direction, thanks to Christa Davis Acampora's picking up my point and offering a more extensive discussion of its salience measured against previous readings. See her essay, "On Sovereignty and Overhumanity: Why It Matters How We Read Nietzsche's *Genealogy* II, 2," in Acampora, ed., *Nietzsche's* On the Genealogy of Morals, pp. 147–161.

line with the modernist notion of liberation from custom and tradition (*Sitte*), and therefore it is closer to the modern construction of rational morality (*Moralität*), and the term Nietzsche generally uses for morality is *Moral*. We should note that it is Kant who would declare rational autonomy and moral custom to be mutually exclusive. Finally, later in the same passage, the sovereign individual is described as claiming power over fate, which surely does not square with Nietzsche's insistence on *amor fati*. If we recall the bird of prey passage from the First Essay (13), "autonomy" is something that Nietzsche would trace to the inversion of master morality; freedom in this sense means "responsible," "accountable," and therefore "reformable" – all in the service of convincing the strong to "choose" a different kind of behavior.

In the text at hand, Nietzsche calls the sovereign individual "master of the *free* will," and it is well known that Nietzsche often rebukes the notion of freedom in this sense. In *Beyond Good and Evil* 21, freedom of the will is dubbed a *causa sui*, or self-causation, which he calls a "self-contradiction" stemming from "the desire to bear the entire and ultimate responsibility for one's actions oneself," and from the audacity "to pull oneself by the hair out of the swamp of nothingness into existence." And in *Daybreak* 112, Nietzsche specifically connects the "error" of free will to the social phenomenon of promising, "the *capacity* to promise certain things and bind ourselves to perform them." And the sovereign individual is the *culmination* of "the paradoxical task" facing nature; it is the ripe fruit of "a man with his own independent, enduring will, whose *prerogative it is to promise*."

In Section 3 the climax of the sovereign individual's self-regulation is the development of conscience, which, as we will see, is an internalization of an earlier, external "technique of mnemonics" that "burned" into the self a moral memory by way of brutal physical torments visited upon wrongdoers. He adds that "the whole of asceticism belongs here as well," with its self-castigating practices that no longer *need* external pains to provide a regulatory force. At the end of Section 3, this internalization process develops into a "gloomy thing," the capacity of reason and *reflection* to "master" the emotions. The start of Section 4 names that "other 'gloomy thing,'" the bad conscience, which becomes a central question in Nietzsche's critique of asceticism and morality. The point is that the sovereign individual seems to be linked *with* this problematic development in the context of Nietzsche's analysis, rather than being a Nietzschean ideal.

A text relevant to this matter can be found in *Beyond Good and Evil* 32, which presents the following historical sequence: (1) a pre-moral (*vormoralische*) form of valuation based simply on the consequences of action; (2) a moral period that shifts from assessing consequences to assessing "intentions" based on a principle of "self-knowledge," which Nietzsche calls a "prejudice" dominant up to the present day; and (3) a "post-moral" (*aussermoralische*) period currently possible, a threshold upon which "we immoralists" stand, and which will no longer take values as grounded in consciousness or intention. I believe that this passage adds weight to the idea that the sovereign individual in the *Genealogy* is not a coming phenomenon, and that the "supra-moral" character of the sovereign individual is similar to the second stage above, because as we have noted the German term is *übersittlich*, and *sittlich* can match what the *BGE* passage calls pre-moral, and thus it might be designated as "ethical," not moral.[3] So the coming phenomenon forecast by Nietzsche in *Beyond Good and Evil* is not something like the sovereign individual, who is supra-ethical in being rationally, or autonomously, moral; the coming sense of valuation is post-moral in being post-rational, post-autonomous, post-sovereign.

If my analysis is on target, why has the sovereign individual so often been misread? There are three reasons, I think. First, we noted that the word *übersittlich* can appear to describe a Nietzschean advance beyond morality, but I hope I have shown a more careful way to read this term. Second, there is a common tendency to interpret Nietzsche as some kind of individualist, but his sense of individuality also takes some care in getting right. Nietzsche is not an individualist, if that concept is tied in any way to traditional models of a substantive "self" that stands behind its actions as a cause or unity (see *BGE* 17, 19–21). In fact at one point Nietzsche calls the self a *Dividuum*, to contrast it with the literal sense of "individual" (*Individuum*) as something "undividable," as a nonpluralized, rigid singularity (*HAH* 57 and 618). Consequently the self, for Nietzsche, cannot be understood as

---

[3] The Cambridge University Press translation has merit, therefore, in rendering *übersittlich* as "supra-ethical."

a discrete, atomic individual (*TI* 9, 33; *BGE* 12). Even consciousness, as a typical locus of individual selfhood, is critiqued as stemming from the need for social acts of communication by way of common, public linguistic signs (*GS* 117, 354), and so genuine "individuality," in the sense of something unique, is even called "incalculable," which would not square with the background of the *Genealogy* passage at hand.

In addition, for Nietzsche the self is not a stable unity, but an arena for an irresolvable contest of differing drives, each seeking mastery (*BGE* 6, 36). There is no single subject, but rather a "multiplicity of subjects, whose interplay and struggle is the basis of our thought and our consciousness" (*WP* 490). Nietzsche's agonistic psychology does not suggest that the self is an utter chaos. He does allow for a shaping of the self, but this requires a difficult and demanding procedure of counter-cropping the drives so that a certain mastery can be achieved (*TI* 9, 41). This is one reason why Nietzsche thinks that the modernist promotion of universal freedom is careless. Contrary to modernist optimism about the rational pursuit of happiness, Nietzsche sees the natural and social field of play as much more precarious and demanding. So according to Nietzsche (and this is missed in many interpretations) freedom and creative self-development are not for everyone: "Independence is for the very few; it is a privilege of the strong" (*BGE* 29). Simply being unconstrained is not an appropriate mark of freedom; being free should only serve the pursuit of great achievement, a pursuit that most people cannot endure.

You call yourself free? Your dominant thought I want to hear, and not that you have escaped from a yoke. Are you one of those who had the *right* to escape from a yoke? There are some who threw away their last value when they threw away their servitude. Free *from* what? As if that mattered to Zarathustra! But your eyes should tell me brightly: free *for* what? (*Z* I, 17)

That most people are bound by rules and are not free to cut their own path is not regretted by Nietzsche. The "exception" and the "rule" are *both* important for human culture, and neither one should be universalized. Although exceptional types further the species, we should not forget the importance of the rule in *preserving* the species (*GS* 55). The exception as such can never become the rule, can never be a model for all humanity (*GS* 76). Absent this provision,

Nietzsche's promotion of creative individuals is easily misunderstood. The freedom from constraints is restricted to those who are capable of high cultural achievement. Nietzsche therefore believes that freedom is a privilege of rank and should not be generalized to all individuals: "My philosophy aims at an ordering of rank: not at an individualistic morality. The ideas of the herd should rule in the herd – but not reach out beyond it" (*WP* 287).

So the creative individual in Nietzsche is a relative, contextual term that cannot be generalized to all selves, because it is essentially a conflicted relation to normal selves and normal selfhood (in *HAH* 225 Nietzsche directly calls the free spirit a "relative concept"). Because some readers have assumed that the creative individual can be generalized to all humanity, at least as a possibility, they have also hoped that such a reading can disturb or even invalidate the interpretation of Nietzsche as an elitist, especially with his apparent anti-democratic posture. Since the sovereign individual does seem to share some intimations of the liberal conception of selfhood, the hope is that we can explore ways to accommodate Nietzsche's philosophy with a more democratic outlook.

Well, indeed these intimations of liberal selfhood are, as I have argued, precisely what the sovereign individual *does* represent. But since I believe that the sovereign individual is not a version of Nietzsche's "free spirit" or creator, the hoped-for accommodation will not succeed. It might succeed if we stressed more the central feature of promising in Nietzsche's discussion, because promising is a core requirement in modern political contract theories. But again, this would have to imply that the "promising individual" is a Nietzschean ideal. It *is* a liberal ideal, but it is not Nietzsche's central ideal. For my part, I have also tried to accommodate Nietzsche's philosophy with democratic politics, but *not* on the basis of liberalism and its attendant assumptions about human selfhood (more on this in Chapter 8).

Nietzsche calls the sovereign individual the "master of the free will." The meaning of freedom in Nietzsche's thought is not at all clear, but it *is* clear that it does not reflect the modern ideal of "free will." At the same time, Nietzsche does not opt for a mechanistic determinism either. In *Beyond Good and Evil* 21, Nietzsche rejects both free will and unfree will: the former because of his dismissal of atomic individualism, and the latter because of his voluntaristic alternative to mechanistic causality (he does, however, affirm the distinction between "strong" and "weak" wills). Nietzsche's self-creating individual cannot be associated with autonomy in the strict sense. The dictum, "Become what you are" (*GS* 270, 335), is ambiguous regarding the freedom–necessity scale: *achieving* "what one is" is an active power that nevertheless cannot be called an autonomous, self-activated creation. It may be that the figure of the sovereign individual does foreshadow in *some* way Nietzsche's creator type, but I doubt such a connection, because of the meaning of "sovereignty," its textual association with morality, and Nietzsche's critique of modernist freedom and individualism.[4] It should be stressed that Nietzsche questions *any* sense of "sovereignty" or self-sufficiency in accounting for human action (in keeping with *amor fati*): "Nothing is self-sufficient, neither ourselves nor things" (*KSA* 12, p.307); "we are not the work of ourselves" (*HAH* I, 588). Moreover, in *BGE* 62 Nietzsche twice uses the word "sovereign" (with emphasis) to describe the exclusive posture of life-denying religions.

One possible problem for my reading must be addressed. The sovereign individual can seem to resonate with Nietzsche's own predilections because the figure is described as having a superior, even disdainful attitude toward "non-sovereigns."

This man who is now free, who actually has the *prerogative* to promise, this master of the *free* will, this sovereign – how could he remain ignorant of his superiority over everybody who does not have the prerogative to promise or answer for himself. . . and how could he, with his self-mastery, not realize that he has necessarily been given mastery over circumstances, over nature and over all creatures with a less enduring and reliable will? The "free" man, the possessor of an enduring, unbreakable will, thus has his own *standard of value*: in the possession of such a will, viewing others from his own standpoint, he respects or despises; and just as he will necessarily respect his peers, . . . so he will necessarily be ready to kick the feeble, unreliable dogs (*schmächtigen Windhunde*) who make a promise when they are not able to do so, and will save the rod for the liar who breaks his word in the very moment it passes his lips.

---

[4] David Owen offers the best attempt, I think, to argue for the sovereign individual as a Nietzschean ideal. See "Equality, Democracy, and Self-Respect," and "Nietzsche, Re-evaluation, and the Turn to Genealogy," in Acampora, ed., *Nietzsche's On the Genealogy of Morals*, pp. 39–56. My reservations involve an undue fitting of the text into standard philosophical terms and issues, a recoiling from Nietzsche's elitism, and the assumption of a universal model of moral agency.

Such a rendering of contempt for inferiors might suggest a Nietzschean disposition toward lower types, but this need not be the case. First of all, any perspective on life, for Nietzsche, will be an expression of power over some other perspective deemed to be inferior. Also, this rendition is still voiced in terms of the power to make promises, and it is not clear to me why a Nietzschean "individual" would be stressing such a power and its deficiencies in others, especially since "forgetting" is not intrinsically problematic in the *Genealogy*, nor is "lying" in Nietzsche's thought generally.

Finally, since I am convinced that the sovereign individual is expressive of the free rational individual so indigenous to modern morality and political philosophy, it is quite possible that the disdain of this individual toward inferiors can give voice to a dirty little secret of modern liberal rationality: not only its judgment of the inferior status of those who do not exercise autonomous reason – witness Kant's classic critique of "self-imposed tutelage" in "What is Enlightenment?"[5] – but also the very real presence of racial and gender biases in modern thinkers who champion "universal" reason while demoting those who do not or cannot live up to this ideal, such as women and non-European peoples (more on this in Chapter 8). Contemporary liberal political theory may have moved past these particular categorial judgments, but there remains a continuing generalized judgment of citizens who are not "rational" enough in political life. As I have said, for Nietzsche any perspective tends to downgrade others, and so the elitist tone of the sovereign individual can indeed refer to the modern rational subject (and also uncover its complicity in paternalistic tyranny). I am not suggesting that Nietzsche would side with any dispossessed "Other" in the face of liberal abuses. I am simply following a Nietzschean diagnosis that unmasks concealed or suppressed forms of power in a political theory that presents itself as a universal model of emancipation, and that therefore does not own up to its own exclusionary or controlling effects.

---

[5] Apart from the docility of most people, Kant says, "only a few, by cultivating their own minds, have succeeded in freeing themselves from immaturity and in continuing boldly on their way." The text is "An Answer to the Question 'What is Enlightenment?'" in *Political Writings* (Cambridge University Press, 1991), p. 54.

CONSCIENCE (SECTION 3)

At the end of Section 2, Nietzsche caps his treatment of the sovereign individual in the following way: The pride and privilege of autonomous responsibility, the sense of "this rare freedom and power" over oneself and fate, has penetrated so deeply into the sovereign individual that it has become a "dominating instinct." The name for this new power of the self is "conscience" (*Gewissen*).[6] In Section 3 Nietzsche elaborates on the "long history" of cruel practices that made something like conscience possible. Conscience is the capacity and prerogative to proudly be answerable to oneself, to "*say yes*" to oneself. But such a phenomenon could only come about when prepared by the struggle to establish memory in the face of active forgetfulness. This is the role played by cruel punishments and torments – Nietzsche mentions practices such as mutilation, stoning, impaling, flaying, drawing and quartering, boiling alive – which served to "burn" a memory into victims and onlookers, because "pain was the most powerful aid to mnemonics." The battle against forgetfulness was the fight *for* memory's capacity to regulate time and preserve a norm against the transitory nature of experience. The "dreadful" history of early penal customs is

a measure of how much trouble it had in conquering forgetfulness, and *preserving* a few primitive requirements of social life in the minds of those enslaved to momentary moods and appetites.

I want to emphasize another element in this section that has bearing on the overall trajectory of Nietzsche's text. The consequences of fixing a memory in the self include, as we have noted, "the whole of asceticism," which Nietzsche describes as having the following aim:

---

[6] The connection here between conscience and instinct could be taken as support for reading the sovereign individual as a Nietzschean ideal, given his high estimation of instinct. Yet for Nietzsche, every human capacity is implicated with instinct in some way; even the reflective activity of philosophy is guided by instinct (*BGE* 3). Moreover, Nietzsche says that the power of free responsibility has *become* instinctive, which is different from original instincts that are primal "givens" in natural life. The notion of "becoming instinct" can be consistent with the way in which Nietzsche understands "second nature," where an alteration of given conditions gradually becomes established enough to no longer be needful of the *labor* of alteration (see *UM* II, 3, and *GS* 290).

a few ideas come to be made ineradicable, omnipresent, unforgettable, "fixed," in order to hypnotize the whole nervous and intellectual system through these "fixed ideas" – and ascetic procedures and lifestyles are a method for freeing those ideas from competition with all other ideas, of making them "unforgettable."

Nietzsche is not referring here simply to religious and moral elements of asceticism, but to intellectual aspects as well. We will see in the Third Essay that Nietzsche identifies the ascetic ideal with the general problem of truth. I have indicated that the *Genealogy* concerns much more than morality, narrowly construed. Nietzsche wants to connect a wide range of cognitive powers with the history of morality, because no form of knowledge, for Nietzsche, can be understood apart from normative forces. The "fixed ideas" he associates with asceticism also function in philosophical foundationalism, in efforts to "arrest" time and becoming by way of stable, necessary truths securely lodged in the mind. It should be mentioned in this context that the word "conscience" has both moral and cognitive connotations in its history. In German, *Gewissen* connects with *Gewissheit*, or certainty. In English, both "conscience" and "consciousness" are derived from a common Latin origin that literally means "knowing-with" or "knowing-together," which can indicate either joint knowledge between minds or the unified coming-together of disparate elements in the conscious mind. The priority of consciousness, as the thinking subject, was first crystallized in Descartes, when he posited the self-conscious subject as the only available bedrock for certainty in human experience (the only thing that cannot be doubted is the mental act of doubting itself). Nietzsche's genealogy is moving to situate such philosophical sources, not in some detached contemplation, but in pre-philosophical, social and moral practices that had to "breed" a reliable self by prosecuting forgetfulness and temporality with the arresting evidence of cruel punishments. He wants to convince us that these early social practices made later intellectual developments possible, and that the same problem of "distancing" from more natural life forces persists in these later developments as well. That is why Nietzsche can end Section 3 by linking the moral imposition of memory and promising with the power of *reason*, which aims for the "mastering of emotions," and which Nietzsche summarizes as "this entirely dismal thing called reflection." Reflection in this context is "dismal" because it moves to displace healthy, instinctive, spontaneous energies in life. It cannot be that Nietzsche is aiming to displace this reflective displacement of natural forces; rather, I think he is continually trying to show us the actual history of esteemed cultural powers and how this history points to the lasting costs, omissions, and dangers haunting modern culture.

GUILT AND BAD CONSCIENCE (SECTIONS 4–5)

In Section 4 Nietzsche asks how that "other dismal thing," bad conscience, came forth in human life. Bad conscience is "consciousness of guilt," an inner sense of one's own fault and responsibility for having done wrong. Yet, once again, this is a late moral phenomenon not evident in earlier periods of culture. Guilt and bad conscience are an internalized psychological condition that only arose out of the long process of breeding memory, promising, and responsibility into the human animal. Guilt implies an accountable free will, which Nietzsche says emerged only after a "*high* degree of humanization" had been achieved. He gives attention to the German word for guilt, *Schuld*, which also means "debt," and he claims that the concept of guilt arose out of an earlier concrete sense of debt. The normative notion of a creditor–debtor relation was based in more primal patterns of economic exchange, and so moral debt was first understood in an external, transactional manner, and not in any reference to individual responsibility or free will. Punishment was not originally justified by the conviction that the criminal "could have done otherwise," but rather by anger at having been injured, an anger mollified by a transactional "equivalence," where injury was "paid for" with the pain of the perpetrator.

In Section 5 the "contractual" relationship between creditor and debtor is described in terms of promising, wherein punishment for transgression is implied in any social transaction, and this sanction is secured by the memory of painful penalties that prompts the promise not to transgress. Yet such a compact does not approximate the more formal sense of contracts we recognize, because Nietzsche highlights the more visceral elements in early forms of punishment. The "equivalence" implied in punishment cannot be understood in isomorphic payments in kind (for instance, goods for stolen goods), because Nietzsche insists that the *pleasure* gained from inflicting punishment is central to ancient notions of compensation. Nietzsche claims that nothing like the modern concept of "rehabilitation" could figure in early penal codes because a retributive vengeance was the primal motivation. Yet the pleasure in punishing cannot likely be understood simply as some sadistic pleasure, and Nietzsche's psychology of power can offer a more nuanced explanation (and perhaps it can account for why the impulse for retribution continues to show itself today, despite the discouragement of this impulse in our more "enlightened" times). The pleasure in punishment is "being allowed to exercise power over the powerless without objection or hesitation." Here Nietzsche retrieves the notion of master morality and says that the pleasure in punishment psychologically elevates the creditor over the debtor. Even though the creditor may not be a master type, in punishing he "takes part in the *rights of the masters*," he is enhanced by displaying power over an "inferior." Even if the creditor does not directly administer the punishment himself, the same pleasure can come from "*seeing* the debtor despised and mistreated" (recall the vision offered by Tertullian). Nietzsche summarizes this more original and visceral form of compensation for injury as "a warrant for, and entitlement to, cruelty." It must be kept in mind, however, that the pleasure arising from punishment in this sense is not so much from the infliction of pain per se as from the elevated experience of power given in such practices.

MORALITY AND THE CHANGING FACES OF CRUELTY (SECTION 6)

Section 6 continues the discussion of cruelty by highlighting the "festive" aspect in public displays of punishment. The torment or execution of criminals was not only a public spectacle – unlike our own sequestered executions – but such events were often experienced with raucous enthusiasm and celebration. We tend to be shocked at these occasions in history. The idea of televised executions would be abhorrent to most modern sensibilities, but, if they were televised, think of how we would react if people gathered to watch the program in the manner of Super Bowl parties. Yet that was the spirit of such spectacles in ages past. There may have been some aversion to these events, but Nietzsche is at least right to remind us of how "normal" it was to celebrate public cruelties without hesitation or guilt. The question is: Why was it "gratifying to make someone suffer"? That it *was* gratifying is a historical fact. Nietzsche's psychology of power is an attempt to explain this fact in a manner that might haunt us because it refuses to sanction our moralistic debasement of such practices. Even if we are right in forbidding public cruelty now, we would be intellectually inept if our judgment of the past missed the kinds of insight Nietzsche offers, even if we do not buy them completely. As Nietzsche says, the *pleasure* in cruelty makes the simple concept of revenge (pay-back) insufficient. The social and psychological *benefits* of revenge – not only the maintenance of communal norms, but also the elevated feelings of *power* experienced by witnesses – provide a better account of why public revenge was "festive." In this section Nietzsche offers two parenthetical remarks that indicate the full scope of his genealogical treatment. He refers to *Beyond Good and Evil* 229, where he says he "pointed a careful finger at the ever-growing spiritualization (*Vergeistigung*) and 'deification' of cruelty," which not only "runs through the whole history of higher culture," but in fact "constitutes it in an important sense." In that referenced passage, Nietzsche claims to "take some risk in letting slip a truth" about *relearning* the meaning of cruelty. The pride that humans have in coming to control the "wild, cruel animal" in their nature conceals the forms of self-inflicted "cruelty" that make this control possible.

Almost everything we call "higher culture" is founded on the spiritualization and deepening (*Vergeistigung und Vertiefung*) of *cruelty* – that is my proposition; that the "wild animal" has not been killed off at all, it lives, it thrives, it has simply – made itself divine.

After citing various historical examples of cruel spectacles, he goes on to say that the meaning of cruelty cannot be restricted to "the suffering of *others*." There is also "an abundant, superabundant enjoyment of one's own suffering, of making oneself suffer." He refers to religious practices of self-denial and self-flagellation, which in fact were often experienced with a kind of ecstatic delight. Yet that is not all. Earlier in the passage he had included in higher culture's forms of cruelty "everything that is sublime right up to the most delicate thrills of metaphysics." Then Nietzsche adds the general phenomenon of knowledge, and we should note in the following quote a link with the term "knowers" in the Preface to the *Genealogy*.

Finally, consider how even the knower (*der Erkennende*), in forcing his mind (*Geist*) to discern *against* the inclination of his spirit (*Geist*), and often enough against his heart's desire – namely to say No where he would like to affirm, love, and adore – holds sway as an artist and transfigurer of cruelty; indeed, every acquisition of depth and thoroughness is a violation of, and a desire to hurt, the fundamental will of the spirit (*Geist*), which ceaselessly strives for appearance and superficiality, – already in every will to know (*Erkennen-Wollen*) there is a drop of cruelty. (*BGE* 229)

Returning to the *Genealogy*, we may now be in a better position to understand why Nietzsche is putting so much emphasis on cruelty. From his naturalistic standpoint, Nietzsche will insist that no familiar "spiritual" phenomenon is or was already inscribed in reality (only needing to be discovered by us). Any such phenomenon had to emerge *out of* brute nature, and indeed by way of a struggle with that nature. Because of this agonistic structure, brute nature will always be the starting point and will remain implicated somehow in what emerges out of it. The brutal physical cruelties of early penal codes, therefore, not only shaped the first forms of organized social norms and moral psychology; they also established the setting for *modifications* of these formats through internalization and spiritualization. So according to Nietzsche, later cultural developments are modifications of cruelty, movements from more physical to more spiritual manifestations.

It seems evident that spiritual cruelty is an analogy drawn from physical cruelty, but it also seems that Nietzsche does not want to rest with a purely analogical difference, which would allow us to disregard the historical role played by physical cruelty in cultural development. There is a difference between inflicting pain on another body and inflicting restrictions on sensuous impulses in the domain of knowledge. Yet we will see that Nietzsche puts great importance on asceticism in cultural history, in part because it can mark a space in between outward physical cruelty and inward psychic cruelty when we consider the self-inflicted *physical* cruelties in ascetic practices of self-mortification and self-denial.

In any case, there is a general point to be drawn here about Nietzsche's overall strategy in the *Genealogy*. There is more than a *mere* analogical relation between "higher culture" and cruelty because, for Nietzsche, there is a transitional link that cannot be strictly disengaged (one reason for this being the persistence of *pleasure* and *power* in whatever changes occur). In addition, I think that Nietzsche deliberately (and happily) wants to retain the rhetorical force of the word "cruelty," in order to shake us up and keep us attentive to the naturalistic setting in his historical analysis. I think that the same is true with other rhetorical tropes in Nietzsche's text, such as the slave, the master, the blond beast, and asceticism. I will have more to say about this in the next chapter, where we take up Nietzsche's implication of the ascetic ideal in the development of philosophy and in the very domain of truth. In Chapter 7 I will also try to sketch the ways in which Nietzsche's genealogy critiques and differs from traditional moral theories. There we will have a chance to elaborate on the other parenthetical remark Nietzsche offers in Section 6 of the Second Essay: that Kant's categorical imperative "smells of cruelty."

CRUELTY AND PESSIMISM (SECTION 7)

After having catalogued the gruesome history of cruelty, Nietzsche begins Section 7 by insisting that he does not want his analysis to provide "our pessimists" with support for their "disgust with life." Rather than take such practices as more evidence for the depravity of human existence, Nietzsche turns the tables on pessimism in a provocative way. He claims that a pessimistic attitude could not have been possible in these earlier times, that any disgust we might have about these times is a result of having been "denatured," of having suppressed certain life instincts and become "ashamed" of them. One of Nietzsche's lasting convictions is that pessimism about life is only possible once we have become "liberated" from nature and natural drives. For Nietzsche, pessimism is a luxury of civilization, of the various ways in which we have become more "secured" from natural dangers and contingencies. In earlier, more precarious times (and perhaps in circumstances of upheaval even now), life could not be bemoaned as "meaningless" because life forces would be too busy prompting us to *engage* our difficulties.

It is in this spirit that Nietzsche continues his distancing from pessimism. Since "suffering is always the first of the arguments marshaled *against* life," Nietzsche asks us to consider past ages as counter-examples to this presumption. In those times, he says, "life on earth was more cheerful than it is today." In fact, he says that the cruel infliction of suffering on people was a "seductive lure *to* life." He then ventures to ask if pain in those days "did not hurt as much as it does now." What can this mean? Perhaps a glance at one of Nietzsche's other books could help here.

In *Gay Science* 48, Nietzsche is discussing distress or misery (*Not*) and the greater degree of physical and psychic suffering experienced in previous ages of human life. Our own less distressed condition, which shields us from so much pain, has ironically magnified the painfulness of whatever pain we do experience, because we are much less "educated" in the experience of suffering and so we react to it as a more alien, and therefore more terrible, occurrence. Because "pain is now hated much more than was the case for earlier humans, one speaks much worse of it." Nietzsche then says something dramatic, and we may gain more sense of it if we consider the familiar notion that the *anticipation* of pain is often more stressful than the actual experience of pain. Nietzsche believes that less experience of actual pain can lend more force to *ideas* of pain. This condition goes so far that "one considers the existence of the mere *thought* of pain scarcely endurable and turns it into a reproach against the whole of existence."

It is in this context that Nietzsche zeroes in on pessimism in a manner similar to his account in the *Genealogy*. The passage is worth quoting in full:

The emergence of pessimistic philosophies is by no means a sign of great and terrible misery. No, these question marks about the value of all life are put up in ages in which the refinement and alleviation of existence make even the inevitable mosquito bites of the soul and the body seem much too bloody and malignant, and one is so poor in real experiences of pain that one would prefer to consider *painful general ideas* as suffering of the highest order.

Nietzsche is therefore saying something much more than that comfortable circumstances are a blessing and that we should realize how lucky we are to have our more "civilized" misfortunes. He is making a general claim about how life is valued in relation to experiences of pain. Comfortable circumstances may drift so far from natural life energies that we can be distressed about life without being endangered, indeed *because* we are not endangered. Nietzsche then says that there is a remedy for the "excessive sensitivity" of modern life that generates pessimistic dispositions. He concedes that the remedy "may sound too cruel," but it involves more *experience* of the actual sufferings of life to break the luxurious spell of pessimism. As he states it in another part of the book, Nietzsche counsels us to *"live dangerously,"* which, in not being averse to finitude, is "the secret for harvesting from existence the greatest fruitfulness and the greatest enjoyment" (*GS* 283).

Returning to the text at hand in the *Genealogy*, after the remarks about the pleasure in cruelty and the modern hyper-sensitivity to pain, Nietzsche reiterates the notion that brute cruelty and pain evolved toward a spiritualization of these phenomena, wherein physical suffering was "sublimated and made subtle" and transformed into "imaginative and psychic" states. What he says next is quite important for the course of his overall analysis. The continuum between overt and imaginative appropriations of pain shows that suffering is *always* subjected to meaning-formation in one way or another. As Nietzsche puts it: "What actually arouses indignation over suffering is not suffering itself, but the meaninglessness of suffering." Whether it be the Christian belief in suffering as a path toward salvation or the pagan model of human suffering as a spectacle for divine onlookers, it is evident that human life is compelled to find *some* sense in suffering (*what* that sense might be is the more acute question addressed by Nietzsche). The upshot here is that the cornerstone of pessimism, the belief that suffering and life in general *are* meaningless, is in some respects an impossible thought, if it is impossible to *live* without some sense of meaning. As we will see later, this "paradox" in pessimism will be articulated further in Nietzsche's treatment of Schopenhauer and nihilism, which will be crucial for understanding Nietzsche's complex genealogical critique of the tradition and his own ideal of life-affirmation.

DEBT AND COMMUNITY (SECTIONS 8–9)

After his foray into the question of pessimism, in Section 8 Nietzsche gets back to the historical course of his investigation.[7] Guilt first emerged in creditor–debtor relationships. The transactional structure of such practices gave the first truly *social* shape to human life: "here person met person for the first time, and *measured himself* person against person." With such transactional measures, humankind staked out the realm of "values" and discovered itself as "the valuing animal as such." These "most rudimentary forms of person-claims" were then *transferred* to the "roughest and earliest social complexes" that gave rise to "social forms of organization and association." According to Nietzsche, in time there arose a more general insight stemming from these transactional formats, namely that "*everything* can be measured in terms of compensation." This is where the general concept of "justice" found its soil, out of which ideals of "equity," "good will," and "objectivity" came to displace sheer self-interest and to mark the more exalted sphere of a *social* being.

In Section 9 Nietzsche focuses on the primal social character of early cultures. The creditor–debtor relation shifted from a person-to-person setting to a community-to-person measure, where the benefits of social life constituted the "debt" that individuals owed to the group. And Nietzsche does not underestimate these benefits: the suffering, harm, and hostility outside the protective peace of society are precisely the threat that motivated the individual's compact with social norms. Nietzsche claims that the offense of violating that compact cannot be reduced to particular misdeeds. The offender has not only broken a promise to comply with particular norms, he has offended and broken his allegiance to the social realm *as a whole*, to its very shaping of the individual's advantages in peace and protection. The injured "creditor" is the social world as such, and the penal response to the

---

[7] The *Genealogy* in general, and the Second Essay in particular, often shifts from its purported historical project to various interludes that take up broader philosophical or cultural reflections. This makes for a choppy text that can appear to lack focus or cohesion. Yet the title of the Second Essay does indicate "related matters," and I think we should recognize that the text aims for much more than a cohesive historical study of the past. Nietzsche aims for a historical sense of how *we* have come to be shaped *presently* by such sources, and how the history of morality is implicated in the widest possible range of cultural and intellectual forces.

violator involves more than just deprivation of social benefits: "he is now also reminded *how important these benefits are.*" With its anger and cruelty visited upon the violator, the community "gives him back to the savage and outlawed condition from which he was sheltered hitherto." Because of the criminal's fundamental break with the social whole, the community responds as if meeting a threat from "the wild." Cruel punishments are at once a defense and a "celebration" of the community's value and power. That is why, as Nietzsche says, the criminal "has not only forfeited all rights and safeguards, but all mercy as well."

In Section 10 Nietzsche says that when a community grows in power and self-confidence, "its penal law becomes more lenient." The less an individual's transgression is perceived as a threat to the social order, the more that order can lessen its anger and cruel responses to transgression. Nietzsche surmises that it is even possible to imagine a society "*so conscious of its power,*" that it could allow itself the noblest luxury available to it – that of letting its malefactors go *unpunished.*" Justice, we are told, can "sublimate itself" and move from punishment toward *mercy,* which therefore moves beyond the initial mercilessness of punishment cited in Section 9. I think we should notice in mercy a possible instance of the "active forgetting" of moral offense that was offered earlier as implicated in Nietzsche's discussion of forgetting. In any case, the idea that justice and law are not reducible to retribution for injury is articulated further in the next section.

In Section 11 Nietzsche critiques attempts to find the origin of justice (*Gerechtigkeit*) in revenge (*Rache*), which he connects with resentment. In such accounts (as in the case of Dühring), justice is based in "*reactive* affects," in feelings of being wronged, accounts which Nietzsche says themselves are based in resentment, owing to their animosity toward "*active* affects" such as avarice and the lust for mastery, which Nietzsche takes to have more value than reactive feelings. We are told that justice is not based in reactive sentiments because such feelings are "the *last* territory to be conquered by the spirit of justice." Echoing Section 10, Nietzsche then talks about a high development of the spirit of justice, where a just man remains just toward someone who harms him – a *"positive* attitude" to be distinguished from indifference, a "clear objectivity both penetrating and merciful" that does not diminish even in the face of injury or scorn. Nietzsche calls this attitude "a piece of perfection, the highest form of mastery to be had on earth," which is more likely to emerge in active types: "The active, aggressive, over-reaching man is still a hundred paces nearer to justice than the man who reacts." The active type has "a *clearer* eye, a better conscience on his side," as opposed to the "false and prejudiced assessment" and the "bad conscience" of reactive sentiments.

Nietzsche claims that a historical consideration of justice shows that it did not originate in reactive feelings against injury, but rather "with the active, the strong, the spontaneous, and the aggressive." Justice emerged as a battle waged by active forces *"against* reactive feelings," by types who "expended part of their strength in trying to put a stop to the spread of reactive pathos, to keep it in check and within bounds, and to force a compromise." Wherever justice is practiced and maintained, the *stronger* power aims to end "the senseless ravages" of resentment among inferior individuals or groups. I think that one of the main elements in Sections 10 and 11 is that a strong person is not motivated by resentment and revenge, and that Nietzsche is here augmenting his genealogy of values by claiming that, as in the sphere of morality, the *political* value of justice emerged first not in the interests of weak types but in the active power of strong types. In Nietzsche's account of the political sphere, we likely have a more developed social condition than the rougher sphere of "master" types controlling "slave" types. If we recall that Nietzsche adds to the slave-setting the phrase "and dependents of every degree" (*BGE* 260), we could read the sphere of justice as pertaining to a more settled and advanced hierarchical society in which lower orders are prone to revenge within their *own* ranks, a disruptive force prompting a response from the ruling order. Nietzsche describes the response as multifaceted experiments with justice that aim to remove the *target* of resentment from "the hands of revenge." These include substituting for revenge "a struggle against the enemies of peace and order," creating compensations for injury, and "elevating certain equivalences of harms into a norm," a reciprocal order that resentment "from now on" will have to accept as the rectification of offenses. This analysis can be seen to follow from remarks in Section 8, where Nietzsche says that justice at its "first level" was expressed among more powerful types who are "roughly equal" in their power and in their advantages over lower types. They can *afford* to arrive at agreements among themselves to settle disputes without violence. And with respect to less powerful types who lack such affordance, the powerful are able "to *force* them to reach a settlement among themselves."

Then Nietzsche announces a culmination of the process he is describing, its most "decisive" development, which occurs when the ruling authorities are "strong enough" to counter "the stronger power of hostile and sympathetic feelings" by setting up a legal system (*Gesetz*). Nietzsche's point seems to be that political law has a genealogical history comparable to his treatment of morality. The establishment of law is not grounded in some metaphysical warrant of "right" (whether divine, natural, or human) because it arises as a *modification* of prior conditions of social power for the purpose of addressing the problem of vengeful dispositions. With a legal system, the ruling authorities create an "imperative declaration" of what counts as just and unjust "in their eyes." Laws, especially in written form, provide a more formal reference for justice and injustice than the more immediate settings of harmful behavior and effects. Nietzsche says that in a legal system – when human offenses are now "crimes," or violations of the law set up by the ruling authority – what is "offensive" about injury can be modulated beyond the injured parties themselves toward the broader sphere of the legal order. In this way the vengeful feelings of subordinate, reactive types can be "distracted" (*ablenkt*) from the immediate damage done to them. Nietzsche claims that such distraction is able to counter the force of revenge by shifting the estimation of injuries away from the narrow perspective of the injured party toward an "evermore *impersonal* assessment of the action." The idea of the impersonal force of law is very much in keeping with modern legal conceptions, but Nietzsche embeds this idea in more natural forces of power relations, rather than in any larger notion of "natural law" or rational principles of justice intrinsic to human nature. We could say that, for Nietzsche, the law aims for an impersonal *effect*, but it is not based in any exalted principle of "impersonal reason."

Nietzsche tells us that "justice" and "injustice" only arise when a legal system is in place rather than in any pre-legal settings of human injury. Moreover, he says that any concept of justice *as such* is "meaningless," because natural life "functions *essentially* in an injurious, violent, exploitative, and destructive manner." From the standpoint of natural life, legal principles of justice are "*exceptional conditions*," in being exceptions to brute nature. Yet given Nietzsche's analysis, this would not "falsify" legal conditions, any more than other valuable cultural forms that emerge from and modify natural forces. Indeed, Nietzsche goes on to describe the law in ways that resonate with his treatment of the agonistic structure of Greek culture in *Homer's Contest*. Legal conditions are "partial restrictions" of natural forces of power, yet not on this account something "other" or even "lesser" than natural power. Legal provisions are called "particular means" serving life-powers, and Nietzsche adds: "as a means toward creating *greater* units of power." In other words, legal culture *adds* dimensions of power that nature alone does not exhibit. Nietzsche concludes by contrasting this agonistic conception of law in the midst of nature with the conception of law as "sovereign (*souverein*) and general" – as something secured in its own sphere over against finite life, and especially as a means "against conflict (*Kampf*) in general" and toward egalitarian equanimity – which Nietzsche calls something "*hostile to life*" and "a secret path toward nothingness." For Nietzsche, the law is not a force that strictly speaking secures an end to power and conflict, because it serves and participates *in* an ongoing "conflict of power-complexes." This interesting discussion of law has received little attention; in Chapter 8 I will try to explore some of its implications.

PURPOSE AND POWER (SECTION 12)

In this section Nietzsche advances some significant reflections on historical thinking. In considering the "origin" of punishment, we must not assume, he says, that a "purpose" of punishment is identical to its origin. This is a critique of teleological thinking, wherein the emergence and development of a thing are guided by a purpose that is intrinsic to the nature of that thing. Referring again to other genealogists, he says that they naively inject a purpose of punishment (for instance, revenge) at its starting point. But Nietzsche claims that a purpose for law should not be assumed when considering the "historical emergence" of law. Indeed he generalizes beyond the specific case of law by saying that "the cause of the emergence of a thing and its usefulness in the end, its actual employment and incorporation into a system of purposes, are totally separate." Nietzsche says of this idea "that there is no more important proposition for every sort of history."

It should be noted that Nietzsche is not utterly rejecting the idea of purposes, because such meanings do come to pass in history; rather he is rejecting the traditional teleological principle of purposes being built into the very manifestation of things from the start. What Nietzsche goes on to say next is an elaboration of this critique from the standpoint of will to power. Given a plurality of competing power-complexes, there can be no single coherent "line" of development in temporal movement. The natural competition of power sites – with no overarching arrangement – gives forth continual breaks and disruptions. Nietzsche offers that *any* emergent condition is "continually interpreted anew, requisitioned anew, transformed, and redirected toward a new purpose by a power superior to it." Surprisingly, he includes "everything in the organic world" in this dynamic of "overcoming and mastering," in which any existing meaning and purpose must be suppressed or destroyed by "new interpretations." Such is the scope of will to power (and interpretation) that it encompasses both natural and cultural phenomena (in this account he joins together physiological organs, legal institutions, social and political customs, art forms, and religious rites).

Nietzsche continues that any *current* understanding of a phenomenon's "usefulness" cannot be traced back without a break to its original emergence. Here he is not simply considering some particular entity in experience, but the history of a general cultural phenomenon that can go by a single name, such as "morality." Genealogical history shows the ruptures and shifts that make for only a *nominal* unity in the word "good," for example. Any particular concept we grasp is not an enduring, substantive essence, but an "indication" (*Anzeichen*) that "points" to an *emergence* in a field of competitive movements. As Nietzsche says about the will elsewhere, willing "is a unity only as a word" (*BGE* 19). We should notice in Section 12 a confirmation of the radically agonistic structure of will to power, that no form of power is immune from being overcome by other forms of power (this structure also figures in Nietzsche's idea of "perspectivism," as we will see). That is why master morality was subjected to overcoming by slave morality. The history of a moral concept, therefore, is "a continuing range of indications, continually revealing new interpretations and adaptations," wherein an instance of "will to power has achieved mastery over something less powerful, and has impressed upon it its own meaning." Therefore the development of a cultural phenomenon cannot be a single "*progressus* toward a goal." Rather, such a phenomenon is "a succession of more or less profound, more or less mutually independent processes of overcoming something." Right away Nietzsche says that *added* to all forms of overcoming are "the resistances used against them every time," the defensive reactions and "the results, too, of successful countermeasures." No form of power, therefore, can ever prevail in complete dominance over time. Moreover, this agonistic structure shows that emergent developments are not simply "changes" but consequences of a struggle between ascending and descending life forces, so that degeneration and a reduction or loss of meaning always figure in "the will and way to *greater* power." All told, this is why Nietzsche insists that any form or meaning is never fixed but "fluid."

Nietzsche stresses such a dynamic concept of will to power as "a major viewpoint of historical method" because he believes that modern sensibilities recoil at any suggestion that "*power of will* is acted out in all that happens," owing to our "democratic idiosyncrasy of being against anything that dominates and wants to dominate." Such a disposition even shows up in the sciences, and the example Nietzsche cites is the evolutionary concept of adaptation, "the inner adaptation to external circumstances." He finds this concept insufficient because it is a bifurcated, second-order "reactive" effect of a more original will to power, which is an energy-field of *activity*, of "spontaneous, aggressive, expansive, newly-interpreting, redirecting, and forming forces." What we call adaptation is therefore simply a resultant condition of an organism, a narrow focus that misses the *force* of an organism's drive-in-the-midst-of-counterforces, which precedes and makes possible any achieved condition that we identify "in" an organism.

THE ORIGINAL MEANING OF PUNISHMENT (SECTIONS 13–15)

In Section 13 Nietzsche returns to the historical analysis of punishment, but now informed by the broader excursion taken in Section 12. He says we must distinguish between the "relative permanence" of an established set of penal customs and procedures and the "fluidity" of the phenomenon, its "meaning, purpose, and expectation, which is linked to the carrying out of such procedures." Nietzsche claims that a particular established concept of punishment emerges *out of* the earlier fluid dynamic, and this is why he objects to a moral and legal genealogy that presumes the procedures to be invented *for* a discrete purpose of punishment.

Then Nietzsche focuses on the historical fluidity of "meaning" in the concept of punishment. The current stage of culture in Europe has inherited from the past "not just a single meaning but an entire synthesis of 'meanings'" regarding punishment. But the meaning of punishment has become "crystallized" into a kind of unity that cannot abide the diversity of its history. I think that Nietzsche is again addressing the difference between the nominal unity of a concept (a single *word* gathering different meanings) and the actual disunity of penal practices and their background energies in history. And if "definition" indicates a stable unification of a concept's meaning, then Nietzsche can say that the concept of punishment is "wholly *indefinable*." The nominal unity of a word may tempt us to assume a unified meaning, but with respect to historical phenomena this is an illusion: "All concepts in which an entire process is semiotically concentrated defy definition; only something that has no history can be defined." Then Nietzsche finishes the section by cataloguing the different elements in punishment that he had previously covered, among them: rendering harmless, payment of a debt, inspiring fear, rooting out degeneracy, festivity, a prompt for memory, and war against threats to peace and order. He does not think there is any unified sense in these disparate elements, because one and the same nominal procedure (punishment) "can be used, interpreted, and adapted for fundamentally different projects."

In Section 14, in view of his historical treatment of punishment, Nietzsche takes aim at the *supposed* benefit of punishment that we have come to assume: that punishing someone is meant to arouse a feeling of guilt and bad conscience in wrongdoers. He believes that his genealogy undermines such an assumption. Throughout history and even now, he says, the "pang of conscience" is very rare among criminals. In fact, he makes the provocative claim that punishment "makes men harder and colder, it concentrates, it sharpens the feeling of alienation, it strengthens the power to resist." One reason Nietzsche gives is that criminals experience punishment as simply the *sanctioned* form of abusive treatment for which they have been prosecuted, that penal justice is simply power and violence practiced with a "good conscience." So Nietzsche concludes that, whatever bad conscience may be, it did not grow out of the soil of penal practices. In Section 15 he claims that the best we can say of a mental state created by punishment is not remorse or self-reproach ("I should not have done that"), but rather a kind of fatalistic sense of bad luck ("Something has gone terribly wrong here"). We might recognize this attitude in a familiar form of self-criticism: "I got caught," or in the moral dodge we often hear today from professional or official wrongdoers: "Mistakes were made."

THE EMERGENCE OF BAD CONSCIENCE (SECTIONS 16–17)

In Section 16 Nietzsche offers his own theory on the origin of bad conscience. What proceeds is actually a reiteration of the master–slave narrative, now with more concentration on psychological aspects. The "illness" of bad conscience arose after humankind was domesticated out of its wilder origins into "the confines of society and peace." The unconscious life instincts of a wilder condition had to be sacrificed to social organization and a more conscious reflection on the workings of its orders. Yet Nietzsche claims that the older instincts for power and struggle against danger did not actually disappear when life became safer in society. These forces simply turned inward and opened up the new landscape of the psyche:

All instincts that are not discharged outwardly *turn inwards* – this is what I call the *internalization* of man: with it there now evolves in man what will later be called his "soul." The whole inner world, originally stretched thinly as between two layers of skin, was expanded and extended itself and gained depth, breadth, and height in proportion to the degree that the external discharge of man's instincts was *obstructed*.

With the advent of social norms and punishment, the wild instincts were "turned backwards, *against man himself.*" This, Nietzsche claims, was the origin of bad conscience, the "declaration of war" against original vital instincts. Yet the ambiguity in Nietzsche's analysis of this "sickness" is shown when he adds the following modification:

> on the other hand, the fact of an animal soul on earth turning against itself, siding against itself, was something so new, profound, unheard of, puzzling, full of contradiction *and full of a future*, that the whole character of the earth changed in an essential way.

Moreover, we are told that the end of this momentous transformation is yet to be seen. What must always be kept in mind is that Nietzsche's critique of the self-inflicted battle against natural instincts cannot be read as an utter denigration. The paths of high cultural development were forged out of this natural "civil war," and Nietzsche's own possibilities as a thinker are an inheritance of that transformation. As he says three sections later, bad conscience is no doubt a sickness, but it is "a sickness in the manner that pregnancy is a sickness" (*GM* II, 19).

Section 17 reiterates the claim that the first organized societies that made bad conscience possible, the first political organizations of law and punishment, did not originate in a "contract" between equal parties but in the imposition of force by powerful types over weaker types. These masters were "unconscious artists" who created *living* modes of domination and submission through sheer exertion of active power in their environment, without the internalization of self-reflection. The original political masters, Nietzsche tells us, knew nothing of guilt, responsibility, and bad conscience, but the social forces they set up made the growth of bad conscience *possible* by way of a domesticating repression of natural drives.

BAD CONSCIENCE AND CREATIVE CRUELTY (SECTION 18)

Now Nietzsche elaborates on both the ambiguous value of bad conscience and the notion of "spiritualizing" cruelty he had referred to in Section 6. The analysis gets decidedly complicated at this point. Despite the illness of bad conscience, Nietzsche says we must guard against disparaging this phenomenon as a *whole*. In fact he claims that the emergence of bad conscience is at bottom "the same active force" as that exhibited by the masters. The "negative ideals" emerging from bad conscience are no less a form of will to power, Nietzsche tells us, except that here power is not exercised in an external, "eye-catching" manner on *other* humans; rather, bad conscience directs the same cruelty, the same "formative and rapacious nature of this force" on man himself, on "his entire animal old self." The contemptuous No to animal nature, the labor of "a soul voluntarily divided against itself," is not an utterly negative phenomenon because it is an *affirmation* of other cultural dimensions (Nietzsche mentions ideality, imagination, even beauty).

The virtue of this analysis, Nietzsche proclaims, is that we are no longer puzzled about how such self-consuming energies could be experienced with so much *pleasure*. The pleasure of self-denial is simply the re-routing of the natural pleasure in cruelty now directed toward the self rather than toward others. This redirection of pleasure amounts to Nietzsche's naturalistic account of how and why nature would divide against itself in a path toward higher cultural possibilities. The energy and power of such developments could only have arisen and been *animated* if they were *modifications* of original natural energies.

The puzzle in this section is that Nietzsche describes this redirection of pleasure and cruelty as "*active* bad conscience." In the setting of master and slave morality, Nietzsche had differentiated the two into active and reactive dispositions, respectively. If bad conscience is an outgrowth of slave morality, why is it now understood as active rather than reactive? I think an answer might be found in another distinction made in the earlier analysis, that between the priest and the slave. Whatever *meaning* can be found in slave morality has to be actively created, and so the slave mentality itself can have its own version of the master–slave distinction when it comes to those creative types who take the lead, so to speak, in fashioning the inversion of master morality. The priest figure can serve to name this special ability within the realm of subjugated types. As a creator of values, the priest's power would be analogous to the master's power, except the latter is confined to external, more physical manifestations. We will have more to say about this matter in analyzing the Third Essay, because there I believe the specific figures of the priest, the ascetic, and variations of the two are confirmed as examples of what is meant by *active* will to power in the domain of reactive departures from the more original active will to power of the masters.

THEOLOGY AND CONSCIENCE (SECTIONS 19–23)

In these sections Nietzsche attempts to trace the way in which religious beliefs figured in the development of moral norms and the advent of bad conscience, with the ultimate consequence being the Christian denial of natural life in the light of a supernatural God. Nietzsche continues to employ the creditor–debtor relation to shape this discussion. He claims that theology grew out of the more natural phenomenon of ancestor worship, which was a gesture of the reverence present generations had for their forebears, to whom they owed their place and success in the world (19). The more successful societies became, the more glorious the stature of ancestors became, to the point where they took on the character of "gods," of beings with super-human attributes.

The debt toward a deity was magnified to the extreme with the Christian God, "the maximal god yet achieved" (20). Nietzsche then mentions the possibility that an ascendance of atheism might liberate humanity from this kind of indebtedness and thus provide a kind of "second innocence" (20). But he also suggests that such a liberation will not likely succeed (21). Why? Because of the two-track development of religion joined with "moralization," with the internalization of debt and guilt culminating in bad conscience. I think Nietzsche is drawing a distinction between mere religious "belief," which might succumb to the force of modern atheism, and moral-religious *values* that are not a matter of mere cognition but the full shaping of a meaningful way of life. The development of bad conscience, the productive civil war of nature against itself, is so powerful that it blocks any easy liberation from religious "beliefs" because of the pleasures and benefits of anti-natural forces. With Christianity the power of bad conscience is given its highest and most ingenious cosmic framework (21). The original ancestor (Adam) is not a revered forebear, but the site of "original sin," the fall of humanity out of paradise into a life of woe. Because of human responsibility for sin, debt and guilt are intrinsic to human life and can never be rectified on earth. Christianity's "stroke of genius" is that salvation is only possible when God sacrifices himself for man's debt in the person of Christ.

Nietzsche's point seems to be that the self-dividing character of bad conscience is given its most complete expression in the binary divisions of reality in Christian thought: not only the division between the supernatural and the natural, but also the moral division between divine perfection and an intrinsically sinful earthly life that cannot be redeemed on its own terms. In this way the good–evil binary in slave morality is maximized in cosmic forces of God and Satan, and in the perfect rectifications of Heaven and Hell. With such cosmic binaries, the power of "fixed ideas" is perfected and secured (22), and the finitude of natural life has received its most acute antithesis. This is why it can be said that the Christian attitude toward earthly life *as such* is one of pessimism, that without a transcendent resolution natural life *is* meaningless.

Section 23 concludes Nietzsche's account of the link between theology and human "self-crucifixion and self-abuse," but he adds an interesting clarification about divinity. If we look to the Greek gods, he says, we will see that the notion of divinity does not *as such* necessarily reflect the kind of deterioration he has described. Greek religion was a "nobler" manner of depicting gods that did not run contrary to natural life in any fundamental way. The life-like characteristics of Greek gods that were perceived as "immoral" by later religious standards (and by many Greek philosophers) are, for Nietzsche, a sign that the early Greeks "deified" the "*animal* in man," thereby resisting a descent into bad conscience. Recalling the discussion of early Greek religion in Chapter 3, we can see why its life-immanence can stand on more "natural" ground by Nietzsche's standards.

CAN BAD CONSCIENCE BE OVERCOME? (SECTIONS 24–25)

Section 24 concludes the Second Essay with great force, and some elements elude easy comprehension. Here we get a sense for the full scope of Nietzsche's genealogy: much more than simply a critique of traditional morality narrowly construed, Nietzsche is targeting an entire (moralistic) world-view that he claims cannot come to terms with natural life as such. His aim is to overcome this alienation and open the door for an affirmation of life on its own terms, an opening that is framed by way of some surprising and perplexing remarks about bad conscience.

Nietzsche begins by posing a question that a reader might put to him: Is he setting up an ideal or destroying an ideal? The gist of his response is to displace the either–or binary with a both–and construction that follows the agonistic structure of will to power. He says that the establishment of "*every* ideal on earth" requires the displacement, vilification, and sacrifice of another ideal already in place: "If a shrine is to be set up, a *shrine has to be destroyed.*" Then Nietzsche moves to the ideal of bad conscience and the question of whether it can be overcome. Modern humans, he says, have inherited the long history of bad conscience and its civil war against nature. This inheritance has become so habitual that our natural inclinations themselves have become thoroughly "intertwined" with bad conscience. Against the force of this legacy, Nietzsche says that "a reverse experiment should be possible *in principle.*" The experiment would involve "an intertwining of bad conscience with *unnatural* inclinations," with all the traditional ideals that have been hostile to natural life. Nietzsche's proposal is confusing: If the unnatural inclinations stem from bad conscience, then the remedy of bringing bad conscience to these inclinations amounts to curing bad conscience with bad conscience. If Nietzsche's target is bad conscience, how can it also be the weapon?

One way to resolve the difficulty would involve recognizing different senses of "bad conscience" operating in Nietzsche's analysis. We have already been prepared for such a possibility in Sections 12 and 13, where Nietzsche insisted on the radically historical nature of cultural concepts, the meaning of which is fluid and susceptible to unexpected shifts. In this way the remedial bad conscience suggested by Nietzsche would not be identical to the bad conscience targeted in the rest of the *Genealogy.* This may work, although there are complications in such a reading, which I will get to shortly.[8]

---

[8] Ridley, in *Nietzsche's Conscience*, gives very careful attention to the mixed uses of "bad conscience," although I think the classification of "good" and "bad" forms covers up important ambiguities, and permutations of these classifications can become taxing, as in "a bad form of the *bad* bad conscience" (p. 97), which Ridley admits is a bit "baroque." A very helpful essay is Mathias Risse, "The Second Treatise in *On the Genealogy of Morality*: Nietzsche on the Origin of the Bad Conscience," *European Journal of Philosophy* 9/1 (2001), 55–81.

We can continue along these lines by recalling the notion of "active" bad conscience considered earlier, which is implicated in creative advances as distinct from sheer slavish resentment. Also applicable here could be the way in which "degeneracy" operates in creative departures from the norm, which was discussed in Chapter 3. Accordingly, bad conscience in *some* contexts – *relative* to the established power of social norms, for example – can play a positive productive role in opening up new possibilities out of its "weakness" relative to established strengths. In other words, bad conscience in a broad sense is a manifestation of *any* incapacity for, or violation of, existing orders. For support we can look right at the beginning of Section 24, at Nietzsche's claim that every ideal has emerged at the expense of an existing ideal, which in part involves "how much conscience had to be troubled" in such transitions. Also relevant here would be Nietzsche's remark in *BGE* 212: that the philosopher by nature is at odds with current ideals and assumptions, that philosophers for this reason are "the bad conscience of their times."

We could say, therefore, that bad conscience can be understood in two ways: in the specific targeted sense of life-denying attitudes, and in a "neutral" sense of alienation from any established beliefs, which Nietzsche also insists is required for *any* new advance, and which would have to include his own appeal for life-affirmation. That is why Zarathustra, in calling for the redemption of earthly life, must experience the "great contempt" for mankind, for its life-negating beliefs that have heretofore marked the human world (*Z* I, Prologue 3). Yet in Section 24 Nietzsche says that slavish bad conscience has entirely permeated the modern world; and note that he speaks of "*we* moderns," so it seems that he is not excluding himself from this affliction. Accordingly, an attempt to overcome bad conscience must be a self-overcoming, prepared by the self-disturbance of alienation from the modern world (and *its* alienation from natural life). Similar to Nietzsche's point about degeneration, this self-alienating distance can appear as bad conscience, as "immoral" from the standpoint of established modern norms. That is why Nietzsche says his "reverse experiment" would come across as a travesty: "We would have none other than the *good* men against us."

Whatever the sense of the reverse experiment proposed by Nietzsche, he concludes that it may be possible only in the future, because "we would need *another* sort of spirit (*Geist*) than we are likely to encounter in this age." Such a spirit would have an agonistic virtue that thrives on strife, a spirit "for whom conquest, adventure, danger, and even pain have become a need," who "would require a sort of sublime malice" against our protective sense of moral goodness. Nietzsche calls this a "*great health*" that may not be possible today. Such a spirit would be "the *redeeming* man of great love and contempt," a phrase drawn directly from *Zarathustra* (III, 5), which shows that a Yes toward life requires a contemptuous No toward our life-denying tradition. What is needed is a "creative spirit" who renounces anything "outside" or "beyond" natural life, who is thoroughly "immersed" in this life (Nietzsche actually uses the term "reality" here), who can "redeem it from the curse put on it by the former ideal." Nietzsche concludes by echoing the crisis that follows the death of God:

> This man of the future will redeem us, not just from the former ideal, but also from what *had to arise from it*, from the great nausea, from the will to nothingness, from nihilism . . .

Such a human of the future will give back to the earth its "goal" and to humankind its "hope." Nietzsche exhorts that "this antichrist and anti-nihilist, who has overcome both God and nothingness – *he must come one day* . . ."

NIHILISM, GENEALOGY, AND TIME

The ending of the Second Essay is powerful and complex. In order to enrich our understanding of Nietzsche's vision of a "future" condition that can overcome God and nihilism, it might be helpful to pursue further the question of nihilism in Nietzsche's thought, as well as the relationship between genealogy and time. As we have seen, Nietzsche believes that traditional constructs are *implicit* forms of nihilism because they negate the life-world; the denial of traditional beliefs (without revaluation) is simply *explicit* nihilism, which concludes that there is no meaning, value, or truth in life. For Nietzsche, nihilism is beneficial only as a transitional stage that overcomes the tradition and opens a space for something new – a form of thinking that is liberated from both the tradition and its nihilistic core (whether implicit or explicit). Those capable of such thinking will accomplish a "redemption" of the life-world, which would overcome both "God and nothingness."

I think it is important to recognize that the overcoming of nihilism, for Nietzsche, cannot mean the elimination of the ever-looming *possibility* of nihilism, because finite life *is* meaningless in a global sense; therefore affirmation is not the same as an "optimistic" attitude that finds meaning securely inscribed in reality. Life-affirmation is more a *tragic* conception that can embrace a meaning that is nevertheless ultimately consumed by life. The possibility of nihilism is something that must be confronted existentially if true affirmation is not to be a dodge of tragic limits. We may be able to connect the necessity of confronting nihilism with the "double reverse" of bad conscience in Section 24, in such a way that there is an intrinsic ambiguity there that cannot reflect clear and clean distinctions between the targeted and the remedial senses of bad conscience.

We can explore this idea further by a brief consideration of the figure of Zarathustra, to whom Nietzsche directly points in Section 25 as a model for the possibility of redeeming life. *Thus Spoke Zarathustra* is not a philosophical treatise but a narrative of Zarathustra's existential *task* of announcing and achieving life-affirmation. Zarathustra is not some prophetic sage who comes to us from the standpoint of achieved wisdom to announce a task that *we* must undergo; he himself must go through the task and experience the full range of its difficulties. The main drama of the text is Zarathustra's own experience of nihilism, not because of the loss of traditional doctrines, but because of the impact of eternal recurrence as the test for genuine life-affirmation. With eternal recurrence, everything in life will return in endless cycles of identical repetition. Zarathustra realizes that this dictates the eternal repetition of that which *he* most despises: weak humans and their life-*denying* character. This thought fills him with disgust and nausea. Yet he tells his followers that such despair is inevitable and must be experienced if life is to be truly embraced (*Z* II, 19).[9] In *Ecce Homo* Nietzsche identifies himself with Zarathustra's task (*EH* III, Z, 8), and he gives a roughly similar portrait of his own encounter with nihilism. He tells us that he has experienced

---

[9] See my discussion of the drama of Zarathustra in *Nietzsche's Life Sentence*, pp. 67–83.

decadence and pessimism to their depths (*EH* I, 1–3), and that such experience was *necessary* for opening up "reverse perspectives" beyond nihilism.

Since all experience, for Nietzsche, is a mix of "crossing" effects that cannot be separated into clear binaries, the task of overcoming nihilism must include the fact that we moderns are thoroughly shaped by the legacy of bad conscience, that we cannot throw off this legacy like a suit of clothes. If there is a possibility of altering this legacy in the direction of life-affirmation, it will involve an internal *self-recognition* of bad conscience and the potential for a self-reversal. Such a potential can be actualized only if the tension between natural life and culture is recognized *as* a tension that generates alienation, and this alienation must be *experienced* as such for any alteration to be possible. The potential for a self-reversal of bad conscience may have been what Nietzsche alluded to in Section 16, where he described bad conscience as "full of a future . . . the end of which is not yet in sight," and as "a great promise."

The question at hand can be linked to Nietzsche's larger historical narrative surrounding the death of God. I have maintained that the question of meaning in life is Nietzsche's core concern as a philosopher. Even though he accuses the European tradition of denigrating the meaning of natural life, the *death* of this tradition's figurehead and the crisis that follows may provide the sharpest and most acute possible recognition of the meaning-question, precisely *because* of the tradition's polarized posture toward natural life. Because of this binary "clarity," the recession of God in the modern world provides the deepest form of the meaning-question by way of the stark choice that Nietzsche emphasizes: *either* nihilism *or* a revaluation of life on its own terms.

The limits of human meaning are intrinsic to finite existence; therefore no honest estimation of natural life can seal off or conceal a looming meaninglessness in the human condition. Greek tragic culture was fully attentive to the radical finitude of life without surrendering to pessimism. Yet tragic poetry came to surrender its cultural status to rational philosophy, which together with Christianity shaped an entire subsequent history of the West that suppressed the tragic by force of its more optimistic principles. In *The Birth of Tragedy*, Nietzsche was hoping for a rebirth of tragic culture, but such a prospect could not simply be a retrieval of Greek culture. This is why the death of God and its consequences came to play such a central role in Nietzsche's later thinking. Because of the West's wholesale struggle against natural life, the death of God presents an internal deconstruction of its optimistic assumptions, and I think that Nietzsche finds importance in the post-Greek tradition for the following reason: The Christian God was both a symbol of transcendence and a *total* picture of reality and life that swept everything up in its story of the *complete* victory of "spirit" over "nature" (see *TI* 9, 5). With the deconstructive effect of God's death, the tradition's binary totalism allows for an *unprecedented* clarification of, and concentration on, the stark problem of meaning in life. More than any other period in history, we confront this problem in its most comprehensive and unadorned form: either nihilism or revaluation, with nothing in between. With the death of God, bad conscience can *experience* itself in the most acute manner for what it is, but this can also prepare the possibility of the most decisive way in which life *can* be meaningful and affirmable on its own terms.

Also relevant for this discussion is a consideration of Nietzsche's genealogy in relation to time and history. It is not the case that Nietzsche is simply condemning past beliefs and aiming to utterly replace them with some new set of beliefs in the future. Since the tradition had been marked by an antagonism toward becoming, time, and history, genealogy goes further than merely considering past, present, or future beliefs; it presupposes the radically temporal and historical character of beliefs as such, including Nietzsche's own philosophical ventures. I think that Nietzsche's genealogical method entails the following temporal structure: We cannot help but think presently in terms of our inheritance of the past. No human thinking or experience can be absolutely new in the strict sense. In addition, the past had to achieve a certain stability in order to *be* an inheritance, to sustain itself over time and across generations. The mistake is to take this stability as a secure truth that is immune to change. Genealogy alerts us to history in its dynamic complexity, contingency, and movement. Our past is *given* to us in time, and these past beliefs at one time challenged and replaced other beliefs that had achieved a certain stability. Therefore our present appropriation of past beliefs cannot presume them to be "givens" in the sense of self-evident truths. Genealogy disturbs self-evidency by revisioning the past – and our present reliance on the past – as something *questionable*, as intrinsically open to question.

The questionable character of historical inheritance should not be confused with radical skepticism or wholesale refutation, both of which actually imply detachment from history, as though we could somehow divorce ourselves from the past. Genealogy simply *revises* beliefs into something less stable, something inherently alterable. We can see this even more clearly if we realize that genealogy, for Nietzsche, not only concerns the present and the past, but the future as well. Our past was once a present engaging its past in the context of future possibilities, some of which came to alter those current appropriations of the past. Our own present appropriation of the past is never a dead repetition but a setting for movement toward our own future possibilities, some of which may alter our present world. If our past, our tradition, were truly self-evident and beyond question, this would have to be the first time in history that such was the case. Nevertheless, we can be inclined to cover up *historical* existence under the dogmatic cloak of "permanent" truths. Yet in this way we are blind to the value of past creative incursions into stability that we now rely on for stability. With sheer stability, the future would be nothing more than a repetition of present patterns. If *our* past had been of this sort it would not have produced the innovations that we now rely on. Genealogy, therefore, also concerns our own time, its past *and* its future, a future that can be genuinely open if we heed the *questionable* character of our past and thus of our present.

Nietzsche's text is itself an enactment of the temporal structure of genealogy; it shows how our present life is shaped by its past, but a questionable past that calls for a creative future prompted by disturbances to our current certainties. Nietzsche's specific venture is to uncover the nature-suppressing dangers in our cultural history, as well as the dramatic crossroads we face with the death of God and a looming nihilism. This is where the turn to the future – the "man of the future" in the *Genealogy* and "philosophers of the future" in other texts – fills out the temporal scope of genealogy. Yet it is not clear what this figure of the future represents. Is it some specific person or type that will deliver some "new" vision of the world, which will replace past visions, or resolve historical errors, or bring an end to cultural decline? Our recognition of the ambiguities in Nietzsche's critiques and his understanding of historical time would have to put such a picture in doubt. It is surely the case that Section 24 expresses an anticipation of something to come in the future. But perhaps what is to come is less a "what" and more a "how," less a new condition to replace old conditions and more the *capacity* to live and think in an affirmative posture toward a natural life of time as such. Nietzsche's "philosophers of the future" may be distinguished primarily by *how* they think and not merely what they think. Their thinking may not reflect something utterly different, but rather their ability to withstand and overcome the crisis of a looming nihilism, and thus to get over the time-suppressing character of traditional philosophy that moved toward this crisis in the first place. The philosopher of the future will be able to affirm life by affirming the radical temporality of existence. If we recall a previous reference to philosophers as the bad conscience of their time, as ever at odds with current ideals, the passage in question also describes the philosopher as "*necessarily* a man of tomorrow and the day after tomorrow" (*BGE* 212). The last part of this phrase suggests an *ongoing* reach beyond the present and the past, even beyond the tomorrow that will next become a present. Can we say, then, that the philosopher of the future is less a figure *in* the future that will bring some task to completion, and more a philosopher *of* the future in the genitive possessive sense, a philosopher possessed and animated *by* the power of the future as such, the futurial *movement* of a radically temporal life?

CHAPTER 5

The third essay: What do ascetic ideals mean?

The third essay offers an answer to the question whence the ascetic ideal, the priests' ideal, derives its tremendous *power* even though it is the *harmful* ideal *par excellence*, a will to the end, an ideal of decadence. Answer: not, as people may believe, because God is at work behind the priests but *faut de mieux* [lacking something better] – because it was the only ideal so far, "For man would rather will nothingness than *not* will." – Above all, a *counterideal* was lacking – until *Zarathustra*. (*EH* III, GM)

Before beginning the tour of this essay, it is necessary to establish something about the first section in relation to a remark in the book's Preface, Section 8. There Nietzsche calls the Third Essay an example of what he means by "the art of interpretation (*Auslegung*)." The essay, he says, "is a commentary (*Commentar*) on the aphorism that precedes it." It had almost always been assumed that the aphorism in question is the epigraph drawn from *Thus Spoke Zarathustra* (*Z* I, 7) that precedes Section 1: "Carefree, mocking, violent – this is how wisdom wants *us*: she is a woman, all she ever loves is a warrior." In recent years, however, John Wilcox, Maudemarie Clark, and Christopher Janaway have shown conclusively that the aphorism in question is actually Section 1.[1] Wilcox also notes that *Auslegung* can mean "explication" as well as "interpretation," and that the use of "commentary" in the Preface suggests that the Third Essay is an "exegesis" of Section 1. Accordingly, this section provides clues about how the entire essay unfolds.

---

[1] For a discussion of this question, see John T. Wilcox, "That Exegesis of an Aphorism in *Genealogy* III: Reflections on the Scholarship," *Nietzsche Studien* 27 (1998), 448–462.

SECTION I AND THE THIRD ESSAY

With the corrected orientation to this section, its terms can provide tracking points for the course and structure of the full essay that follows. The section outlines different ways in which the ascetic ideal can manifest itself (note the plural in the essay's title): in artists, scholars, philosophers, women, priests, and saints. I am indebted to Christa Davis Acampora for suggesting the following possible course of the essay's sections in the light of Section 1: Ascetic ideals exhibited in artists (2–4), in philosophers (5–8), in the priest (9–13), in women and unhealthy types (14), then the priest again as a healing force for unhealthy types (15–17), then a "rumination" expanding upon the previous sections (17–21), then the question of science as an inadequate opponent of ascetic ideals (23–24), then art as a possible opponent (25), and finally the general possibility (held in suspense) of the ascetic ideal's *self*-overcoming and what such a future course might involve (26–28).

I think such an outline can be very helpful for reading the essay, and in rough terms my commentary accords with it, although my own sections and treatment will follow a thematic sequence that is not entirely framed as a specific tracking of the terms in Section 1. I do want to stress, however, the multiple ways in which the ascetic ideal appears in the essay. Religious practices of self-denial are surely the connotation associated with "asceticism," and yet Nietzsche applies the term to many non-religious domains. This is a complicated question, but I think we can take note of a previous point about the historical fluidity of cultural concepts. Nevertheless it still seems odd that Nietzsche would associate the ascetic ideal with areas such as philosophy and science. Yet we should also recall a previous suggestion about Nietzsche's rhetorical choices. Even though science, say, seems to have little in common with religious asceticism, Nietzsche is happy to retain the rhetorical force of asceticism because it keeps alive the fundamental question at the heart of the *Genealogy*: the value and meaning of natural life. Religious asceticism would likely admit its opposition to natural existence as such. Subsequent cultural developments might conceive of themselves as not religious in this sense, as not conflicted with natural life. Yet Nietzsche insists that these developments *continue* in different ways to harbor a disaffection with core natural forces, and the retention of "asceticism" is meant to force the question of life-denial on our attention throughout the essay. This is why the little "dialogue" at the end of Section 1 is also important, because it highlights the problem of nihilism and life-affirmation. According to Nietzsche, the ascetic ideal shows that the human will "prefers to will *nothingness* rather than *not* will." This is a complex point that plays itself out in the essay, and Nietzsche suggests in the dialogue that it is a "new" point that could elude the reader's comprehension. So, he says, "let us begin again." It seems that the Third Essay is a recapitulation of preceding elements of the *Genealogy*, yet now from a sharpened perspective that puts the full force of life-affirmation, life-denial, and the problem of nihilism on the table for the remaining part of the book (note that the line about willing nothingness is repeated in the very last sentence of the book).

ART AND THE ASCETIC IDEAL (SECTIONS 2–4)

The question of art and asceticism is an intricate one. The first line in Section 1 holds that with artists the ascetic ideal means "nothing, or too many different things." It is hard to fathom what this means, but at least there is an ambiguous relationship between art and asceticism, as we will see. In any case, in Section 2 Nietzsche cites Wagner as an example of an artist who can come to renounce sensuality on behalf of chastity. The tension between sensuous passion and dispassionate ideals, between "animal and angel," need not be anti-life, Nietzsche tells us; in fact, it can be a "precarious balancing act" that is an *enticement* to life, as in the case of Goethe.

In Section 3, however, Nietzsche takes up Wagner's opera *Parsifal* as an art work dangerously prone to asceticism, as a celebration of sexual renunciation in the form of Christian love. Such would be the case if the opera is taken seriously, yet Nietzsche wonders if it might be meant as a comedy, as a kind of parody of renunciation. He nevertheless dubs a comic interpretation of *Parsifal* as more a wish on his part. If the opera is meant to be serious, then it surely succumbs to a Christian hatred of "knowledge, spirit (*Geist*), and sensuality," which would wind up being Wagner's own self-denial of the original aim of his art to be "the highest spiritualization (*Vergeistigung*) and sensualization." The point seems to be that the most life-serving art can be seduced into ascetic life-denial.[2]

In Section 4 Nietzsche takes up the relation between artists and their work. He claims that an artist is simply the womb and soil for the work, who therefore should be "forgotten" if the work is to be enjoyed. Moreover, we should not "identify" an artist with what is portrayed in the work; here Nietzsche is challenging the familiar idea that art is the expression of the artist's own character or intentions. Yet Nietzsche is more than simply denying the "authority" of the artist when it comes to the meaning of a work; he says that artists would not be able to *create* a work if they were identical to the world of their work:

> Homer would not have created Achilles and Goethe would not have created Faust, if Homer had been an Achilles and Goethe a Faust. A perfect and complete artist is cut off from the "real" and the actual for all eternity.

It is not clear what Nietzsche is up to here, because it would seem obvious that an author is not *identical* to a character in a work (except in an autobiography). I think that Nietzsche is retrieving something that goes back to *The Birth of Tragedy*, namely that art is essentially "appearance" rather than "reality" in the strict sense. And yet the reference to Homer and *an* Achilles makes me wonder if there is also an echo here of the notion we encountered earlier in the text about master and slave types and the "degeneracy" of creativity, in that creative types are not fully absorbed in the "reality" of their world and are withdrawn from the spontaneity of fully active types. We can say at least that an Achilles would not have had the "distance" from his world to be able to create, or even want to create, something like the *Iliad*.

At any rate, Nietzsche seems to find in Wagner's *Parsifal* an exhibition of fatigue over the "unreality" of art, and an inclination to penetrate what is forbidden to art, namely "*real* being." Yet since such an inclination runs counter not only to art but to the conditions of becoming in natural life, Nietzsche detects in Wagner an intimation of Schopenhauerian pessimism and nihilism, and thus an

---

[2] See Sarah Kofman, "Wagner's Ascetic Ideal According to Nietzsche," in Schacht, ed., *Nietzsche, Genealogy, Morality*, pp. 193–213.

acute form of the ascetic ideal. We will have more to say about the way in which art might be a counterplay to asceticism, especially in terms of artistic "appearance" over against metaphysical "reality."

ART AND PHILOSOPHY (SECTIONS 5–6)

In Section 5 Nietzsche continues a rather ambiguous depiction of art. Repeating his claim that ascetic ideals mean nothing to artists (or so many things as to amount to nothing), Nietzsche decides to "put artists aside for the time being" (the significance of art will thus return in the text). It is not at all clear what "nothing" or "too many things" signify. But the ensuing discussion may be a clue. It seems that the ascetic *ideal* is a high-order form of thought, and it is here associated with philosophy. Despite the creativity of artists, Nietzsche says that they are still beholden to forces in the world for support, that they are not "sufficiently independent" to provide the deepest insight into the questions at hand. He claims that Wagner needed the support of Schopenhauer's philosophy to give him the "*courage* for an ascetic ideal."

Although Nietzsche always celebrates the significance of art, he does not find art *as such* to be sufficient for addressing the questions he is pursuing. He seems to claim a special kind of freedom for philosophy, for its *conceptual* departure from any particular area of culture, which opens up the deepest possible articulation of the meaning of human culture and its most far-reaching questions. For background, we should take a look at how Nietzsche exhibits this outlook even in *The Birth of Tragedy*, which purportedly champions art and tragedy against the advent of Socratic philosophy. In that book Nietzsche celebrates tragic myth as being more profound than both a rational model of existence (*BT* 23) and a tendency to ossify myths into a kind of "juvenile history" (*BT* 10), or what we would call a religious fundamentalism that conflates mythical images with actual realities. Tragic drama undermines this kind of religious literalism in two ways: (1) theatrical artifice is recognized as a form of creative appearance; and (2) Dionysian deformation "takes back" all forms through the force of negative fate. The Apollonian–Dionysian confluence in tragic drama at once *displays* and *limits* the formation of cultural meaning. This is why Nietzsche thinks that in tragic art "myth attains its most profound content" (*BT* 10). Tragic myth *presents* a finite world of meaningful appearances that, despite being "apparent," are *not* renounced in favor of transcendence or abnegation. Tragic appearances have a "reality" because they tell us: "Look there! Look closely! This is your life" (*BT* 24).

At the same time, Nietzsche admits that the *meaning* of tragic myth "never became transparent in conceptual clarity to the Greek poets," which is one reason why tragedy did not have the strength to survive (*BT* 17). He tells us that "the structure of the scenes and the visual images reveal a deeper wisdom than the poet himself can put into words and concepts," and that Nietzsche's own conceptual efforts are pursuing a philosophical account of that wisdom (*BT* 17). It should be clear that tragic poetry by itself would not suffice for Nietzsche's intellectual tasks. Philosophical concept formation (e.g., "the tragic") provides a deepened and enhanced comprehension of the meaning and purpose of cultural phenomena. Yet as a reflective enterprise, philosophical understanding has to "distance" itself from pre-philosophical, pre-conceptual cultural forms. Such distance harbors the danger of philosophical alienation from, even hostility toward, pre-conceptual culture. The advent of Socratic philosophy in the Greek world is the original case study of this danger, wherein concept formation resisted the force of becoming to create structures of "being" that could quell or govern flux for the purpose of secured knowledge and conscious mastery of life.

In *The Birth of Tragedy* Nietzsche aims for much more than a historical analysis of Greek culture; he is meditating on the very nature of philosophy and its future prospects, indeed the coming of a new tragic age (*EH* III, BT, 4). Philosophy must always draw on pre-conceptual sources – in terms of pre-existing artistic cultural productions and by way of philosophy's own creative impulses that cannot be reduced to its conceptual products. The problem, as Nietzsche sees it, is that Platonic philosophy and its inheritors represent an antagonistic, eliminative disposition toward pre-conceptual, aesthetic, tragic origins. In *The Birth of Tragedy* Nietzsche poses the question of whether this antagonism between the theoretical and the tragic world-view is inevitable and beyond resolution (*BT* 17). He thinks not, and suggests an image for reconciliation in the figure of an "artistic Socrates" (*BT* 14, 15, 17), a thinker who is not averse to aesthetic modes, who indeed can employ such modes in the practice of philosophy.

It is not enough, however, to coordinate conceptual and artistic production in philosophy. Such coordination implies a tragic limit because of the indigenous abyss at the heart of philosophy (indeed all cultural production) owing to its "creative," rather than "foundational," base. Reflecting back on *The Birth of Tragedy*, Nietzsche claims that in this work he had discovered the *concept* of the tragic, and that he sees himself as "the first *tragic philosopher*," the first to offer a "transposition of the Dionysian into a philosophical pathos" (*EH* III, BT, 3). In that book philosophy has a higher status than tragic art, and yet it is drawn *from* tragic art in retaining a *self-limiting* check on the "reality" of philosophical concepts. This is why Nietzsche applauds Kant and Schopenhauer for initiating the *self-overcoming* of reason by way of their limiting rational constructs to "appearances" that cannot comprehend noumenal "reality" (*BT* 18). In this way, philosophical optimism dies at its own hands; such self-limitation even amounts to a "Dionysian wisdom apprehended in concepts" (*BT* 20). The path is now open for a more comprehensive wisdom that can embrace the whole of life, including the terrors of nature. The self-limitation of reason causes the theoretical mind to shudder before an abyss. But Nietzsche thinks that such a self-imposed anxiety harbors the healthy prospect of overcoming optimism and cultivating a tragic disposition that can *recover* pre-philosophical origins in a new way.

Yet anxiety before the abyss can also prompt pessimistic despair and nihilism, as in the case of Schopenhauer, which gets us back to Section 5 and the way in which philosophy can become implicated with the ascetic ideal. Nietzsche considers Schopenhauer to be a "genuine philosopher," who possesses the independence to stand by himself without the need for support from other authorities, unlike the artist Wagner who needs the philosophy of Schopenhauer to shape his thinking. Yet Schopenhauer succumbed to the ascetic ideal, especially in his thoughts on music, to which he gave special significance as the most direct expression of "reality," the "in itself" of the Will behind all appearances. This very impulse to penetrate a reality behind appearances is what turned Schopenhauer's philosophy and Wagner's art into a *metaphysics*, which Nietzsche tells us here is the deepest spirit of the ascetic ideal, the urge to pass beyond, and pass over, the appearances of natural life.

Section 6 seems to be a diversion into aesthetic theory, but it actually articulates further Nietzsche's association of art and philosophy with the ascetic ideal. He takes up Schopenhauer's apparent agreement with Kant's theory of beauty and aims to show something very different going on in Schopenhauer. Kant had tried to demonstrate that beauty, whether in art or nature, could be understood in a universal manner, despite its being a "subjective" occasion rather than an objective fact. For Kant, beauty is a perception of pleasure without "interest," without any of the normal motives in the cost–benefit business of life. The pleasure of beauty comes from disinterested contemplation, where features of the object strike us independently of any relation to our needs. So the beauty of a tree, for example, is perceived "for its own sake," its presence freed from any utility, and even from the project to gain knowledge of the tree.[3]

Nietzsche takes two paths in critiquing this Kantian inheritance in Schopenhauer. First, he thinks that Kant is trapped in a "spectator" theory of beauty that is too narrow in omitting the standpoint of the creative artist. And once the *experiences* of artists are brought into the mix, we find that "disinterest" is a strange concept, given that artists exhibit "a fund of strong personal experiences, desires, surprises, and delights in the field of beauty." Second, Nietzsche thinks that Schopenhauer's appropriation of Kant departs from the latter's theory in a fundamental way. Here Nietzsche is highlighting the role that art plays in Schopenhauer's pessimism: The disinterested contemplation of art provides not only access to universality, but also a respite from the normal striving of the will, and this respite is a pleasurable release from the unending (and futile) cycle of pleasures and pains in life. Since Schopenhauer's philosophy does not countenance any transcendent or worldly deliverance from this cycle, art gives us a temporary glimpse of why renouncing the will to live is the only mark of wisdom and mode of salvation. According to Nietzsche, in this way Schopenhauer betrays Kantian aesthetics because he displays

[3] See Immanuel Kant, *Critique of Judgment*, trans. Werner Pluhar (Indianapolis, IN: Hackett Publishing, 1987), Sections 20–22.

a profound *interest* in art as an alleviation of pain. Nietzsche claims that Schopenhauer's outlook cannot suffice for a theory of beauty and art because it only addresses "one effect of beauty, that of calming the will." Nevertheless Nietzsche draws from this outlook a "hint" for answering the question of how and why a philosopher would honor the ascetic ideal: "he wants *to free himself from torture.*"

A NATURAL PERSPECTIVE ON ASCETICISM (SECTION 7)

We come to an important part of the Third Essay that begins to make good on the line in Section 1 about willing nothingness. Nietzsche offers the remarkable claim that Schopenhauer was not actually a pessimist, even though he wanted to be one. What can this mean, given that Schopenhauer identified his philosophy as a pessimistic denial of meaning in life? On top of the discussion of Schopenhauer's ascetic pain-killing maneuver, Nietzsche alerts us to "the other side of the account," which amounts to a naturalistic perspective on Schopenhauer's pessimism: In other words, independent of Schopenhauer's metaphysical position on the nature of "reality" and its meaninglessness, Nietzsche asks about Schopenhauer's own personal posture as a pessimist, about what it means to *live* in that posture. He begins to articulate how even pessimism from this standpoint is a form of will to power that gives meaning to life in an agonistic relation to antithetical forces (in Schopenhauer's case, sexuality, women, and Hegel). Nietzsche claims that Schopenhauer *needed* these enemies to *avoid* becoming a pessimist. How so? The full implications of unadulterated pessimism would seem to subvert any impulse to *participate* in a meaningless existence; yet Schopenhauer lived a long, engaged, productive life of vigorous opposition to "optimism," especially a life of writing sophisticated books for a reading public, of bringing the wisdom of pessimism to bear on how people should think and live. This is why Nietzsche says that Schopenhauer's enemies "held him tight and kept seducing him back to existence." As a result, Schopenhauer was able to cure sheer nausea and find his own kind of "happiness." Such, I think, is Nietzsche's naturalistic redescription of pessimism that begins to articulate the distinction he made in Section 1 between *willing* nothingness and *not* willing.

Nietzsche then moves beyond the "personal case" of Schopenhauer to consider philosophers in general (which he calls coming "back to our problem"). He claims that "as long as there are philosophers on earth" they exhibit an "irritation and rancor against sensuality." Owing to this posture against the immediacy of natural experience – whether it be in the service of transcendent aims or simply the more modest project of bringing conceptual order to sense experience – Nietzsche says that philosophers have always been partial to the ascetic ideal, to the self-castigation of natural sensuality. He even makes the seemingly reductive claim that a *genuine* philosopher is marked by such ascetic tendencies, without which one is only a *so-called* philosopher (we leave aside for the moment the difficult question of whether Nietzsche is including himself in this typology, a question that I think echoes the ambiguities in earlier discussions of bad conscience).

Nietzsche then completes his naturalistic account of the seem- ingly *anti*-natural impulses in philosophy. These impulses are simply another form of will to power. Like all animals, the "*bête philosophe*" instinctively aims for optimal conditions of power in the midst of obstacles to these conditions. The agonistic structure of will to power accounts for a philosopher's *aversion* to sensuality (and things like home life) in the service of a stimulating *freedom* for a life of thought. The ascetic *ideal* names precisely this kind of power over natural forces that opens up the power of thinking. As in the case of Schopenhauer, the ascetic ideal in philosophers is not actually a form of life-denial, but an *affirmation* of a life marked by "the highest and boldest intel- lectuality (*Geistigkeit*)." Nietzsche adds, however, that affirmation here only applies to a particular kind of life, because the philosopher "affirms *his* existence and *only* his existence."

There emerges in this section an important problem that I will postpone addressing until the treatment of Section 13. In claiming that pessimism and asceticism, from a naturalistic perspective, are not actually a form of life-denial, we run up against two daunting questions: (1) What are we to make, then, of Nietzsche's frequent charge that these postures *are* a form of life-denial? (2) If these postures are not life-denying, what, if any, is the difference between their form of "affirmation" and Nietzsche's own ideal of life-affirmation? The text must surprise us at this point, and these perplexing questions have not, I think, been adequately recognized or engaged in the scholarly literature. Later I will try to suggest answers to these questions.

THE PHILOSOPHER AND THE ASCETIC IDEAL (SECTIONS 8–10)

Now Nietzsche begins to sketch the ways in which philosophy is correlated with ascetic self-denial. In Section 8 he catalogues various dispositions of intellectual life that by nature run against normal goods. The development of intellectual powers (*Geistigkeit*) has required a "desert" of freedom from sensuality and common practices, a psychic desert that renounces most of what the world values in order to think differently and deeply. Nietzsche describes a set of seclusions, routines, and austerities of a thinker's life, and he includes an autobiographical reference, which shows that he *is* including himself in this depiction of philosophers. I think that the account here mirrors the treatment of "we knowers" in the Preface, whose "absent-minded" alienation from natural experience echoes what Section 10 will call "the peculiarly withdrawn attitude of philosophers." A philosophical disposition, therefore, bears a resemblance to classic ascetic values: poverty, humility, and chastity. But Nietzsche adds that philosophical "chastity" should not be understood as a hatred or sheer denial of sexuality. He claims that philosophical production is simply a re-routing of sexual energy in other directions, so that the "disinclination" to sex is actually a "transfiguration" of erotic drives into intellectual work. Indeed, Nietzsche associates philosophical chastity with a kind of pregnancy and "*maternal* instinct" that bring forth "a different progeny than children."

Section 9 summarizes Nietzsche's discussion by saying that "a certain asceticism" is both a precondition for, and a consequence of, the "highest spirituality (*Geistigkeit*)." The link between philosophy and the ascetic ideal has been so close and strong that he concludes: "it was only by the *leading-strings* of this ideal that philosophy ever learned to take its first little steps on earth." This is so because the drives and virtues of philosophers – doubt, analysis, research, investigation, risk, non-partisanship – began as violations of primary and prevailing modes of morality and conscience. Measured against the morality of custom, philosophy was a kind of outlaw phenomenon, and philosophers themselves sensed their heretical status. If philosophy is now considered a worthy pursuit, Nietzsche reiterates his genealogical principle that "all good things used to be bad things at one time." Every advance on earth was originally a struggle against existing forces that could only unfold by way of "spiritual and physical torment." Every significant cultural *change* was originally perceived as dangerous, immoral, and ruinous; and the profound changes brought by philosophers were perceived no differently.

Section 10 rehearses an earlier discussion of the "degeneracy" of creative types when measured by established codes. According to Nietzsche, reflective contemplation was originally so different from an active, warlike world that it had to arouse a certain fear of its deviancy in both the community and contemplatives themselves. Philosophers in the beginning had to struggle against their own *resistance* to their posture against existing ways of life. In other words, philosophical thinking was both an internal and external struggle; it was a fight against its world, but it had to fight *for* its deviant power within the living psyches of philosophers. They had to use terrible means of self-castigating cruelty against the forces of custom and tradition in their own selves, so that "they could *believe* in their own innovations" as something worthy and achievable.

At this point Nietzsche establishes a historical relation between philosophers and religious ascetics. Although philosophers were not identical to ascetic priests, the posture against normal life in both types had similar or analogous features. That is why Nietzsche says that philosophers had to pattern themselves on previously established religious types in order to get their bearings or appear in an already familiar form. Since philosophy *is* a struggle against normal modes of life, it took its cues, or found its inspiration, from the life-denying disposition of ascetics. Although Nietzsche is not entirely clear here, he claims that philosophy would not have been historically possible without the precedence of the ascetic ideal. Why? Because philosophy developed and had to sustain itself in "conditions of crisis" that needed something like the ascetic ideal to shape and valorize its radical bearing.

At the same time, Nietzsche is at pains in this section to differentiate the philosopher from religious asceticism. The historical function of the ascetic ideal in philosophy's development is called by

Nietzsche an outward appearance, a mask, even philosophy's own self-misconception. Although philosophy always bears a certain struggle of natural life against itself (thus showing some resemblance to the ascetic ideal), Nietzsche nonetheless wants to keep open the possibility of a liberation of philosophy from the ascetic ideal – despite the fact that this ideal "has been maintained until most recently" as the guiding spirit of philosophy. Even though the ascetic priest had been the prevailing model for philosophers in the past, he asks: "Have things *really* changed" in our "more enlightened world?" He wonders:

Is there enough pride, daring, courage, self-confidence, will of spirit, will to take responsibility, *freedom of will*, for "the philosopher" on earth to be really – *possible*? . . . [4]

THE ASCETIC PRIEST (SECTION 11)

Nietzsche now zeroes in on the ascetic priest as the essential prototype for understanding the meaning of ascetic ideals, whatever form they may take. I have indicated that Nietzsche's emphasis on this type is largely for rhetorical impact in forcing us to engage life-denying elements in the Western tradition – rather than a strict identification of various ascetic tendencies (like philosophy) with religious forms of self-denial. Yet here Nietzsche's discussion of the priest is more substantive because it aims to show why such tendencies ever took hold in natural life, why nature could produce successful counter-natural movements. To that end Nietzsche turns his naturalistic eye on the kinds of power and interest that ascetic priests stood for in their *lives*.

Nietzsche stipulates his opposition to the ascetic ideal as well as an admission that the ascetic priest is a formidable adversary. He also says, somewhat oddly, that the priest is not the best defender of his ideal, and that we (opponents) must "help him . . . to defend himself well against us." This gesture is not easy to understand.

---

[4] This passage would lend the most support for the idea that the sovereign individual is a Nietzschean ideal (or at least bears some relation to it). Yet I still believe that the discussion in the Second Essay bears too much weight against the idea.

Surely it cannot be a defense of asceticism's metaphysical project (a transcendent reality). Rather, I think it advances a naturalistic account of how and why such an ideal would succeed in natural life – because, as Nietzsche insists, the ascetic ideal is far from a historical "exception and curiosity," it is a historical *reality*, indeed "one of the most widespread and long-enduring facts there are."

The contest enjoined by Nietzsche is "the *valuation* of our life by the ascetic priests," their opposition to the natural world of becoming on behalf of an utterly different reality. But since natural life excludes any such reality, what would be the naturalistic explanation of why an impulse toward this reality could arise at all, much less prosper? To appreciate the distinctiveness of Nietzsche's approach, we can compare it with two alternatives: A metaphysical defense of ascetic tendencies could point to psychological disaffection with life as a kind of evidence that we are not meant for this life. Surely human existence is difficult to bear, and why couldn't our disaffections be a kind of "lure" from a transcendent reality? On the other hand, a naturalistic critique of ascetic tendencies (in the manner of scientific naturalism) would attribute them to cognitive errors or psychological deficiencies. Nietzsche also targets the psychology of asceticism, but I do not think that he rests his critique on the "falsehood" of religious beliefs. *His* naturalistic approach avoids the "hand-waving" dismissal of religion on cognitive grounds by wondering how such phenomena – despite their being *metaphysical* errors – could ever *take hold* in history with such force and success to the degree that they have in the West. At some point, an "error" becomes way too big to be easily dismissed (and besides, as Nietzsche maintains, religious "errors" have been implicated in the full range of Western intellectual developments, including science). So in a way Nietzsche is granting a measure of deep respect to something he nevertheless opposes, and he is attempting to uncover how the ascetic ideal could become so *powerful* in natural life.

The ascetic priest's hostility to life has continually "grown and prospered" *in* life. Consequently Nietzsche's life-philosophy cannot rest with an utter rejection of its importance or an over-confident critique of its truth. The prosperity of the ascetic ideal must stem from "a necessity of the first rank." Despite the fact that "an ascetic life is a self-contradiction," its "necessity" must be found in its being a form of *life*. Indeed, Nietzsche concludes that *"life itself must have an interest* that such a self-contradictory type not die out." It is crucial to recognize the dramatic features of Nietzsche's analysis and how it figures in the rest of the text. Since there is no vantage point *outside* natural life-phenomena, then even a phenomenon that "opposes" life must somehow figure in the "interest" of life. This is the complicated puzzle driving Nietzsche's genealogical study, and we have already noticed that such self-opposed tendencies figure in both the further-ance of certain (weak) types of life *and* the opening up of valuable cultural possibilities that expand human existence beyond the setting and sheer force of brute nature.

In any case, Nietzsche closes the section with a significant descrip-tion of what makes the ascetic priest's power different from other forms of will to power. The priest displays a degree of resentment that goes global: The will to power of asceticism "wants to be master, not over something in life, but over life itself and its deepest, strongest, most profound conditions." Here, Nietzsche says, "an attempt is made to use power (*Kraft*) to obstruct the sources (*Quellen*) of power." The ascetic priest turns against the beauties and joys of carnal life, and yet a *new* kind of satisfaction unfolds: "pleasure is *looked for* and found in failure, decay, pain, misfortune, ugliness, voluntary depri-vation, self-destruction, self-flagellation, and self-sacrifice." From the standpoint of nature, this amounts to "a conflict that *wills* itself to be conflicting," that exalts in itself proportionate to the degree in which its *natural* life capacities are *diminished.*[5]

Before we move on to the next section, I want to repeat for emphasis two important features of Nietzsche's discussion of the ascetic ideal: (1) Nietzsche does not dismiss the value of the ascetic ideal – even though he is standing against it – because it is a *life*-phenomenon that must be understood in terms of how it brings meaning to certain kinds of life and how it figures variously in a wide range of cultural developments. (2) The ascetic ideal exhibits a unique form of will to power in that it seeks oppositional power over *all* of natural life; this is different from other instances of power *within* natural existence

[5] For an excellent discussion of ascetic cruelty and will to power, see Ivan Soll, "Nietzsche on Cruelty, Asceticism, and the Failure of Hedonism," in Schacht, ed., *Nietzsche, Genealogy, Morality*, pp. 168–192.

that seek to overcome specific life-phenomena to further *other* life interests. We have noted the reciprocal, agonistic structure of will to power as a dynamic *field* of becoming, which correlates any instance of meaning with finite limits and resistances. In effect, ascetic will to power aims to overcome natural will to power as such, because it seeks to escape the agonistic structure of becoming into a realm of secured "being." The ascetic ideal amounts to a natural paradox in that ascetic power is a self-consuming drive to escape will to power itself – in other words, to overcome the field of overcoming. Yet such a paradox would be injurious only for the *metaphysical* project of asceticism, not the specific life interests it can serve. As we proceed, the two elements I have identified here will figure significantly in our attempt to comprehend Nietzsche's coming discussions and central elements of the text as a whole.

THE ASCETIC IDEAL AND TRUTH (SECTION 12)

This section comes across as something of a digression, but I believe it advances an essential feature in Nietzsche's *Genealogy*: the question of truth. He returns to the phenomenon of philosophy and asks: What happens when ascetic self-denial, its "will to contradiction and counter-nature," becomes philosophical? It expands its vision beyond mere "personalized" (*leibhaften*) life matters to larger matters of truth and reality. Ascetic philosophy turns the table on what natural experience finds to be "true and real." Philosophy now finds "*error* precisely where the real instinct of life most surely posits truth." Corporeality, pain, and plurality are now "illusions." Similarly the senses, appearances, and one's own personal selfhood are renounced in favor of a super-sensible truth. Ascetic philosophy can push denial so far that it even excludes human reason from this higher truth. In this regard Nietzsche directly points to Kant, whose critical philosophy limited reason to "appearances," and who therefore rendered noumenal "reality" inaccessible to human knowledge.

It is clear from this passage that Nietzsche is countering an ascetic view of truth with a natural sphere of truth and reality. What kind of truth is Nietzsche advancing here? It cannot be the same as standard models of truth in the philosophical tradition, which even if more worldly than ascetic transcendence have relied on fixed standards of certainty and universality. To begin, Nietzsche says that we "knowers" (*Erkennende*) should have some gratitude for ascetic "reversals of familiar perspectives and valuations," because in principle "to see differently, and *want* to see differently" is valuable (this recalls the ambiguous virtue of bad conscience). Indeed, Nietzsche says that such differential practice "is no small discipline and preparation of the intellect for its coming 'objectivity.'" What does Nietzsche mean here by objectivity (put in scare quotes)? It is not the traditional standard of "disinterested contemplation," which Nietzsche calls an absurdity, owing to its pretense of knowledge disengaged from human interests and values. Rather, his sense of objectivity, while indeed an expanded horizon beyond narrow perspectives, nevertheless remains within an agonistic *field* of perspectives that is continually navigated and gathered in a manner that does not come to rest in any fixed or universal measure. Nietzsche calls it an ability or power (*Vermögen*), in the exercise of which:

one's Pro and Con are *under control* and alternately displayed and retracted (*sein Für und Wider in der Gewalt zu haben und aus- und einzuhängen*), so that one knows how to use the *differences* in perspectives and affect-interpretations for knowledge.

Nietzsche here declares what has come to be named his "perspectivism." He calls upon philosophers to henceforth be on guard against the dangerous conceptual fictions of "pure reason" (a reference to Kant), a "pure, will-less, painless, timeless subject of knowledge" (a reference to Schopenhauer), "absolute spirit" (a reference to Hegel), or "knowledge in itself." Such notions propose something impossible for natural, embodied, situated beings: "an eye turned in no direction at all" (what has come to called "the view from nowhere"), where "the active and interpretive powers are to be suppressed, absent, yet through which seeing is first and only a seeing-something." To rescue the natural sphere of interpretive powers, Nietzsche announces his perspectival model of knowledge, which also fills out the sense of objectivity he had just mentioned:

There is *only* a perspectival seeing, *only* a perspectival "knowing." And the *more* affects we are able to bring to words about a thing or matter (*Sache*), the *more* eyes, different eyes we are able to use for this same thing, the more complete will be our "concept" of the thing, our "objectivity."

The importance of this moment in the *Genealogy* cannot be over-estimated. Yet its meaning and implications are not given much extended discussion in the text. Accordingly, it would be helpful to supplement our treatment with a venture into the question of truth in Nietzsche's overall thought.

INTERLUDE: THE QUESTION OF TRUTH IN NIETZSCHE'S PHILOSOPHY[6]

Nietzsche replaces the notion of an absolute, uniform, stable truth with a dynamic perspectivism. There is no free-standing truth or purely objective, disinterested knowledge; rather, we can only think according to the perspectives of different and differing instances of will to power. Accordingly, motifs of knowledge and truth are better rendered in terms of an open field of "interpretations" (*GS* 374). Nietzsche has often been assumed to be denying any sense of truth or advancing a kind of relativistic phenomenalism. There is much ambiguity on the question of truth in Nietzsche's texts (and some shifting in the different periods), but I think it is plausible to say that he accepts and employs motifs of truth, as long as truth has been purged of metaphysical foundationalism and limited to a more modest, pluralized, and contingent perspectivism. Even if knowledge, for Nietzsche, is variable, historical, and born of human interests, this does not make it false, arbitrary, or uncritical.[7] For one thing, Nietzsche's frequent judgments of so-called life-denying perspectives in favor of life-affirming perspectives would seem to rule out a crude relativism. Moreover, his reference to a kind of pluralized objectivity – wherein the more perspectives one can take up, the more adequate one's view of the world will be – suggests a certain measure for thought. Yet such a measure cannot deliver a settled standard of

[6] Much of what follows is drawn from my discussion in Ch. 6 of *A Nietzschean Defense of Democracy*.

[7] For extended treatments, see Schrift, *Nietzsche and the Question of Interpretation*, especially Chs. 6 and 7, and Maudemarie Clark, *Nietzsche on Truth and Philosophy* (Cambridge: Cambridge University Press, 1990). Clark is especially good on perspectivism (Ch. 5), although there is on over-estimation of positive constructions of truth and science, which is presumed to be an abandonment of Nietzsche's early "denial" of truth. Another good source on perspectivism is Peter Poellner, "Perspectival Truth," in Richardson and Leiter, eds., *Nietzsche*, pp. 85–117. In this same volume is Ken Gemes, "Nietzsche's Critique of Truth," pp. 40–58, which is a nuanced analysis claiming that Nietzsche rejected *theories* of truth in favor of how truth operates in life.

certainty; in fact, it is predicated on a *critique* of certainty in favor of an intricate expansion of thought into a variegated field of outlooks.

I will try to sort out the various and seemingly conflicting references to truth in Nietzsche's thought by way of the following distinctions: (1) a global, negative truth that Nietzsche affirms; (2) a positive, foundational model of truth that Nietzsche denies; and (3) a modified sense of perspectival truth that strikes a balance between the first two conditions:

(1) Throughout his writings, Nietzsche affirms a dark, tragic truth of becoming, in that conditions of becoming must be accepted as a baseline notion that renders all forms and structures contingent and ultimately groundless (see *BT* 21–22, *TI* 3, 2 and 6, and *WP* 708). In this way we can understand various references in the texts to a difficult truth that must be appropriated to counter our myopic fixation on life-promoting structures of thought.

> A thinker is now that being in whom the impulse for truth and those life-preserving errors clash for their first fight . . . the ultimate question about the conditions of life has been posed here, and we confront the first attempt to answer this question by experiment. To what extent can truth endure incorporation? That is the question; that is the experiment. (*GS* 110)

> Something might be true while being harmful and dangerous in the highest degree. Indeed, it might be a basic characteristic of existence that those who would know it completely would perish, in which case the strength of a spirit should be measured according to how much of the "truth" one could still barely endure. (*BGE* 39)

Nietzsche names a "fundamental insight," the tragic recognition that "there is no pre-established harmony between the furtherance of truth and the well-being of mankind" (*HAH* 517).

(2) Because of Nietzsche's commitment to the truth of becoming, positive doctrines of truth that presuppose foundational conditions of "being" are denied, indeed they are often designated as "appearances" or "falsehoods" (see *WP* 616, 708). Our knowledge structures are based upon a filtering process that screens out strange and unusual elements that disturb our sense of stability (*GS* 355). Although such structures are life-preserving, they must still own up to their dependence on falsification and error (*BGE* 24).

(3) Even though the truth of becoming gives Nietzsche some ammunition for designating traditional truth conditions as appearances and errors, he notices a trap that befalls us in trafficking with the binary oppositions of reality and appearance, truth and error. Falsification is simply the flip-side of verification. If traditional truth conditions are renounced, then "errors" lose their substantive measure and hence their deficiency.

> The true world – we have abolished. What world has remained? The apparent (*scheinbare*) one perhaps? But no! *With the true world we have also abolished the apparent one.* (*TI* 4, 6)

There are a number of ways to supplant the negative connotations of "appearance" that have been set up by traditional measures of "reality." We can notice, for example, a positive connotation of appearance – "the actor appears on stage" – which indicates a temporal condition of *appearing* that is anything but deficient, and that could easily fit Nietzsche's scheme of things. A notebook entry suggests just such an idea: Appearance (*Erscheinung*) is countered by the word *Schein* (which could be rendered as "appearing" or "showing"), where *Schein* is a condition of reality (*Realität*) that opposes any transformation into an imagined truth-world (*KSA* 11, p. 654). Another entry describes appearance as a nonmetaphysical *reality*, which makes possible the constructed forms of meaning that, while ultimately groundless, are necessary for life.

> "Appearance" itself belongs to reality (*Realität*): it is a form of its being; i.e., in a world where there is no being, a certain world of *identical* cases must first be created through *appearance*: a tempo at which observation and comparison are possible, etc. Appearance is an arranged and simplified world, at which our *practical* instincts have been at work; for *us* it is perfectly real (*recht*); that is to say, we live, we are able to live in it: *proof* of its truth for *us* ... the world, apart from our condition of living in it ... does *not* exist as a world "in itself," it is essentially a world of relations: possibly it has a different aspect from every point: its being (*Sein*) is essentially otherwise (*anders*) from every point: it presses upon every point, every point resists it – and the sum of these is in every case entirely *incongruent*. (*WP* 568)

Here Nietzsche posits two levels of appearance: the primal, formless flux of becoming, and the subsequent gathering of this flux into livable forms. Since both are designated as appearance, there is no other "reality" against which either one could be called "apparent" in a deficient sense. So we can locate in this discussion two levels of truth: the tragic truth of becoming and the livable truth of meaning-perspectives. When it comes to truth, we do not have to confine ourselves to the choice between sheer flux and sheer being. In different ways, Nietzsche provides avenues for discerning a modified, contingent, pluralized array of truths that are neither utterly unhinged nor fixed: "There are many kinds of eyes... and consequently there are many kinds of "truths," and consequently there is no truth" (*WP* 540).

There are several motifs in Nietzsche's writings that can indicate a nonfoundational, pluralistic sense of truth that is disclosive of the world and yet open and non-reductive:

(1) *Art.* As we have seen, art becomes a primal metaphor for Nietzsche, since it is a presentation of meaning without the pretense of a fixed truth. Moreover, the meanings disclosed in art are what give human existence its bearings in the midst of the tragic truth of becoming: "We possess *art* lest we *perish of the truth*" (*WP* 822; see also *WP* 853 and *GS* 107). Art provides an effective setting wherein we can overcome a naive realism in philosophy and come to understand the *creative* dimension in thought (*GS* 58). In fact, truth can then be redescribed as an open-ended *process* of creative formings that can never itself become fixed or closed (*WP* 552). More on this in the next chapter.[8]

(2) *Perspectival interpretation.* Even though Nietzsche insists that the world cannot be reduced to a stable or uniform measure, that there are only interpretations from different perspectives, we need not banish the terms "knowledge" and "truth," as long as they do not connote the reductive mistakes of the tradition.

> In so far as the word "knowledge" has any meaning, the world is knowable; but it is *interpretable* otherwise, it has no meaning behind it, but countless meanings. – "Perspectivism." (*WP* 481)

---

[8] For an important and influential reading of Nietzsche that stresses the relationship between perspectivism and art, see Alexander Nehamas, *Nietzsche: Life as Literature* (Cambridge, MA: Harvard University Press, 1985), which serves as a guide for understanding major themes in Nietzsche's thought and his nonfoundational approach to truth. The emphasis on aesthetics and self-creation, however, tends toward an undue compression on individuation.

Are these coming philosophers new friends of "truth"? That is probable enough, for all philosophers have so far loved their truths. But they will certainly not be dogmatists. It must offend their pride, also their taste, if their truth is supposed to be a truth for everyman. (*BGE* 43)

Nietzsche's opposition to hardened "convictions" is also associated with an interest in truth; indeed, "convictions are more dangerous enemies of truth than lies" (*HAH* I, 483). With respect to the question of truth, something very significant must be recognized about Nietzsche's perspectivism. It would be entirely wrong to assume that Nietzsche equates perspectivism with "subjectivism" (the idea that truth is relative to individual beliefs). Usually when he is discussing different perspectives, it is not in terms of different *individual* takes on the world, but different *settings* for how the world can be understood – in art, science, history, etc. Also significant is Nietzsche's frequent use of the first person plural (we, our) in the depiction of knowledge (notice this form in the passage on perspectivism from Section 12).[9] Especially relevant here is something we noted earlier: for Nietzsche, individual self-consciousness is in fact an internalization of language, which is essentially a *social* network of communication that requires commonality of expression. Accordingly, no form of language – including the "internal" language of consciousness – can ever be separated from a social base (*GS* 354). Certainly individual creativity is essential for Nietzsche, but only *relative* to common patterns, as innovative disturbances of an established setting. Moreover, creativity, for Nietzsche, is primarily in the service of culture-formation rather than mere "self-creation." Finally, since interpretation as will to power is a process of becoming, one cannot even ask "Who interprets?" because even "the subject" is an interpreted creation meant to simplify and "define" the process (*WP* 556).[10] The point is that Nietzsche's perspectivism cannot be understood apart from extra-individual spheres, where therefore it allows for certain constraints on merely "subjective" states.

---

[9] On this important point see Daniel W. Conway, "*Wir Erkennenden*: Self-Referentiality in the Preface to *Zur Genealogie der Moral*," *Journal of Nietzsche Studies* 22 (Fall 2001), 116–132.

[10] In *BGE* 34, both the object and the subject are called fictions. With less hyperbole, Nietzsche claims that the inner world is no less an interpretation than the outer world (*WP* 477).

(3) *Experimentalism.* Nietzsche connects an experimental attitude with truthfulness (*GS* 51) and he calls his new philosophers *Versucher,* "experimenters" (*BGE* 42). He is not in favor of unbridled thought or an abandonment of intellectual discipline, but rather continual self-assessment.

> ... we others who thirst after reason are determined to scrutinize our experiences as severely as a scientific experiment – hour after hour, day after day. We ourselves wish to be our experiments and guinea pigs (*Versuchs-Thiere*). (*GS* 319)

Even with the inevitable ambiguities and uncertainties of a finite existence, Nietzsche has no favor for those who lead an uncritical life, who do not continually question and give reasons for their beliefs (*GS* 2). Good arguments and good reasons are not ignored or devalued (*GS* 191, 209). In sum, then, Nietzsche's so-called repudiation of truth is best referred to traditional models of truth and knowledge, since his philosophy allows for several senses in which the word "truth" can function *in between* sheer becoming and sheer being – as long as contingency, contextuality, and agonistics continually check the tendency to elevate findings to an unimpeachable status.

With this proposal of a nonfoundationalist sense of truth, we should confront the nagging problem of self-reference that attaches to such gestures and that would affect everything from Nietzsche's judgments of life-denying perspectives to the very assertion of perspectivism itself. If Nietzsche is right about an ungrounded, perspectival field of thought, why should we put any stock in his many critical judgments? Why should we accept his perspectivism? His judgments and his perspectivism would themselves only amount to a certain perspective. Has not Nietzsche committed a performative contradiction (as Jürgen Habermas would put it) in advancing his ideas while at the same time denying a foundation for ideas? Is not some decisive sense of truth and validity needed to make any philosophical advance, even a nonfoundationalist one?[11]

---

[11] See Habermas, "The Entwinement of Myth and Enlightenment: Rereading *Dialectic of Enlightenment,*" *New German Critique* 26 (1982), 13–30. For discussions of the problem of self-reference in Nietzsche's perspectivism and engagements of the various responses to this problem, see Schrift, *Nietzsche and the Question of Interpretation,* pp. 181–194, and Clark, *Nietzsche on Truth and Philosophy,* pp. 138–158. See also the group of essays by Robin Alice Roth, Babette E. Babich, and Daniel W. Conway in *International Studies in Philosophy* 22/2 (1990), 67–109.

I want to engage this problem by arguing that Nietzsche's various judgments and his perspectivism can be sustained without succumbing to the charge of self-referential inconsistency. I will begin by citing a passage in which Nietzsche seems to *affirm* the fact that a perspectival approach could be thrown back at itself and be subject to self-referential limitation. After challenging the scientific picture of a law-governed world with the counter-interpretation of an unregulated field of will to power, Nietzsche closes with this remark:

> Supposing that this also is only interpretation – and you will be eager enough to make this objection? – well, all the better. (*BGE* 22)

Notice that Nietzsche is saying something quite dramatic here – "all the better" (*um so besser*). In other words, it is *better* that his stance only be an interpretation, that it be self-referentially limited; it would be *worse* otherwise. The philosophical problem of self-reference that has been directed at Nietzsche's position seems to be completely dissolved by such a remark, which refuses to see self-reference *as* a problem by expressing a preference for its conditions. Let me attempt to work from this remark and sort out the various dimensions of Nietzsche's thought that would have to be addressed in accordance with this unusual response to self-reference.

Nietzsche is willing to offer judgments against weak, life-denying perspectives in favor of life-affirming perspectives. Nevertheless Nietzsche also indicates that *global* evaluations of life cannot be given any veridical status, since they stem from perspectival interests (*TI* 2, 2).[12] Evaluations of life, then, are local estimations that serve the interests of certain perspectives but that cannot stand as a global measure to cancel out other estimations. This would not be inconsistent with Nietzsche's texts; although he vigorously opposes what he calls the perspectives of the weak, nevertheless these perspectives have their value. Life-denying perspectives serve the interests of certain types of life, who have been able to cultivate their own forms of power that have had an enormous effect upon the world.

Nietzsche *does* have a "global" philosophical position, namely *perspectivism*, in the sense that the life-world is a field of perspectives, each willing its own life interests; as perspectives in a field of becoming,

---

[12] A notebook entry from the same period reads: "The total value (*Gesamtwert*) of the world can not be evaluated" (*WP* 708); the word "total" makes Nietzsche's point more clearly, I think.

however, none can pose as the "truth." Nothing here would forbid Nietzsche from making judgments about perspectives that *he* thinks are deficient estimations of life. Yet, as we have seen, since overall estimations of life can have no veridical status, Nietzsche's critique cannot amount to a project of refutation or erasure, but rather a challenge and provocation from the side of different interests. Nietzsche's own perspective is the *affirmation* of the perspectival *whole*, of all the finite conditions of life without exception – the "necessity" of all life conditions that is dramatically portrayed in the notion of eternal recurrence, wherein every aspect of life repeats itself again and again in exactly the same way. Here Nietzsche opposes himself to other perspectives that would be repulsed by such repetition, that seek conditions of being, order, and stability to overcome finite limits. Nietzsche's global perspectivism, however, acknowledges that these perspectives are at least affirming their own life interests. What they cannot affirm is the agonistic whole – and this becomes Nietzsche's particular battle to wage in the perspectival field.

Perspectivism, for Nietzsche, is not equivalent to radical skepticism or to the relativistic notion that differing viewpoints are equally valid. Although Nietzsche considers all knowledge and value to be perspectival, he advocates *commitment* to one's own perspective over others; a detached condition or an absence of resolve or a skeptical reserve are diagnosed by Nietzsche as forms of weakness. The "objective" person who strives for "disinterested" knowledge is deficient in having no specific stand to take or judgments to make.

His mirror soul, eternally smoothing itself out, no longer knows how to affirm or negate; he does not command, neither does he destroy . . . neither is he a model man; he does not go before anyone, nor behind; altogether he places himself too far apart to have any reason to take sides for good or evil. (*BGE* 207)

Our mistake has been "confusing him for so long with the *philosopher*." Likewise we tend to assume a connection between philosophy and skepticism.

When a philosopher suggests these days that he is not a skeptic – I hope this is clear from the description just given of the objective spirit – everybody is annoyed . . . It is as if at his rejection of skepticism they heard some evil, menacing rumbling in the distance, as if a new explosive were being tried somewhere, a dynamite of the spirit . . . For the skeptic, being a delicate creature, is frightened all too easily; his conscience is trained to quiver at every No, indeed even at a Yes that is decisive and hard, and to feel as if it had been bitten. Yes and No – that goes against his morality; conversely, he likes to treat his virtue to a feast of noble abstinence, say, by repeating Montaigne's "What do I know?" or Socrates' "I know that I know nothing." (*BGE* 208)

Skepticism, in fact, is here identified with a certain "nervous exhaustion and sickliness," and notice how the skeptic's deferral of Yes and No would violate the orchestration of Pro and Con in Nietzsche's measure of perspectival "objectivity."

Throughout his texts, Nietzsche gives attention to the positive contributions that various perspectives have given to human culture – including, as we have seen, perspectives that Nietzsche vigorously challenges. One finds support for perspectives such as a hardnosed physics (*BGE* 14), a contemplative reflection (*GS* 301), and even a religion of sin and eternal punishment (*GS* 78). As we saw in Nietzsche's run-up to his notion of objectivity, life-denying outlooks contributed habits of denial and departure from accustomed perspectives that help shape the discipline needed to prepare the intellect for its orchestration of different perspectives for the project of knowledge. Nietzsche's new philosophers will exhibit both creativity and an adequate knowledge of the world, according to the extent to which they can be polyperspectival, that is to say, take up the various vantage points that human culture affords and has afforded in the past, indeed "almost everything" in that past (*BGE* 211). Even asceticism and puritanism will be useful in the development of mastery over common human attachments (*BGE* 61). Accordingly, familiar assumptions about the "constancy" of a philosophical outlook must be challenged.

We usually endeavor to acquire a *single* department of feeling, a *single* attitude of mind towards all events and situations in life – that above all is what is called being philosophically minded. But for the enrichment of knowledge it may be of more value not to reduce oneself to uniformity in this way, but to listen instead to the gentle voice of each of life's different situations; these will suggest the attitude of mind appropriate to them. Through thus ceasing to treat oneself as a *single* rigid and unchanging *individuum* one takes an intelligent interest in the life and being of many others. (*HAH* I, 618)

What makes Nietzsche's perspectival pluralism different from other proposals that affirm a variety of "truths" is that Nietzsche insists on an *agonistic* pluralism – neither an atomistic aggregate of unrelated perspectives, nor a potential harmony of interrelated perspectives, but rather a plurality that is constituted by conflict, both between and within perspectives. This does not mean that truth is lost, only that it will have to be converted from traditional criteria so as to include conditions of conflict and their various movements, conditions that are no less real or disclosive if we attend to competing differences within particular perspectives such as art, ethics, religion, and even science. Also relevant are tensional differences *between* perspectives, especially when we have to traverse orientations that tend to repel each other in certain ways. Significant examples are found in situations that move between facts and values, the empirical and the religious, the instrumental and the aesthetic, the customary and the novel – the list can go on. We do not simply inhabit various perspectives; engaging different perspectives in life situations involves elements of dissonance, since what is evident in one perspective can be absent, even deliberately suppressed, in another perspective. And yet we must continually dwell with this oscillating dynamic in circumstances that interlace different contexts. Relevant here is a passage from *Human, All Too Human* (276), where Nietzsche likens the individual to a hall of culture large enough to accommodate conflicting powers of the spirit such as art and science. And Section 251 declares that a higher culture needs a "double-brain," a division of science and non-science, where both are important and should not be confused with each other.

THE ASCETIC IDEAL AND LIFE-ENHANCEMENT (SECTION 13)

After his excursion into the question of truth and perspectivism, Nietzsche returns to his treatment of the ascetic ideal and its relation to life. This section actually provides the most pointed clarification of his nuanced analysis of asceticism (if clarification is the right word). He says that the "self-contradiction" of an ascetic "life *against* life" is only an apparent contradiction, only a provisional expression and interpretation, indeed a "psychological misunderstanding" of the *reality* of the situation, which is presented as follows: Even though the ascetic ideal may perceive itself as against life (this would be its metaphysical vision), from a naturalistic standpoint he claims that this ideal "*springs from the protective and healing instincts of a degenerating life*, which uses every means to maintain itself and struggles for its existence." In other words, when some forms of life are degenerating, are losing a more original natural vitality, life itself will engender different strategies (of power) to prevent an utter abnegation of life (suicidal despair, for instance). That is why Nietzsche says that the ascetic ideal is only a *partial* depletion of life instincts, the *deepest* of which "have remained intact" and continually fight against sheer depletion "with new remedies and inventions." The ascetic ideal is "one such remedy" that struggles against a death-wish and thereby works "for the *preservation* of life." Proof of such a preserving force, we are told, is the historical success of this ideal that came to rule humanity with extensive power, especially whenever civilizing developments brought a "taming" of the human animal.

This section also confirms, I think, that the ascetic priest is the creative form of *active* bad conscience discussed in Section 18 of the Second Essay, a force distinct from the slave mentality per se because it provides the formation of meaning that gives cultural power to slave consciousness. Nietzsche calls the ascetic priest "the incarnate wish for being-otherwise, being-elsewhere." But the *power* of such wishing is distinct from something "elsewhere" because it is a "binding" to life that makes the priest an *instrument* for life, for creating "more favorable conditions for being-here and being human." The priest's power makes him the creative champion and leader of the herd by shaping their life-resentment into a meaningful form of existence. This is why Nietzsche says that the ascetic priest is only an "apparent enemy of life." His negating posture "actually belongs to the really great *conserving* and *yes-creating* forces of life."

Before finishing with this section, now would be the time to take up the question I postponed in the treatment of Section 7: What is the difference between ascetic "affirmation" (yes-creating forces) and Nietzsche's own ideal of life-affirmation? Addressing this question will also provide another angle on the continuing ambiguity of Nietzsche's critique of life-denying values. The problem at hand is that Nietzsche stands for life-affirmation, and, at the same time, throughout his writings he discusses other beliefs that are life-preserving, life-enhancing, life-promoting, and even yes-saying, while these beliefs are often the ones he attacks as life-denying. What is going on here? For the sake of economy, I want to suggest a distinction between *life-affirmation* and *life-enhancement*, where the former is Nietzsche's ideal and the latter can be attributed even to ideals that are life-denying in Nietzsche's sense.[13]

In order to build this distinction I must back up a bit and reiterate the complex genealogy of master and slave values, where *both* are instances of creative will to power; indeed, where the slave mentality seems to be a prerequisite for spiritual cultivation (*BGE* 188) and the creation of an advanced culture. As we have seen, the master–slave distinction may have clear delineations at first, but it begins to get complicated in the context of cultural creativity and Nietzsche's brand of higher types, who could be understood as an "interpenetration" of master and slave characteristics combined in a "single soul" (*BGE* 260). To be precise, most slave instincts are simply forms of brute resentment, and so Nietzsche singles out *creative* slave instincts as instruments of culture; only certain individuals will carry slavish elements in a higher direction. The priest type, for instance, is weak in a worldly sense, but strong in will to power by *creating* values that promote the sick and castigate the healthy (*GM* III, 15).

From the standpoint of creative will to power, there is a notable overlap between master and slave; indeed, as has been noted, the creative conflict between master and slave forces is called the most decisive mark of a higher, more spiritual nature (*GM* I, 16). Consequently, even the "evil" that designated the destructive threat of the master is now recapitulated in creative disruptions of established conditions.

The strongest and most evil spirits have so far done the most to advance humanity: again and again they relumed the passions that were going to sleep – and they reawakened . . . the pleasure of what is new, daring, untried . . . Usually by force of arms, by toppling boundary markers, by violating pieties – *but also by means of new religions and moralities* [my emphasis]. In every teacher and preacher of what is *new* we encounter the

---

[13] Two textual instances of these terms can be noted: enhancement (*Erhöhung*) in *BGE* 257, and affirmation (*Bejahung*) in *EH* III, Z, 1. Nietzsche does not offer a precise, formal distinction along these lines in his discussions. Yet I believe that the distinction is clearly implied in the texts.

same "wickedness" that makes conquerors notorious, even if its expression is subtler and it does not immediately set the muscles in motion, and therefore also does not make one that notorious. What is new, however, is always *evil*, being that which wants to conquer and overthrow the old boundary markers and the old pieties. (*GS* 4)

Innovators are the new object of hatred and resentment (*Z* III, 12, 26), they are the new "criminals" (*TI* 9, 45), the new "cruel ones" (*BGE* 230), the new perpetrators of "war" (*GS* 283). In sum, cultural creativity is made possible by a "crossing" of master and slave characteristics, so that not everything in the latter is "slavish" and not everything in the former is "noble." In the end, therefore, the creator–herd distinction is *not* equivalent to the master–slave distinction; there are overlaps, but the crude domination found in the original condition of the master cannot be considered the primary focus of Nietzsche's analysis of creative types.

We need to recognize a general insight operating here: For Nietzsche, *any* development of culture out of natural conditions and any innovation will require a dynamic of discomfort, resistance, and overcoming, i.e., a contest with some Other. Nietzsche asks us not only to acknowledge this dynamic but to be wary of its dangers, which are indicated in traditional constructs and their *polarization* of a conflicted field into the oppositions of good and evil, truth and error. The ascetic ideal in the end represents the desire to escape the difficulty of incorporating the Other (*as* other) into one's field of operation. Affirmation, for Nietzsche, is anything but comfortable and pleasant; it means taking on the difficulty of *contending with the Other without wanting to annul it.* The bottom line in Nietzsche's genealogy, then, is that *every* perspective is mixed with its Other, because a perspective needs its Other as an agonistic correlate, since opposition is part of a perspective's constitution. Conflict, therefore, is not simply to be tolerated; affirming oneself requires the affirmation of conflict, since the self is not something that is first fully formed and then, secondarily, presented to the world for possible relations and conflicts. The self is formed *in* and *through* agonistic relations. So in a way, openness toward one's Other is openness toward oneself.

Life-affirmation, in Nietzsche's strict sense, requires an affirmation of otherness, which is consistent with the agonistic structure of will to power, and which is consummated in coming to terms with eternal recurrence: the endless repetition of every instance of life, including those that one opposes. Life-denial stems from a weakness in the face of agonistic becoming, an incapacity to affirm the necessity of otherness. Yet life-denying perspectives are life-*enhancing* because they further the interests of certain types of life who have cultivated their own forms of power that have had an enormous effect on world history. So, for example, Christianity is life-enhancing (see *A* 34–35, 39–40) but not life-affirming. Life-denying perspectives exhibit *local* affirmations of their form of life; this is why the ascetic priest can still be called a "yes-creating force." As we have seen, even philosophical pessimism is a stimulus for (a certain kind of) life. The sheer absence of life-enhancement would amount to *suicidal* nihilism (*GM* III, 28). Short of suicide, then, all forms of life aim to will their meaning, even if that meaning is a conviction about the meaninglessness of (natural) life. This helps explain an interesting fact: Religions that yearn for a deliverance from earthly life still forbid suicide. Even Schopenhauer, who saw life as an absurd error, argued against suicide.[14]

Nietzsche's conception of life-affirmation goes far beyond life-enhancement; it aims for a *global* affirmation of all life conditions, even those that run counter to one's interests. We will have more to say about this matter shortly, but to keep our bearings we need to keep in mind the following distinctions: (1) that between life-enhancement and suicidal nihilism, and (2) that between life-affirmation and life-denial. Nietzsche can extol the value of life-denying perspectives because of their life-enhancing power.[15] But he can challenge these perspectives as falling short of life-affirmation.[16]

Returning to Section 13, the last topic we will engage is Nietzsche's association of the ascetic ideal's life-enhancing power with human "sickliness" (*Krankhaftigkeit*). At first there seems to be a clear indication here of Nietzsche's critical posture against "degenerating life"

[14] Arthur Schopenhauer, *The World as Will and Representation*, Vol. I, trans. E. F. J. Payne (New York: Dover Publications, 1958), pp. 398–402.
[15] Moreover, within life-enhancement Nietzsche tends to distinguish *healthier* forms (e.g., the Greeks, the Renaissance) from *sicker* forms (e.g., Christianity). The former are closer to Nietzsche's sense of life-affirmation, but not necessarily up to its full demands.
[16] Simon May, in *Nietzsche's Ethics and His War on Morality* (Oxford: Clarendon Press, 1999), conflates Nietzsche's usage of life-affirmation and life-enhancement, and then finds a problem in Nietzsche because the two terms should not be conflated (p. 120). But I maintain that Nietzsche all along does not conflate the two.

that is consummated in the ascetic priest. Indeed, the historical success of ascetic power is called proof that the prevailing model for human existence "up until now" has been a symptom of sickness and alienation from natural life. As usual, however, this polemical position is not without ambiguity. The yes-creating power of asceticism provides life-enhancing meaning for a "sick animal." In fact mankind is *the* sick animal compared with all other animals. The implication is that animal life is normally a more natural health and that the human animal develops a kind of natural illness. Then Nietzsche asks: What *causes* this sickness? Here is where things get complicated.

Nietzsche begins by correlating, even identifying, human sickness with something valorous: Humans are more sick in being more uncertain and changeable; also in being *unfestgestellter*, which can be translated in several ways – as more undetermined, indeterminate, unsecured, unestablished, or unrealized. In *Beyond Good and Evil* 62, Nietzsche calls humankind *das noch nicht festgestellte Thier*, which can be rendered "the animal yet to have an identity." Given Nietzsche's predilection for conditions of becoming, such characterizations can hardly be problematic in principle. In fact, Nietzsche connects human sickness with seemingly admirable qualities (viewed from his standpoint):

> He is *the* sick animal: where does this come from? Certainly he has dared more, innovated more, braved more, and has challenged fate more than all the rest of the animals taken together: he, the great experimenter with himself . . .

Nietzsche then calls humankind the "eternal-futurist," whose strength (*Kraft*) is an unstoppable urge to the future that "inexorably digs into the flesh of every present like a spur." Right away Nietzsche adds: "How could such a courageous and rich animal not also be the most endangered, the most profoundly and extensively sick of all the sick animals?"

What are we to make of this intricate mix of characterizations, especially when it includes elements that seem to accord with Nietzschean virtues (daring, innovation, experimentation)? I think the reference to the future and its "injury" to the present gives us a clue. The temporality of experience seems to dictate the courage that elevates humans over other animals. Surely animals are *in* time, but humans seem to be aware *of* time in a special way. Animal life appears to be more immersed in the immediacy of present circumstances and instinctive behavior. For humans, the "non-being" of the future and the past have a *presence*, as shown in our capacity to anticipate and recall events that are not yet or no longer present. The ability to perceive *otherwise* than the present accounts for human innovation and experimentation, but it also calls for an abiding courage to withstand the continuing force of negation entailed by temporal awareness. Human experimentation also carries a comprehension of the possibility of failure, and so our projects can be haunted by finitude in a way that instinctive behavior is not. More generally, the awareness of death in the midst of life – even without any present threat – gives human existence a special burden. The condition of animals is also mortal and thus tragic in the end, but humans are *conscious* of tragic mortality, even at times of safety and success, and so they can incorporate a tragic awareness into their very sense of life, for better or worse.

I believe that such an orientation on time explains why Nietzsche combines bravery, endangerment, and sickness in his account of human existence. Unlike other animals, humans are "set loose" from the instinctive immediacy of brute nature by "exceeding" the present in a perception of past and future conditions – the creative potential in this excess recalls the remark (in *GM* II, 19) that bad conscience is a sickness in the manner of pregnancy. Yet temporal experience in this way is infused by negations of present "being," and so the human animal is marked by an intrinsic *insecurity* that registers at every level of life. For humans, temporal becoming is not just a fact of nature, it is also a tragic burden pressed upon our experiences and sense of meaning.

Nietzsche concludes the section with a reiteration of the life-enhancing power of the ascetic ideal. The burden of temporal experience can produce epidemics of being "fed up" with existence, which can threaten to obviate human participation in life. Yet Nietzsche claims that such a despairing condition can exhibit so much power that it becomes a new "fetter" to life. The No to life "brings a wealth of more delicate Yeses" that compels the ascetic type to *live* (in a different way). Perhaps we can summarize Nietzsche's analysis in the following manner: Humans are first and foremost embedded in the *first nature* of animal life. The *second nature* of temporal experience engenders both the greater capacities of the human animal and the burden of tragic awareness. This burden can produce the *counter-nature* of the ascetic ideal, through which "life struggles with death and *against* death." Yet from a naturalistic standpoint, even this ideal can be driven by primal life drives to find alternate routes of power and life-enhancing strategies in a counter-natural posture. We must keep in mind, however, that within this "positive" analysis of ascetic life-enhancement there remains Nietzsche's own critical counter-posture of life-affirmation, which comes to reassert itself in subsequent sections.

THE DANGER OF THE ASCETIC IDEAL
FOR LIFE (SECTIONS 14–15)

Nietzsche's naturalistic account of the life-enhancing power of the ascetic ideal amounts to the "better defense" suggested in Section 11 – better than the ideal's own self-conception and its metaphysical vision. After this rendition of its power and value for life, however, Nietzsche now shifts gears and launches a full-throttle polemic against the life-*denying* elements in the ascetic ideal. In effect Nietzsche is advancing a rhetorical opposition that pits an *affirmation* of natural life against an *enhancement* of life that is nevertheless predicated on life-denying impulses. In accordance with our analysis of perspectivism, we could say that the previous account was in the spirit of a global perspectival pluralism (acknowledging the virtues of different perspectives), while the coming polemic reflects Nietzsche's particular perspective of life-affirmation (challenging the overt or covert fugitive tendencies in other perspectives).

In Section 14 Nietzsche stipulates that "sickliness" has become the human norm in history. Yet now the analysis shifts from the powers engendered by this illness to its "danger for the healthy." Since sickness is the norm, then cases of health – "spiritual-corporeal powerfulness" (*seelisch-leiblichen Mächtigkeit*) – are rare and a matter of luck for humanity. The health in question here cannot be confined to a natural animal health preceding human sickness, or to the health of original master types. Nietzsche's polemic is primarily aiming to make room for the high-cultural health of *creative* types, who accordingly must exhibit *some* of the "sickness" that culture-creation requires, but who can also overcome or resist ascetic tendencies of life-denial. This is why Nietzsche reconnects his discussion with the problem of nihilism. Without the possibility of some kind of life-affirming health in human culture, Nietzsche warns against a looming "will to nothingness" that can grow out of two correlated dispositions: (1) *compassion* for human suffering, which is moved to alleviate or prevent the pains of life, but which thereby diminishes or suppresses the productive vitality made possible by suffering; and (2) *nausea* at human existence, either by way of disgust with a finite world of suffering *or* as a consequence of the *depleting* effects of a hyper-compassionate refuge from productive suffering. The danger, as Nietzsche sees it, is that compassion and nausea "might some day mate," which would magnify the danger of asceticism into a full-force depletion of life energies and a deadening of the human spirit.

The rest of Section 14 and Section 15 are pretty much a recapitulation of Nietzsche's psychological critique of slave morality and the ascetic ideal: a layout of the rancorous and vengeful dispositions that weak types launch against the strong to valorize their own impotence and incapacitate the powerful. Two aspects of his treatment deserve some emphasis. First, Nietzsche reiterates the historical power of ascetic illness by finding it implicated "almost everywhere in Europe," in all its cultural spheres: "You can look behind every family, every corporate body, every community: everywhere, the struggle of the sick against the healthy." Such an assault can even be found in "the hallowed halls of science." The reason for stressing this extension of ascetic power is that it captures the ultimate aim of Nietzsche's genealogy: a critique of modernity and its inheritance of life-depleting forces from earlier times. The important difference is that modern cultural institutions have *actual worldly power* (in politics, for instance) – unlike slave morality's original condition of a merely *imagined* power in religious fantasy. The modern world is therefore more dangerous because it has shifted slavish and ascetic tendencies beyond psychological dispositions into real positions of power that now *govern* natural life.

The second aspect to emphasize is the effect of ascetic power on healthy types. In Section 14 Nietzsche singles out the "ultimate, finest, most sublime triumph of revenge," which reaches its peak when people who by nature are happy, successful, and "powerful in body and soul" become infected by bad conscience and "begin to doubt *their right to happiness.*" Section 15 repeats how the ascetic priest persuades the sick to find the source of their *suffering* in themselves, in an internalized guilt. Yet Section 14 seems to target the different problem of healthy types developing guilt about their *happiness.* We could call this a (life-enhancing) medicine given to the wrong patient. Nietzsche names it the "world turned upside down," and he calls for protection against this reversal in a dramatic way: "it is essential that the healthy remain *separated* from the sick." The healthy should not even think it their task to be "nurses and doctors" for the sick; they require a "pathos of distance" for their task of ensuring a future for humanity.

Nietzsche suggests something here that may feed into certain elements of his later thought that seem to propose a radical social program dedicated to the ascendancy of the healthy over the weak, and even a kind of authoritarian political order run by the strong at the expense of lesser types. We will take up this question in Chapter 8, but for now we should notice that Nietzsche's analysis seems to shift markedly from a complex, nuanced genealogical treatment to a rather polarized division of human types that may even require segregation to foster the healthy and protect against a looming nihilism. And yet the end of Section 14 intimates something other than a social program. It seems more like a rallying cry for life-affirming creative types to steel themselves against the forces of illness, to band together in "good company" and "good air" to hold off corruption. The last line of the section – where Nietzsche includes himself with the use of "we" – broadcasts the call for cultural segregation and its task (which, taking note of a qualifying phrase, may still be in mortal danger):

So that we, my friends, can actually defend ourselves, at least for a while yet, against the two worst epidemics that could possibly have been set aside just for us – against *great nausea at man*! Against *deep compassion for man*!

THE THERAPEUTIC EFFECTS OF THE ASCETIC IDEAL
(SECTIONS 16–18)

This portion of the text shifts back to examining the enhancing effects of the ascetic ideal for depleted types, though now with echoes of the preceding polemic. Moreover, the next block of sections I will group together (19–22) will shift again to a polemical mode against the dangers posed by ascetic life-enhancement for a life-affirming health. We may indeed be vexed about a lack of organizational discipline in the text or an undue redundancy, but it seems that Nietzsche wants to sustain a shifting back and forth between such perspectives. This kind of interpretive plotting at least forces readers to continually engage the ambiguities and tensional complexities in Nietzsche's genealogy.

In the sections at hand, I think that readers have been prepared to digest Nietzsche's recapitulations, so I will focus on certain distinctive features in these passages. Section 16 retrieves the healing power of the ascetic priest for the sick, but Nietzsche restricts the priest's "medicine" to *affects*, which he says "cannot possibly yield a real *cure* of the sick in a physiological sense." The bulk of the section is a long concluding set of remarks set off from the rest of the text by brackets. Here he sketches a presumption that would be a prerequisite for the right kind of reader: that the "psychic" element in the ascetic perspective – concerning the conjunction of suffering and guilt – cannot be a "fact" but only an "interpretation" of a fact, which is a *physiological* disturbance.

Here we find a more pointed aspect of Nietzsche's naturalism: the priority given to the body and physiological forces (such references abound in his writings). That the priest targets the "soul" of sufferers is an ingenious interpretation that can provide meaning and power for those sufferers. The implication of Nietzsche's remarks, however, is that the targeted types *cannot* be cured of the *natural* condition that requires amelioration in the first place – their physiological makeup (which thus seems to be beyond any basic alteration). Nietzsche adds that the condition of the sufferer in question "does *not* stem from his psyche, to speak crudely; more likely from his stomach . . . " The mention of the stomach should be read in the spirit of rhetorical effect, because right away he says that this "crude" formulation is not intended to be *understood* crudely. He continues that well-formed and ill-formed people "digest" their experiences as their stomachs digest food. So the "indigestion" of the ill-formed is indeed physiological, but he adds: *as much* as other factors, or often as a consequence of other factors. This qualification is enough to show Nietzsche's resistance to "crude" physiological explanations having the only say. Indeed, he continues: With the orientation announced here, "we can, between ourselves, still be the severest opponents of all materialism." We thus notice more evidence for why we should be cautious when interpreting Nietzsche's naturalism. In deploying physiology, he does not mean to exile what we typically take to be psychological states of mind; nor would he side with contemporary physicalism (in the mind–body debate), which usually explains (away) psychic states by reducing them to brain physiology. For Nietzsche, physiology is a matter of complex natural forces and experiences, and the "cruder" formulations should be read more as a rhetorical provocation against mentalistic or spiritualistic assumptions. We should keep in mind that science too is an interpretation, for Nietzsche (*GS* 373).

After the discussion of physiology, Nietzsche proceeds in Sections 17–18 to describe further the enhancing effects of the ascetic ideal. Putting ourselves in the priest's own *perspective*, he says, there is much to admire in its techniques for alleviating suffering. Even though this perspective is ignorant of the true physiological basis of aggrieved types, its "psychological-moral" strategy is indeed capable of relieving lethargy and depression. Within its own interpretive sphere, its prescription of self-denial discovered "a real deliverance" from depression; therefore it would be wrong to castigate its *intention* to starve natural desire "as symptoms of insanity" – as clumsy "free thinkers" tend to do. Even though asceticism's *own* interpretation of its program is "fantastically false" (from a naturalistic standpoint), nevertheless the *will* to this interpretation produces enormous life-enhancing effects. The religious impulse toward "salvation" may be delusional, but Nietzsche insists that we "pay due respect" to its program. For those who cannot abide suffering, the hypnosis of self-denial is the most direct worldly route to alleviating suffering. For those who are incurably depressed by life, worldly self-negation "*must* be valued positively"; it is even deemed as "*the* positive itself." This is why salvational schemes have given the name *God* to what is actually a will to nothingness.

In Section 18 Nietzsche tracks the same kind of narcotic strategy in more mundane and practical spheres: Depression and suffering can be alleviated by "mechanical activity," by giving oneself up to routines of work, regularity, and obedience; also by the pleasure that comes from altruistic behavior toward others; also by the "will to reciprocity" that forms the "herd" of a community. We are told that while strong types are much less prone to such self-abnegating collectivities, nevertheless the healing pleasures of such things for others cannot be denied.

THE ASCETIC IDEAL AND GUILT (SECTIONS 19–22)

Now Nietzsche shifts back to a polemical mode, and much of the discussion is a reiteration of previous critical stances in the book, particularly with respect to guilt. I will look past these elements, which readers should now be able to comprehend, and emphasize those elements that will enhance our understanding further, especially when it comes to the final sections of the Third Essay. In Section 19 Nietzsche targets the "dishonesty" of the ascetic ideal and its consequences. Today's "good people," who are "moralized root and branch," cannot face the *truth* of their condition and their values (from a naturalistic standpoint); they continue to believe in their values as straightforward representations of a moral reality, rather than as *fugitive* bearings toward natural reality (which Nietzsche's rhetorical emphasis on "ascetic" attitudes is trying to unmask).

In Section 20, before reiterating the healing effects of guilt and bad conscience – all predicated on turning cruelty back on the self – Nietzsche hints at something that we have already surmised: that the effects of the ascetic ideal are so pervasive as to be present even in those who seek to overcome it. Ascetic guilt about human nature may infect even "we psychologists of today," who:

cannot get rid of a certain mistrust *toward ourselves*... probably we too are still the victims, the prey, the sick of this contemporary taste for moralization, much as we feel contempt toward it, – it probably infects *us* as well.

We should keep in mind that such an admission can be read in terms of Nietzsche's ambiguous accounts of slave morality and bad conscience, in which the harmful effects of life-aversion may contain the seeds of their own self-overcoming.

In Section 21 Nietzsche claims that he does not deny that ascetic medication has improved humankind, but he wants to make sure that the costs of such improvement are equally recognized (its weakening of natural forces). Moreover, when it comes to the acutely sick types in particular, the ascetic program actually "makes the sick patient *more* sick in every case, even if it makes him 'better'." Ascetic self-castigation may have enhancing effects, but the "violence" of its counter-natural power only increases an alienation from nature proportionate to its success. Since Nietzsche is convinced that the ascetic ideal has indeed gained monumental historical success, then the danger of *increased* sickness and alienation takes on world-historical proportions. The ascetic ideal "has inscribed itself, in a terrible and unforgettable way, into the whole of mankind," and so Nietzsche names it "*the real catastrophe* in the history of the health of European man."

Section 22 provides another swipe at the ascetic ideal in its Christian manifestation. In general, "the ascetic priest has ruined psychological health wherever he has come to rule," even in cultural "arts and letters." Nietzsche singles out the New Testament and its legacy in this regard, particularly as it bears on a deliberate rejection and debasement of ancient Greek literature. At the same time that Nietzsche confesses his distaste for the New Testament, he also expresses his admiration for the Old Testament (better rendered today as the Hebrew Bible), because there he finds "great men, a heroic landscape and . . . the incomparable naïvety of the *strong heart*." In any case, Nietzsche finds the New Testament "petty" in comparison, with people of much lesser stature who "make such a fuss about their little failings." And he calls their desire for "eternal life" the height of presumptuousness, given their stature: "An 'immortal' Peter: who could stand *him*!" The particular focus of Nietzsche's attack here is the tendency in Christianity to valorize small, even wretched types, giving them and their problems the highest importance by aligning them directly with God's love and concern. In this regard Nietzsche even cites Luther's revolt against the Catholic church – its worldly authority, its priestly and ceremonial mediation – in favor of every individual's direct personal encounter with God. According to Nietzsche, such Christian elements were precursors for a host of leveling tendencies in European history, especially the democratic valorization of each individual having "equal" social status. As he says in another text: "The democratic movement is the heir of the Christian movement" (*BGE* 202).

SCIENCE AND THE ASCETIC IDEAL (SECTIONS 23–25)

These sections represent the climax of Nietzsche's genealogical investigations, especially regarding the reach of the ascetic ideal. They also offer the most dramatic provocations in his approach to the question of truth. These discussions, I think, are perhaps the most difficult to fathom in the book, but I hope that we have been prepared well enough to draw some sense out of them.

Section 23 begins by stressing again Nietzsche's focus on the *meaning* of the ascetic ideal, rather than just its history. The *ideal* of asceticism, its *will*, is a grand, world-forming order of thought, a philosophical vision with enormous historical power. It possesses an overarching *goal* and has succeeded in shaping history according to its goal alone, suppressing any other interpretation. It believes "in its unconditional *superiority of rank* over any other power." Why, Nietzsche asks, has there not been more resistance to the ascetic ideal? Where is there an opposing ideal that can challenge "this closed system of will, goal, and interpretation?" Why is a counterpart *lacking* in history? Yet in the current age, he says, a counter-ideal is presumed *not* to be lacking. Modern science, after all, is considered "a genuine philosophy of reality," and it operates effectively without any reliance on God, otherworldliness, or self-denial. However, Nietzsche derides such "trumpeters of reality," who are unable to deliver anything relevant to his question. He says that "their voices do *not* come from the depths, the abyss of scientific conscience does *not* speak from them." It is at this point that the text demands a careful and close reading. The gist of the subsequent discussion, I think, is as follows. Modern science, for Nietzsche, is not the opponent of the ascetic ideal, for two reasons: (1) Science in the main is not driven by *any* ideal (and the ascetic ideal can only be opposed by a counter-*ideal*); (2) Where science *can* achieve the level of an ideal, it is simply the most current manifestation *of* the ascetic ideal.

Regarding the first point, Nietzsche adduces what amounts to the normal practices of working scientists and scholars, who perform what he calls "much useful work" (he even says that he delights in their work). Yet he describes "the industry of our best scholars" as something lacking in any passion or vision for the *ideal* of science, as a self-anesthetizing hiding place and "*enforced* contentedness" (which might be a version of the "mechanical activity" recounted earlier). In historical terms we could say that what Nietzsche calls the "unreflective diligence" of scientific work is due to the *success* of modern science and the comfort of its establishment – which of course only came about after science had had to *fight* for its status against countervailing cultural forces. And this fight had to be launched from a philosophical level of comprehensive depth to succeed against then-established world-views (Plato and Descartes represent prime examples from the ancient and modern periods). The *joining* of this fight also required of its protagonists the courage and drive to commit themselves to a cultural battle that carried great risks (one thinks especially of Socrates). In any case, if a counter-ideal to asceticism is to be found in science, Nietzsche has in mind *this* kind of philosophical passion, an ideal that has to be *willed*, and which is not to be found simply in the established work of science and scholarship.

In Section 24 Nietzsche considers the "rarer cases" among modern philosophers and scholars who do embody an ideal and who would assume themselves to be opponents of asceticism. These "unbelievers" are critical of any kind of faith or belief of the kind coming from ascetic tendencies. Nietzsche refers here to "we knowers," which can hearken back to the Preface, and which can once again prompt questions about Nietzsche's own participation in this sphere. It does seem that such unbelievers reflect Nietzsche's posture, because he describes their debunking attitude toward any "faith" that becomes dominant; indeed its strength is diagnosed as a sign of intellectual weakness: For instance, faith in salvation cannot admit of any proof and cannot establish truth; in fact it stems from deception. Surely here we have a worthy nominee for Nietzsche's counter-ideal to the ascetic tradition.

Nevertheless, the discussion takes a surprising turn. After the sketch of "we knowers," Nietzsche asks with regard to their nomination: "What about this case?" He then shifts to the *third person* in depicting "these 'no'-sayers and outsiders of today," who demand "intellectual cleanliness," who are the "heroic spirits (*Geister*) constituting the honor of our time." He goes on to list examples of this contemporary ideal:

. . . all these pale atheists, Antichrists, immoralists, nihilists, these skeptics, . . . these last idealists of knowledge in whom alone intellectual conscience dwells and is embodied these days, – they believe they are all as liberated as possible from the ascetic ideal, these "free, *very* free spirits."

And they do seem very much like Nietzschean free spirits, so perhaps we are getting somewhere. But immediately we hear: "and yet, I will tell them what they are not able to see." These "heroic spirits" are themselves manifestations of the ascetic ideal! They themselves are currently its "most spiritualized (*vergeistiger*) product." What is going on here? In nineteenth-century Europe there were surely a host of "free thinkers" of various stripes, whose aim was a liberation from all sorts of cultural constraints, be these religious, moral, political, artistic, or philosophical traditions. Yet Nietzsche is not aligning himself with these "*so-called* 'free spirits,'" because he claims they have not become truly "free" from the counter-natural tradition of the ascetic ideal. Why? These modern figures "are very far from being *free* spirits: *because they still believe in truth.*"

The charge seems strange. How is it that these no-sayers who challenge traditional confidences are still bound by a belief in truth? Nietzsche even says that "precisely in their faith in truth they are more rigid and more absolute than anyone else." Then he adds a personal remark: "Perhaps I am too familiar with all this out of proximity" – again the ambiguity of Nietzsche's own status in this scenario. Nevertheless, there is something emerging in these passages that Nietzsche is trying to distinguish from other modern developments, even when he himself is or has been caught up in them (which in fact accords with his belief that no philosophical move can or should avoid self-examination and even self-criticism). In any case, I believe that Nietzsche's emphasis on certain modern trends targets at least two supposedly liberating forces that nonetheless are not free enough: (1) a scientific liberation from all sorts of beliefs based on custom, religion, passion, etc.; and (2) a philosophical liberation from an even wider range of beliefs – such as moral and political doctrines – to such an extent that it seems to verge into Nietzschean territory (recall the reference to atheists, Antichrists, and immoralists). Yet note also that

Nietzsche tagged this list with the adjective "pale." What is it in these various liberations that prompts him to name them a continuation of the ascetic ideal?

I think the answer lies in the spirit of *confidence* such forces exhibit in their liberating moves, so that whatever that move may be (even if it is a nihilistic denial of meaning), it *replaces* the "errors" of other views, and so the liberated sphere is still in the service of "truth." What renders this problematic for Nietzsche is that it does not accord with his own approach to truth, which is a matter of interpretation and perspective. In this passage he directly counterposes the dynamics of interpretation *against* these modern developments; indeed they are said to *renounce* the spirit of interpretation – which, he says, expresses the ascetic ideal "just as well as any denial of sensuality." Perhaps an example would help us fathom this surprising claim. It is unlikely that modern atheists would be satisfied with calling religion an interpretation, unless it could be called *mere* interpretation; yet this would not fit the radical perspectivism Nietzsche is advancing. And these atheists would not likely be comfortable with their own position being called an interpretation, "mere" or otherwise.

For Nietzsche, it is the drive for a *secured* truth – even in a negative stance toward established truths – that is the core meaning of the ascetic ideal:

... the *compulsion* toward it, the unconditional will to truth, is *faith in the ascetic ideal itself*, although as an unconscious imperative, make no mistake about it, – it is a faith in a *metaphysical* value, a *value of truth in itself* ...

The mention of metaphysical value is an important indication of what may be going on here. We recall that Nietzsche defines meta-physics as "the faith in opposite values" (*BGE* 2), in formulations that *exclude* each other so that concepts can be secured from the infection of otherness. Nietzsche opposes metaphysics in this sense because he insists on a tensional, agonistic, *crossing* dynamic that finds all concepts implicated with otherness; and this is why perspectivism cannot abide any sheer "refutation" of other perspectives. Therefore with respect to Nietzsche's charge against so-called free spirits, we could say the following: If a belief in modern science, or free inquiry, or radical skepticism moves one to champion these orientations as correcting the "errors" of the past, or superstition, or common sense, or mass opinion, or whatever – one is still caught up in a problematic will to truth, as Nietzsche sees it. A discontent with agonistic becoming and an impulse to surmount this tensional force by way of a secured warrant can take many forms, actually *any* form, whether it stems from religion, philosophy, science, skepticism, or even the posture of a "free spirit."

Returning to Section 24, right after the passage quoted above, Nietzsche intimates his own perspectival concept of truth: The idea of knowledge without presuppositions is "unthinkable." Prior to every form of knowledge there must first be a kind of "faith," without which knowledge lacks "a direction, a meaning, a limit, a method, a *right* to exist." To think otherwise, to think that knowledge can be secured against perspectival limits, to think, for instance, that philosophy can be placed "on a strictly scientific foundation," is actually "*to stand on its head* not just philosophy, but also truth itself." Nietzsche then quotes a passage from *The Gay Science* 344, which implicitly connects a modern faith in truth with the ascetic ideal: A faith in scientific truth, for example, "*thus affirms another world* from the one of life, nature, and history." The belief in science "is still based on a *metaphysical faith*." Things are no different, he says, even for "we knowers of today, we godless anti-metaphysicians." It seems that the *anti*-metaphysical posture here would sustain the binary thinking that constitutes a metaphysical faith (while *contending* with metaphysics would be a different story). *Any* form of binary thinking, it seems, would still be beholden to the tradition's ultimate binary opposite to the natural world – God. The *Gay Science* passage closes with a reference to the death of God scenario: The traditional equation of God and truth – including any of its subsequent corollaries – must face the ramifications that follow from God's demise. In the context of Section 24, it seems clear that the modern faith in science and in all sorts of "liberated" standpoints represents one of those "shadows" of God that have not owned up to their lost warrant.

At the close of Section 24, Nietzsche summarizes the problem: The *mastery* of the ascetic ideal over all of European thought is shown, not simply in particular forms of that ideal, religious or otherwise, but essentially in the fact that "truth was not *allowed* to be a problem." In what sense? Certainly not in the problem of "where" truth should be found; there have been long-standing debates about whether truth should be located in sense experience, in reason, in God, etc. The problem that Nietzsche claims has been suppressed concerns the very idea of truth as a decisive standpoint set against "error," its binary opposite. This is the esteemed *value* of truth that Nietzsche targets, the ascetic impulse to screen out any disturbance to a presumed truth, in whatever form a conviction may take, even an anti-metaphysical conviction. Accordingly, a genuine alternative to the ascetic ideal would have to tackle the value of truth at this level:

> From the very moment that faith in the God of the ascetic ideal is denied, *there is a new problem as well*: that of the *value* of truth. – the will to truth needs a critique – let us define our own task with this – , the value of truth is experimentally (*versuchsweise*) to be *put in question*.

This level of interrogation matches the way in which Nietzsche called for morality to be put in question (*GM* P, 6; see also *BGE* 228), which indicates again how the *Genealogy* is not confined simply to morality narrowly understood, because it ranges widely into the *intersection* of the problem of morality and the problem of truth.

   In Section 25 Nietzsche concludes that science is not the *natural* opponent of the ascetic ideal because in the matter of truth it is likewise alienated from the unstable forces of natural life. Such forces would include the energies of creativity, which is why he says that, while science is driven by a certain "value-ideal," it is "never value-creating." He then seeks to clarify how two seemingly different standpoints – asceticism and science – can yet share a common ideal. As we have seen, religious asceticism is simply the most obvious and telling manifestation of the deeper issue animating Nietzsche's philosophy: the diagnosis of life-alienating forces in human culture; *this* is the core meaning of the ascetic ideal, whatever form it takes. Obviously modern science – in both its history and practice – has been antagonistic toward religion and transcendent doctrines in its drive for cultural authority. Yet Nietzsche insists that, even with this contested relationship, science is still a manifestation of the *core* meaning of the ascetic ideal:

> Its opposition and battle are, on closer inspection, directed not at the ideal itself but at its outer-works, its apparel and disguise, at the way the ideal temporarily hardens, solidifies, becomes dogmatic.

Nietzsche then indicates how science is indeed more attuned to life than the transcendent versions of the ascetic ideal: "science liberates what life is in it by denying what is exoteric in this ideal." In other words, science opposes the "overt" manifestations of religion – its doctrines, theologies, and life-styles – that do in fact stand in the way of something like science. Yet with respect to the core meaning of the ideal – which in this context could be called "esoteric" or "covert" – Nietzsche declares: "Both of them, science and the ascetic ideal, are still on the same foundation." And right away he identifies this common foundation with the matter of truth:

> that is to say, both overestimate truth (more correctly: they share the same faith that truth *cannot* be assessed or criticized), and this makes them both *necessarily* allies, so that, if they must be fought, they can only be fought and called into question together. An assessment of the value of the ascetic ideal inevitably brings about an assessment of the value of science.

One way to understand this with respect to science is as follows: Of course science insists on the critical assessment of truth *within* its domain, but the question is whether science would tolerate a critical assessment that puts scientific knowledge *itself* into question. A challenge to the domain of science would be especially pointed, given that modern *philosophy* (from Descartes to Kant) generally presumed the validity of science when it came to the question of knowledge, and that since the modern period there has developed a strong trend toward what has been called "scientism," which assumes that any significant question about the nature of things can be answered by science, and only by science.

After offering a provocative parenthetical remark about art being a better nominee for opposing the ascetic ideal (something we will explore in the next chapter), Nietzsche elaborates on how the alliance of science and asceticism can be understood in specific ways. The discussion focuses mainly on two elements: (1) how the practices and epistemological assumptions in science show a comparable antagonism toward more natural drives; and (2) how certain results of the modern scientific world-view have reinforced or reconstituted a central feature of the ascetic ideal: that natural life on its own terms exhibits no intrinsic meaning.

On the first point, Nietzsche briefly discusses the way in which scientific knowledge must fight off a host of natural dispositions, passions, and instincts in order to shape its aim toward an objective, disinterested understanding of nature, which is presumed to give truth that is independent of human interests and freed from the disorder and contingencies of lived experience. Despite the different spheres of *content* in science and religious asceticism ("natural" and "supernatural" spheres), when it comes to scientific criteria and the "discipline" required for training in science, Nietzsche asks us to notice a form of self-denial that is comparable to an ascetic denial of natural life impulses. This is why Nietzsche says that "science rests on the same base as the ascetic ideal: the precondition of both the one and the other is a certain *impoverishment of life*."[17]

The second point requires some care in interpretation, and I think it is best viewed in light of the death of God, although here there emerges a different angle on its consequences. We have already noted that the eclipse of God in modern thought also threatens its "shadows," the supposedly secular beliefs that in fact have lost their historical anchor. Nietzsche's analysis in the sections at hand compresses this scenario into the problem of truth. According to Nietzsche, scientific truth is simply a modification of theological binaries, and so the modern displacement of God will have to deauthorize scientific confidences about knowledge. Yet in the section presently under discussion, Nietzsche pushes the science–asceticism equation even further, now in the light of asceticism's conviction about the meaninglessness of natural life, on its incapacity to find meaning on life's own terms. Let us see how the remainder of Section 25 addresses this complex and fascinating question.

Nietzsche continues to conflate the supposed differences between science and asceticism by taking up the "famous *victories*" of modern science over theology and religious world-views. There surely *are* such victories, he says, but they do not support the familiar binary-story of "natural science" overcoming and replacing "supernatural" beliefs.

---

[17] With regard to philosophy, the first historical form it took exhibits a more direct relation with religious asceticism in Plato's apparent dualism of spirit and matter, soul and body, eternity and time. Indeed an important influence on Plato was the Orphic-Pythagorean tradition that clearly had ascetic elements. See E. R. Dodds, *The Greeks and the Irrational* (Berkeley: University of California Press, 1968), pp. 140–156 and Ch. 5.

Nietzsche asks: Over *what* has science been victorious? Not the ascetic *ideal* but only certain of its trappings.

The ascetic ideal was decidedly not conquered, it was, on the contrary, made stronger, I mean more elusive, more spiritual (*geistiger*), more insidious by the fact that science constantly and unsparingly detached and broke off a wall or outer-work that had attached itself to it and *coarsened* its appearance.

In what follows Nietzsche elaborates on an *ideal* shared by asceticism and science – despite the "outward" battle between their worldviews – and this ideal has to do with the meaninglessness of finite life, with the nihilistic erasure of meaning in the lived world. How can this be, when science deliberately separates itself from world-transcending beliefs and considers itself to be a highly meaningful endeavor? Nietzsche brings in the example of astronomy and asks if we can truly say that the Copernican defeat of theological astronomy was a defeat of the ascetic ideal. He thinks not, and it is here that the matter of a shared nihilism comes into play and the full complexity of the death of God is shown. If the modern alternative to God's eclipse is simply modern science, then Nietzsche seems to think that the nihilistic core of the ascetic ideal has not only been sustained, but even strengthened, because it can now rest on much more evident and "natural" grounds (and therefore no longer requires a supernatural script).

We might comprehend Nietzsche's move by considering the well-known self-conception of modern science as a radical transformation of how nature is to be understood by way of mechanical physics. The new mechanical model of nature was thoroughly dependent on mathematical measures, which could provide the maximal degree of "objectivity," and which could not be compatible with less measurable or immeasurable matters such as purposes and values (goodness, beauty, goals, etc.). This is the source of the famous fact–value divide, where nature is viewed as a value-free set of measurable facts and values are no longer intrinsic to nature (as they were in ancient and medieval thought). Nature is now simply matter in motion measured by a quantified space-time grid; nature as such has no aim or purpose. The location of *values* therefore had to be redirected to the human subject – whether in the personal subjectivity of "taste" or in the transcendental subjectivity of universal principles intrinsic to any rational mind (as attempted by Kant). Yet in either case, values could no longer be attributed to natural "reality" because they were now "merely" subjective states projected "upon" objective nature (a sunset is not "really" beautiful; it only appears so to us). As a consequence, the status of certain meanings was not only sectioned off but also demoted to the point where it would be possible to say that human life is not "really" meaningful in the sphere of nature. Such, I think, is the context in which we can comprehend Nietzsche's subsequent remarks about astronomy in particular and science in general.

The reason why Nietzsche challenges the victory of Copernican over theological astronomy is that the ascetic departure from natural meaning no longer requires a supernatural story because in effect it has perfected an *immanent* departure from natural meaning *within* a natural setting.

Has man perhaps become less *needful* of a transcendent solution to the riddle of his existence because his existence has since come to look still more arbitrary, more a loitering (*eckensteherischer*), and more dispensable in the *visible* order of things? Has not man's self-diminishment, his *will* to self-diminishment, been unstoppably progressing since Copernicus?

Nietzsche then alludes to the gradual reduction of human self-understanding to the "natural" condition of scientific findings, such as the "animal" characteristics given in biology (perhaps Nietzsche has Darwinism in mind here). He goes on:

Since Copernicus, man seems to have been on a downward path, – now he seems to be rolling faster and faster away from the center – whereto? Into nothingness? Into the "*piercing* sensation of his nothingness"?

We should notice here a clear reference to the language of the madman passage in *Gay Science* 125 that announced the death of God – the loss of a divine center that has the earth unchained from its sun, "straying as through an infinite nothingness." Yet, as I have suggested, the passage in question here pushes the matter further than just the loss of historical warrants in modern thought, which could be called a concealed nihilism; here Nietzsche seems to declare that modern science is a manifestation of ascetic nihilism made more *actual* in a worldly sense. This is why he can say of the growing diminishment of human meaning in modern science: "Well! That would be the straight path – to the *old* ideal."

Here is my take on Nietzsche's position: The original ascetic ideal found natural life meaningless and reached for transcendent relief. Modern science overcame religious transcendence, but with its *reductive* naturalism human meanings were robbed of their previous status and became superfluous in the natural order – despite (or because of) their being rendered "subjective" in modern thought. In this way science provides a *stronger* case for the meaninglessness of natural existence (compared with religious fantasy), and so, within the sphere of natural life alone, *both* religion and science posit a lack of meaning. Moreover, since science restricts thought to the natural world, meaninglessness is now complete and exhaustive, because at least the old ideal provided the *solace* of an imagined deliverance. Nietzsche's argument seems to be that a reductive *scientific* naturalism is no less nihilistic than supernaturalism; it is even more dangerous because it can *consummate* nihilism if science is accepted as the only proper account of nature. What we are circling around here is the important matter of how Nietzsche's naturalism differs from scientific naturalism, and how Nietzsche's approach would be looking for a natural *affirmation* of life-meanings. That is why Nietzsche says that a strictly scientific picture of the world "would be an essentially *meaningless* world" (*GS* 373), and that the question of the *value* of existence lacks "any grain of significance when measured scientifically" (*GS* P, 1).

Nietzsche proclaims that "*all* science" shares with asceticism a "humiliating and degrading effect" on human life by "seeking to talk man out of his former self-respect, as though this were nothing but a bizarre piece of self-conceit" (recall the analysis of guilt). By *all* science Nietzsche means "natural as well as *unnatural*" science. The unnatural form seems to reference Kant's critique of reason, in which knowledge is restricted to modern scientific knowledge, which renders knowledge of things like God, freedom, the soul, and immortality unattainable. Yet Kant recognized the crisis that this constraint represents, especially for human morality. Kant's solution was to limit scientific reason to "appearances," so that something like moral freedom could be posited as *possible* in a sphere of noumenal "reality." At least Kant recognized a crisis that had to be addressed, as opposed to those who take the deflation of human values as *not* disturbing – either by ignoring the issue or perhaps by way of a certain satisfaction taken in debunking cherished beliefs. Nietzsche agrees that the situation *is* a crisis that has to be met head on; but the crisis is *caused* by the presumption that scientific knowledge is the only way to properly understand nature, and the meaning-crisis is in fact the consequence of an ascetic inheritance in science and even the consummation of that ideal's nihilism. Without confronting that ideal as such, no solution to the crisis can be found; some evidence of this barrier is Kant's noble but tortured attempt to both justify *and* limit scientific knowledge, which wound up simply positing a further binary in a postulated "reality" segregated from any direct access in natural experience and knowledge.

In sum we can say that Nietzsche's critique of the ascetic ideal targets every dimension of European thought – theological, philo-sophical, and scientific – owing to a common disposition toward finite life and a common (binary) conception of truth, both of which stem from a failure or inability to find natural existence meaningful on its own terms. In the final sections of the Third Essay, Nietzsche explores the possibility of overcoming the ascetic ideal and its nihilis-tic implications. If there is any way to do this (and Nietzsche seems tentative) it will have to follow from an *affirmative* posture toward natural existence.

OVERCOMING THE ASCETIC IDEAL (SECTIONS 26–28)

Before Nietzsche takes up the possibility of overcoming the ascetic ideal, in Section 26 he takes a final swipe at other indications of this ideal. He has particular scorn for the "'objective' armchair scholar," who embodies a modern turn toward "descriptive" and "contempla-tive" thought, a non-judgmental orientation that Nietzsche derides as incapable of any affirmation or denial, and thus disengaged from any value-formation. Such disengagement is a species of ascetic nihilism, but it is pale and inert compared to the more robust passion shown in more moralistic versions of the ascetic ideal. In this regard Nietzsche says something of surprising interest: "I have every respect for the ascetic ideal *in so far as it is honest*! So long as it believes in itself and does not play any tricks on us!"

Why is this significant? For one thing it fits Nietzsche's perspectival approach to truth, which does not countenance sheer "refutation" but rather *contention*. And as in competitions generally, there can be a measure of respect between opponents. Moreover, Nietzsche's genealogy of the ascetic ideal has paid a lot of attention to the life-enhancing value of its orientation. With life-affirmation as *his* perspective, however, Nietzsche will vigorously contest the ascetic ideal. Yet the remark about honesty adds an intriguing element to Nietzsche's perspectival contest. His naturalistic approach does not rely on refuting the ascetic ideal, but rather *exposing* its anti-natural tendencies. If it were to *admit* these tendencies, Nietzsche might be satisfied. The historical problem is this: Classic asceticism would readily admit its life-aversion but do so on behalf of a (fantasized) supernatural sphere; scientific asceticism renounces the supernatural but hides its ascetic tendencies behind a presumed naturalism. From the standpoint of *Nietzsche's* naturalism, *both* forms exhibit a "dishonesty" that needs to be exposed: the fantasy of "another life" in classic asceticism, and the presumption of a non-ascetic affirmation of "this life" in scientific asceticism. It seems that if either orientation would simply confess to its disaffection with natural forces – and therefore accept a perspectival retraction of its presumption to possess *the* truth – then perhaps Nietzsche would express much less antagonism. He might even affirm them in a way: these perspectives would not have to renounce or cease activating their values; they would simply have been exposed as having willfully cut off certain natural energies in the course of their commitments. I confess to speculation here, but Nietzsche's remark about honesty seems to imply something along these lines.

Section 27 confirms two things about the *Genealogy*: The gathering theme and climax of the book is the problem of truth; and the primary aim of the book is not the past or even the present, but the future, and the possibility of overcoming the exclusive dominance of the ascetic ideal. Nietzsche says rather starkly that currently there is no alternative to the ascetic ideal (keep in mind that an "ideal" is important because it embodies a deep philosophical commitment to meaning and value). Modern atheism will not suffice: it appears to be a renunciation of all high-blown ideals, "*except for its will to truth.*" And Nietzsche reiterates that atheism's will to truth is in fact the core expression of the ascetic ideal. It is "that ideal itself in its strictest, most spiritual (*geistigsten*) formulation, completely esoteric, stripped of all outer-works, and thus not so much its remnant as its *kernel.*"

Nietzsche next offers a final complication (as if things were not complicated enough) in his genealogical analysis, which has to do with the notion of self-overcoming. We already know that will to power involves movements of self-overcoming when prompted by "internal" conflicts and obstacles. According to Nietzsche, this is how atheism is the continuation of the ascetic ideal with respect to the will to truth. For a host of reasons, the Christian-ascetic truth-ideal eventually came to undermine its own theological foundations (especially with the development of modern science, which Nietzsche claims simply redirected the same will to truth):

Unconditional, sincere atheism (– *its* air alone is what we breathe, we more spiritual men of the age!) is therefore *not* opposed to the ascetic ideal, as it appears to be; instead, it is only one of the ideal's last phases of development, one of its final forms and inner consequences, – it is the awe-inspiring *catastrophe* of a two-thousand year discipline in truth-telling, which finally forbids itself the *lie entailed in the belief in God.*

Nietzsche quotes a passage from *Gay Science* 357, which describes this situation in the following way: The Christian moral conscience of truthfulness (especially in the confession of sins) was translated into the scientific conscience of "intellectual cleanliness at any price," which in time found religious models less and less warranted and believable. Now theology has been thoroughly replaced by science, which is what Nietzsche means by the death of God. The quoted passage continues by naming this outcome "Europe's most drawn-out and bravest self-overcoming." Included is a reference to how this movement fits the general structure of will to power:

All great things bring about their own demise through an act of self-sublimation: that is the law of life, the law of *necessary* "self-overcoming" in the essence of life.

The German term for "self-sublimation" is *Selbstaufhebung*, which can mean both self-annulment and self-preservation, even self-advancement – thus continues the ambiguity of a self-overcoming of asceticism that nevertheless sustains its ideal. The best way to make sense of Nietzsche's argument is to keep in mind that the ascetic ideal has been concentrated by Nietzsche into a life-averse ideal of *truth*, an exclusive binary model that deems any differing condition to be the *opposite* of truth, to be an irredeemable error. *This* is the essence of the ascetic ideal for Nietzsche, as distinct from what *form* it might take (in religion, science, and so on). Now we can better understand how the eclipse of religion by science was at once a self-overcoming and a self-sustaining process. If truth is conceived in the binary fashion noted above, then any conflicts between science and religion in the modern world (and there were plenty) would have to be a zero-sum game. To whatever degree science gained success, to that same degree religion would have to be deemed a failure. It is the truth-ideal *behind* religious trappings that explains how atheism can be called by Nietzsche the self-overcoming of Christian theology (and how the death of God might be called a "suicide"). At the same time, since science shares the *same* ascetic truth-ideal, then the self-overcoming of *religious* asceticism will not mean the overcoming of the ascetic ideal itself. The remainder of Section 27 now intimates Nietzsche's own hopes for the (self-)overcoming of the ascetic ideal as such, in all its forms.

Just as Christian theology and its truth-ideal produced a self-overcoming in the direction of science and atheism, Nietzsche says that the essential pattern of self-overcoming in will to power can produce a self-overcoming of the entire "will to truth" in the ascetic ideal, along with its moral aversion to finite life. Just as the moral conscience of truthfulness destroyed "Christianity *as a dogma*," Nietzsche says:

> In the same way Christianity *as a morality* must also be destroyed – we stand on the threshold of *this* occurrence. After Christian truthfulness has drawn one conclusion after another, it will finally draw the *strongest conclusion*, that *against* itself; this will, however, happen when it asks itself, *"What does all will to truth mean?"* . . . and here I touch upon my problem – again, on our problem, my *unknown* friends (– because I don't *know* of any friends as yet): what meaning would *our* entire being have, if it were not that that will to truth has become conscious of itself *as a problem* in us?

Since Nietzsche claims that this overcoming of ascetic morality and truth will occur "in the same way" as theology's self-overcoming, it seems clear that the prospect he envisions would have to mean the *self*-overcoming of the ascetic ideal. We have already seen how often Nietzsche's critical moves maintain an ambiguous relation with the target of criticism (as in the case of bad conscience). That ambiguity is also indicated in this section when Nietzsche uses the first person in signaling the overturning of the ascetic ideal ("my problem"), while also using the "we" earlier in describing modern atheism ("we more spiritual men of the age") – which is *still* caught up in the ascetic ideal. We might clarify the ambiguity of asceticism's self-overcoming in the following way: The ascetic (binary) model of truth has been the standard in the entire Western tradition, from Christian religion to modern science. Nietzsche says that such an ideal will finally draw its "strongest conclusion" that cancels itself out. The question that Nietzsche cites as guiding this development is: What does all will to truth mean? In the context of the *Genealogy*, the answer would be that it is at bottom hostile to natural life, and therefore nihilistic from a naturalistic standpoint. Nietzsche's diagnosis would amount to this: The ascetic truth-ideal finally discovers the truth about itself. And the self-overcoming involved here would echo the self-overcoming of theology (moved in the direction of science owing to internal conflicts confronting religion in the modern world). The internal conflict that would drive the ascetic ideal (including science) toward a self-overcoming would be posed in Nietzsche's genealogical diagnosis: the anti-natural posture governing even supposedly natural world-views; and the nihilistic implications in supposedly positive concepts of truth and meaning.

Such an analysis, I think, further confirms that Nietzsche's critiques never issue from some separate vantage point; they uncover disturbances intrinsic to the life-phenomena in question. And since the ascetic ideal has been the essential thrust of Western thought, a critique (from a Western thinker) could not be an invasion launched from outside that ideal. We should note that Nietzsche refers to the prospect of Europe overcoming the ascetic ideal as a "great drama (*Schauspiel*)" in coming centuries, a drama "most terrible and questionable." Since *Schauspiel* in German specifically refers to the theater, we cannot help noticing an echo of Greek tragic drama in the "self-destruction" of the ascetic ideal. And yet the tragic, for Nietzsche, need not (should not) entail pessimism, and he closes the section by saying that this terrible drama may be "also the one most rich in hope . . . "

One way to understand Nietzsche's hope from a philosophical standpoint would be that the self-overcoming of the ascetic truth-ideal – its exclusive, binary conception of truth secured from other-ness – could bring forth a non-binary sense of truth that accords with finite life. If ascetic truth were overturned on its own (binary) terms, the result would be the *nihilation* of any sense of truth, and thus nihilism. This is the abyss confronting the West, as Nietzsche sees it. If there *is* to be hope for truth and meaning, the binary model of truth must give way to a non-binary, non-securable sense of truth – precisely the sense of Nietzsche's perspectival, agonistic understanding of truth, which in genuinely "natural" terms can overcome both dogmatic truth and an anti-dogmatic denial of truth. Such an outcome would mirror the call earlier in the text for the overcoming "of both God and nothingness" (*GM* II, 24).

The final section of the essay seems odd from a rhetorical standpoint. In effect it reiterates the historical dominance of the ascetic ideal and how it represents a life-enhancing power of meaning-formation. One would think that the previous section could have been an effective climax, with Nietzsche's expression of hope for a life-*affirming* future. Yet this last section could be an appropriate finale for the declared purpose of the book: a genealogy of traditional morality that tries to explain how and why life-aversive beliefs could have come forth from, and taken hold in, natural existence.

Nietzsche tells us at the start of Section 28 that the "*animal* man" and earthly existence have thus far had no meaning or purpose except for the ascetic ideal. The meaning of this ideal was an attempt to overcome the intrinsic suffering and finite limits in natural life. Nietzsche diagnoses this as an aversion to all the evident elements in life that cannot be secured from suffering and change, which are listed at the end of the section: animal and material conditions, the senses, reason, happiness, beauty, appearance, transience, growth, death, history, and longing. Since natural life is Nietzsche's standard, this aversion amounts to "a *will to nothingness*," the secret core of all the supposed resolutions of suffering in ascetic thought. And yet, staying with a naturalistic standard, Nietzsche takes pains to show that this aversive will "is and remains a *will*!" The ascetic ideal is and remains a form of *life* that shapes a sense of meaning and purpose *in* life.

Here is where Nietzsche mentions "suicidal nihilism," which is important for comprehending Nietzsche's complex effort. Given the very real conditions of finitude and suffering in life, human *awareness* of this tragic reality could quite well spawn an urge for suicidal escape. The ascetic ideal, however, provides a way to serve life, to ward off *suicidal* nihilism through the *productive* nihilism of its counter-natural powers. The only absolute form of life-denial is suicide, and so the ascetic ideal, though not life-affirming, is life-preserving. Ascetic cultural forces provide humanity with a livable meaning by creating alternatives to radical finitude and becoming. Yet since these alternatives have to "fight off" natural forces, asceticism goes so far as to *court* suffering in the self-directed "cruelty" toward these forces in human life – which thus *remains* a participant in life's domain of suffering. This is why Nietzsche repeats earlier remarks that suffering as such is not the problem, but rather the *meaninglessness* of suffering. And the ascetic ideal provided a meaning for suffering that was able to sustain life. Nietzsche declares: "Up to now it was the only meaning; yet any meaning is better than no meaning at all." And he closes with the refrain: "man still prefers to *will nothingness* than *not* will . . . " Since this line repeats a claim from Section 1, another reason for the rhetorical focus of this last section would be Nietzsche's notice that the Third Essay is a commentary on Section 1.

Even as we understand the textual setting of the last section, we should not lose sight of the role that Nietzsche's critical alternative to the ascetic ideal plays in the *Genealogy*. The force of his argument in fact can be located implicitly in the gesture to life-enhancement at the close of the book. Short of nihilistic suicide, all forms of culture, including ascetic culture, aim for some kind of meaning in life. With the death of God – the eclipse of the supernatural – the default criterion is some kind of natural orientation. Nietzsche's fundamental question runs: What would it mean to be truly faithful to the natural world, or, as Zarathustra says, to be "faithful (*treu*) to the earth" (*Z* P, 3)? What would it mean to genuinely say Yes to life? Despite the life-enhancing power of the ascetic tradition, Nietzsche's own project of life-affirmation would gain muscle by diagnosing life-averse elements in alternative models of meaning. Moreover, I think it is important to recognize that Nietzsche does not see his philosophical project as coming utterly from out of the blue, that within Western culture itself there are elements that his critique could be said to *retrieve* in some way. That is why I think the claim in Section 28 – "up to now" existence on earth had no meaning except for the ascetic ideal – would only make sense if the historical framework in question began with Socrates and Plato, who could be called the progenitors of the ascetic ideal. An alienated posture could be noticed in their battle against an earlier *tragic* culture that impressed Nietzsche because it came to terms with the intrinsic finitude of life. In many ways Nietzsche's "prosecution" of the West is also a *defense* of the West's tragic roots, which preceded the traditions targeted by Nietzsche. Even though we cited the resonance of the tragic in Nietzsche's account of the self-destruction of the ascetic ideal, a tragic measure is *Nietzsche's* predilection; the ascetic ideal in all its forms is driven by an aversion to tragic limits. This is why I have said that focusing on the tragic can provide much guidance for comprehending Nietzsche's philosophy, his critique of the West, and how we might assess the relevance of Nietzsche's thought for us. The remaining chapters of this study will try to make good on my assumption.

CHAPTER 6

Reflections on the Genealogy

In this investigation I have tried to offer a close reading of Nietzsche's *Genealogy* that can give readers a sense of the remarkable complexity and range of the book. Now I would like to step back and examine a number of background issues in more detail, which can enhance an understanding of the text. These reflections will prepare the final two chapters, which aim to track how Nietzsche's analysis compares with familiar moral and political theories. Implicit in my commentary has been an attempt to appreciate the philosophical import of Nietzsche's work. But assessing its merits requires some further historical discussions and an engagement with alternative approaches to the issues at hand. In getting started, a summary sketch of the *Genealogy* would help. I will not present a compressed run-through of the book's main elements, but rather a broad scan of the overall philosophical strategy animating Nietzsche's historical treatment of the Western moral and philosophical tradition; such a scan can help set the stage for the discussions to come.

AN OVERVIEW OF THE *GENEALOGY*

I have maintained that the fundamental question underlying the *Genealogy* is: Can there be meaning and value in natural life following the death of God? The eclipse of the supernatural in modern thought is a presumed turn to nature, but Nietzsche insists that this turn is in fact a looping reliance on the theological tradition, and that the eclipse of God forces a more radical naturalistic challenge: If the Western tradition in one way or another is beholden to a nature-transcending or life-averse condition, then the loss of this condition's divine logo and warrant undermines traditional sources of meaning and value, to the point where the West faces the choice between nihilism and a new, affirmative philosophy of nature.

The *Genealogy* is a historical study that fills out the details of the above scenario by trying to show how and why the tradition has been life-averse and cannot be sustained in the wake of modern developments. The genealogical history unfolding in the book is meant to simultaneously clarify and critique the counter-natural drives in European culture, no less in its supposed departures from supernatural beliefs. The First Essay concentrates on debunking our moral confidences by tracing esteemed values to premodern sources in slave morality and Christianity, which were marked by an inability to abide, and an attempt to overcome, the more natural forces of power and value in master morality. In the Second Essay, modern morality is then shown to have inherited slave values and converted them into supposedly worldly, secular norms. The Third Essay focuses on the ascetic ideal as the organizing term for counter-natural values, and the rhetorical force of this term is meant to disturb confidence in what Nietzsche takes to be the deepest, most extensive, and most comprehensive manifestation of the ascetic ideal: the belief in truth. The ultimate target is a belief in an unconditional, binary model of truth that aims for immunity from any taint of otherness, and this model, according to Nietzsche, shows itself in modern science and philosophy no less than in transcendent religious systems.

The trajectory of the three essays (which loops back and forth between them) is meant to undermine modern intellectual confidences by tracing them back to *moral* roots – which injects *values* into supposedly *fact*-based objectivity – and then by tracing modern moral assumptions back to premodern *conditional* moral roots in the slave revolt against master morality – which upends the belief in modern values as universal, exclusive, and fully positive in character. Nietzsche wants this historical narrative to shock us out of complacency, which hides troubling questions that a genealogical treatment may reveal and that Nietzsche is more than willing to launch: Can our intellectual and moral convictions actually stem from life-negating or life-averse conditions?

A naturalistic philosophy, for Nietzsche, can abide nothing outside evident forces of life. Yet since counter-natural movements have in fact emerged in natural life, one cannot presume to dismiss such developments as anti-natural "errors" in the strict sense. There must be some sense in which nature was bound to give forth such cultural phenomena. Nietzsche therefore recognizes the need for a naturalistic account of counter-natural drives. The course of his attempt to provide such an account is filled with the complexities inherent in this seeming paradox – which is resolved by the guiding theme of will to power, the tensional strife indigenous to natural *and* cultural forces.

The ambiguities in Nietzsche's treatment can be gleaned from his insistence on the correlative *tensions* between nature, culture, and meaning. Nature by itself is raw will to power, the ongoing struggle between opposing life forces in the unending cycle of victory and defeat, life and death. By itself, nature has no "meaning," no purpose or value in its blind instinctive energies. Yet out of nature there emerges the human ability to form meaning and value in its *cultural* capacity to exceed the sheer immediacy of instinct, which by way of language is able to develop a reflective sense of time and thus create values that inform the present with past inheritances and future goals.

I think it is clear that, for Nietzsche, *any* meaning must exceed and overcome *sheer* nature, and so there is always a tension between nature and culture. Yet for this very reason Nietzsche aims to show that culture is no less a form of will to power: Cultural forms are simply a redirection of *raw* will to power into "refined" modes of power that overcome brute instinct and violence in the direction of sustainable constructs of meaning. This is why Nietzsche's interest in early Greek culture is so important for understanding his argument. In his reflections on the *agōn* and tragic poetry, Nietzsche identifies an early model of culture that *refined* raw nature – with contests for excellence rather than violent annihilation, and Apollonian art forms rather than wild Dionysian abandonment – and that accordingly achieved a certain "balance" between natural forces and cultural meanings by way of a "crossing" dynamic between the two spheres.

Since culture and nature, for Nietzsche, always exist in *tension*, culture remains a precarious achievement, the vulnerability of which allows for two possible extremes that can undo the balance: (1) nature can overwhelm culture in the direction of barbarity, violence, and chaos, and (2) culture can overwhelm nature by aiming to supersede natural forces with regimes of order, control, stability, or self-denying transcendence. From the standpoint of Nietzsche's preferred balancing-act, he can say that *both* tendencies are nihilistic, the first a reversion to the meaninglessness of brute nature, the second a conversion of culture into a life-denying alienation that finds *any* effect of natural energies to be a threat to meaning, so that even human *cultural* life is meaningless when restricted to natural life. It must be stressed that, for Nietzsche, human life *is* meaning-creating, but the problem turns on how meaning can be lost by either hyper-natural or hyper-cultural extremes.

Against this background, the intricacies of Nietzsche's naturalistic account of life-averse tendencies can be seen in a clearer light. We noticed in the text a mix of polemical critique and appreciation in Nietzsche's discussions of slave morality and asceticism. On the one hand, his life-affirmative posture animates the polemic, while, on the other hand, the life-enhancing value of these movements is recognized as a source of meaning for weaker types and an antidote against suicidal nihilism – such is his naturalistic explanation for why counter-natural ideals emerged, because life itself required this internal conflict for the preservation of certain forms of life, especially when human "domestication" gradually supplanted the more natural powers exhibited in master morality.

The mix of polemic and appreciation exhibits even further complexity when it comes to master morality. The powers of the master type are restricted to the more natural domain of overt action and physical prowess. The internalization of power in slave morality, while problematic, opens up the capacities of imagination and thus the more refined forms of culture-creation that Nietzsche himself celebrates. Therefore, slavish tendencies are not only life-enhancing, they are also not altogether regrettable when mixed with creative power. And since Nietzsche claims that such creative power emerges not through the slavish masses but through special individuals (the ascetic priest type and its offshoots), then here we notice a possible blending of slavish passivity and masterly activity, of the distancing effect of weaker types and the productive effect of stronger types – both coexisting "within a single soul" (*BGE* 260). It seems that higher *culture*, for Nietzsche, would not be possible apart from the creative redirection of power made possible by *natural* weakness. Nietzsche's hope is that future creative types can break through the dominance of ascetic culture to open up a more affirmative, more "naturalized" culture.

Owing to this complex scenario, Nietzsche's future hopes do not, even cannot, embody an utterly antithetical relation to the ascetic tradition – thus the ambiguity of his accounts of the ascetic ideal and bad conscience. First of all, philosophical reflection itself is a consequence of a certain withdrawal and distancing from the spontaneity of a strictly *active* life (recall the position of "we knowers" in the Preface). Nietzsche's own philosophical vision cannot be insulated from *this* kind of life-aversion, but perhaps we could characterize it as a move toward a more *intimate* distancing from nature. Second, the ascetic ideal has been so powerful and pervasive in the West, and its life-averse posture has produced so much high-cultural effect, that any cultural resistance to ascetic culture on behalf of a more naturalized culture would have to issue from a *self*-overcoming of the ascetic ideal, moved by the exposure of its internal conflicts with respect to life.

Whatever difficulties Nietzsche's analysis may present for us, we can at least appreciate its *consistency* with his naturalism in the following sense: If natural life is all there is, nothing in life can emerge from, or be understood by way of, some "external" vantage point, whether this be a transcendent vision *or* an anti-transcendent stance that ignores or belittles "spiritual" beliefs – because nature *has* produced such beliefs and they must therefore have some internal significance in natural life. Nietzsche's naturalism thus cannot abide *any* belief that is purely antithetical to any phenomenon that has taken hold in life. Such is the problem with scientific naturalism taken to a scientistic extreme, which can be provoked in the following way: Why did it take so long for the truth to come out and overturn pre-scientific "errors" if there is nothing outside nature? From what vantage point could such a historical judgment of error be made? Could this judgment be one of those "shadows" of the supernatural, a God's-eye view of nature now mimicked by science? In any case, even the ascetic ideal is not absolutely *anti*-natural, because it has life-enhancing value *and* it has opened up the possibilities of philosophy, which can even engineer the self-transformation of the ascetic ideal into a life-affirming ideal.

With respect to Nietzsche's philosophical ideal, let us now turn to a further discussion of the question of truth.

NATURE, ART, AND TRUTH

In sum, it is clear that Nietzsche understands nature as a complex array of competing forces, which eludes any attempt at unification or exclusive, binary thinking – and this includes the binary of dogmatism and skepticism. For Nietzsche, natural life and natural knowledge exhibit neither strict certainty nor radical uncertainty. Knowledge and meaning, therefore, *are* possible in Nietzsche's approach, but they are constituted by intrinsic natural *limits*, which is why they can be called *tragic* phenomena. And it is my contention that Nietzsche's naturalism has its roots in his early work on Greek tragedy. We have noted that tragedy, for Nietzsche, was far more than a literary form because it presented an early Greek *world-view* that was more faithful (more true) to the finite conditions of natural life than the coming developments of philosophy issued by Socrates and Plato. Early Greek myth and religion did not promote a transcendence of earthly existence toward a timeless eternity or salvation from suffering.

There are two senses in which we can understand the affirmative posture of Greek tragedy toward natural life, according to Nietzsche's interpretation: an aesthetic sense and a religious sense. First, Nietzsche sees the artistic Apollonian elements in tragedy as essential to the life-affirming spirit of the Greeks. The very act of fashioning a beautiful portrayal of a dark truth shows that the Greeks even here were delighting in the power of artistic imagery to display the attractions of the life-world, as opposed to withdrawing into quietism, pessimistic denial, or hopes for another world. For Nietzsche, pessimistic art is a contradiction (*WP* 821). In addition, Apollonian art forms shaped a world of meaning in which the Greeks could dwell, and through which they could bear the terrible truth of Dionysian deformation, thus avoiding the danger of self-abnegation.

Second, the historical association of tragedy with the worship of Dionysus, together with Nietzsche's articulation of a divine dyad at the core of tragedy, indicates that the Greeks (and Nietzsche) understood tragedy as expressive of certain truths about existence that call for a reverent response. In other words, the disclosures of tragedy, stemming from "divine" sources, are not simply "human" meanings, but rather elements of the world *to* which humans must respond, and which they are called to affirm. The effect of tragedy is the simultaneous affirmation of human life and its ultimate limits.[1]

Moreover, a certain extra-human significance would accord with an aspect of Nietzsche's analysis of tragedy that is often ignored, namely his refusal to reduce Apollonian and Dionysian powers simply to human artistic production. Prior to the discussion of tragic art, Nietzsche refers to the Apollonian and Dionysian as "artistic energies that burst forth from nature herself" in natural creation and destruction, birth and death, and the emergence of dream states and frenzied abandon, which are not deliberately intended by humans (*BT* 2).[2] Nietzsche suggests that human artistry is a "mediated" relation to this natural energy, an "imitation" of immediate creative forces in nature. Imitation here could not mean representational simulation, but rather the more performative sense of "impersonating" these energies in artistic practices (impersonation being one of the meanings of *mimēsis* in Greek). Even human artistic production, for Nietzsche, is not grounded in the individual will and subjectivity of the artist: humans are not "the true authors of this art world" (*BT* 5). Such suggestions would certainly fit well with Nietzsche's sympathetic treatment of Greek deities and in a general sense with Nietzsche's emphasis on art as not simply a human artifact, but as disclosive of the *world's* meaning and significance: "for it is only as an *aesthetic phenomenon* that existence and the world are eternally justified" (*BT* 5). What is "saved" by art is not only human meaning, but *life* (*BT* 7). Therefore we can conclude that the "divine" references that exceed humanity and suggest the "true author" of the art world point to primal forces in natural life. This is consistent with Nietzsche's claim that culture arises *out of* nature and it compels us to realize that the

---

[1] This can show an important sense in which Nietzsche's concept of the *Übermensch* can be understood, not as something "super-human" but as a sense of life that is no longer human-centered. See my article "Apollo and Dionysus: Nietzschean Expressions of the Sacred," in *Nietzsche and the Gods*, ed. Weaver Santaniello (Albany, NY: SUNY Press, 2001), pp. 45–56.

[2] It should be said that the Greek word translated as "nature" is *phusis*, which is derived from the verb *phuō*, meaning to grow, to bring forth, to give birth. In Homer, *phuō* usually refers to plant life, with a specific meaning of bringing forth shoots, and earth is commonly called *phusizoos*, that which gives forth life (*Odyssey* 11.301).

baseline reference for Nietzsche is not humanity or even art, but life (*BT* ASC, 2).

Although Nietzsche is not a religious thinker in any typical sense, his work does exhibit a disposition of reverence toward life. For this reason we might not be surprised that he was comfortable celebrating Greek deities, and that he continued to refer to, even align himself with, the Greek god Dionysus (see especially *TI* "What I Owe the Ancients"). Yet Nietzsche was first and foremost a philosopher. Reflecting back on *The Birth of Tragedy*, he says that here he had discovered the *concept* of the tragic, and that he sees himself as "the first tragic *philosopher*," the first to offer a "transposition of the Dionysian into a philosophical pathos" (*EH* III, BT, 3). The same holds for Nietzsche's references to art, which should not be confined simply to "the arts." Nietzsche is advancing an "artist-philosophy," which is a "higher concept of art" (*WP* 795).

With respect to the question of nature and art, we can say that, beginning with *The Birth of Tragedy*, Nietzsche seems to shape his naturalism in part by way of an intimate relationship between nature, art, and tragedy, with the latter presenting an art world that best "impersonates" the surging creative–destructive dynamic of nature. The critique of Socratic rationality in *The Birth of Tragedy* targets its incapacity to tolerate living nature, its refuge in fixed ideas and conscious reflection. For Nietzsche, Socrates and Plato initiated the alienation from finite nature that is consummated in ascetic nihilism. Yet we should remember that the Dionysian *by itself* also represented the danger of nihilism, of abandonment to self-denying ecstasy. In other words, alienation from life can stem from either a static refuge in pure form (Socrates and Plato) or a dynamic refuge in a disintegrating formlessness (we notice something like the dangers of hyper-cultural and hyper-natural extremes discussed earlier). This is why Apollonian art is so important in Nietzsche's account; it provides a meaningful world that avoids both types of nihilism by way of aesthetic "appearances."

There is a clear connection between this early treatment in Nietzsche's work and the later critique of the ascetic truth-ideal, especially with regard to science. In *The Birth of Tragedy*, Socratic reason is associated with the development of science (Sections 15–16); and the later Preface published in 1886 reflects on the book as a confrontation with "something frightful and dangerous . . . a *new* problem – today I should say that it was *the problem of science itself*, science considered for the first time as problematic, as questionable" (*BT* ASC, 2). The same passage coordinates this problem with the alternative of art and its life-serving power. Despite the flaws he now recognizes in his first work, he is still dedicated "to the task that this audacious book dared to tackle for the first time: *to look at science from the perspective of the artist, but at art from the perspective of life.*"

It is notable that Nietzsche signals this 1886 passage in his discussion of science and the ascetic ideal in the *Genealogy* (III, 25), published in 1887. And this signal follows the remark about art that I have postponed discussing until now. In the midst of his exposure of science as a continuation of the ascetic truth-ideal, Nietzsche interjects:

Art, let me say at the outset, since I will deal with this at length some day, – art, in which *lying* sanctifies itself and the *will to deception* has good conscience on its side, is much more fundamentally opposed to the ascetic ideal than science is.[3]

The anticipated work is named in Section 27: *The Will to Power: An Attempt at the Revaluation of all Values*, a book that in fact never came to fruition.[4] Nevertheless, the issue at stake here is one that reaches all the way from the work on tragedy to the *Genealogy*, which I think can be gathered as follows: Tragic art represents a nature-attuned alternative to the counter-natural nihilism of the ascetic truth-ideal.

Although Nietzsche did not specifically follow through on this contrast in a published work, the notebooks show much in this regard, and the published material following the *Genealogy* contains enough intimations of the question to merit some attention

[3] In the same passage Nietzsche distinguishes this perspective on art from the kind he had previously called servile to the ascetic ideal, which he now names a form of "artistic *corruption*." He also mentions Homer in a positive light because of Plato's ascetic objections to his poetry.

[4] Although I have been referring to translated notes under the title *The Will to Power*, it is important to recognize this as a "non-book," because it was compiled not by Nietzsche but his sister. The status of this "book," despite Nietzsche's initial aims for it, is undermined by alterations in later notes and by Nietzsche's apparent suspension of plans to publish such a text. For important discussions of this matter, see Bernd Magnus, "Nietzsche's Philosophy in 1888: *The Will to Power* and the *Übermensch*," *Journal of the History of Philosophy* 24/1 (January 1986), 79–98, and the discussion between Peter Heller, R. J. Hollingdale, Bernd Magnus, and Richard Schacht in *International Studies in Philosophy* 22/2 (1990), 35–66.

(see *TI* 9, 8–11 and 24). What would it mean to say that (tragic) art is a nominee for overcoming the binary model of truth in the ascetic ideal? And since I have argued that Nietzsche's opposition to this ideal does not rule out other senses of truth – one of which I have already associated with art – another question arises: What are we to make of Nietzsche's claim that the virtue of art is its valorization of lying and deception? Would we not be better off ignoring this idea, especially since an extended treatment never materialized? Perhaps. Yet I still believe that the matter of art and truth deserves attention because it gathers together topics that occupied Nietzsche's thinking from beginning to end, and it can prepare a path for understanding how his work presents an alternative approach to standard philosophical questions. For instance, I believe that there *are* plausible and cogent Nietzschean answers to questions about truth and morality; and that such answers stem from a nuanced comprehension of the *tragic* structure of life and thought.

If there are such possibilities for a sense of truth in Nietzsche's philosophy, shouldn't we be troubled by his apparent celebration of lying and deception in the above passage? Indeed, such tropes abound in Nietzsche's writings, so how can this square with any sense of truth? The question is not easy to answer, but we can begin by recalling the ambiguous sense of "appearance" in Nietzsche's thought. There is a positive connotation of appearance as a "happening," which is consistent with a radical becoming; appearance in this sense would have to be distinguished from a "mere" appearance that conceals a "reality," and which thereby is parasitic on traditional standards of being and truth. Recalling a passage we cited in the previous chapter (*TI* 4, 6) – and paraphrasing somewhat – if the traditional "real world" is ruled out, so too is the (merely) "apparent world." Therefore it cannot be the case that Nietzsche's own use of "appearance" would entail something "unreal" or "false," because that would sustain traditional (binary) models of reality and truth by simply flipping them around. I think that the same can be said for his celebration of artistic lying and deception.

It has long been understood that the realm of art – as a creative product of imagination – is something different from "real" things given to us in normal experience; also that art is not to be judged by the usual standards of truth and falsity (and it would be odd to say that one style of art "refutes" another style). As long as art is sectioned off as a sphere of culture from other spheres that do deal with truth (science, for example), then everything seems fine. Yet Nietzsche is challenging this kind of arrangement and even elevating art to a higher status. In doing so, I think it is plausible to say that he will often bank on the traditional *binary* models of reality–appearance, truth–fiction, etc., and advance the *deficient* side of the traditional opposition for rhetorical effect and provocation, for a shock to the system, so to speak. What recommends this rhetorical angle is that the crossing-structure of will to power and perspectivism (Nietzsche's alternative to binary thinking) could not entail simply the exchange of one binary opposite for another. Yet when Nietzsche advances artistic lying and deception, this seems to cross a line that tropes such as appearance or fiction need not draw us across. Is Nietzsche on thin ice here?

Several unpublished notes from the late 1880s repeat the language of *The Birth of Tragedy*, to the effect that art is a "lie" that saves human life from the "truth" of Dionysian disintegration, the ultimate consequence of a world of becoming: "We possess *art* lest we *perish of the truth*" (*WP* 822). Measured against what I have called the tragic truth of becoming, Nietzsche deploys tropes of "deception" for *any* construction of meaning that cannot ultimately be preserved. Artistic deception in this sense marks *all* of human thought:

We have need of lies in order to conquer this reality, this "truth," that is, in order to *live* . . . man must be a liar by nature, he must above all be an *artist*. And he *is* one: metaphysics, religion, morality, science – all of them only products of his will to art, to lie, to flight from "truth," to *negation* of "truth." (*WP* 853)[5]

The critique of traditional thought systems amounts to this: they themselves are (artistic) creations with no ultimate foundation, yet they interpret themselves otherwise – they claim to be *true* and nothing like "art." This is why *tragic* art is distinctive and so central in Nietzsche's critique. Tragic art acknowledges not only its creative character, but also the *abyss* at the heart of a creative model of thought,

---

[5] References such as these and the overall discussion I am advancing challenge the assumption of Maudemarie Clark (and others) that Nietzsche abandoned his early anti-truth talk in favor of a more scientific orientation.

the absence of any secure foundation behind the coming-forth of creative acts – an abyss that prompts the fugitive tendencies in the tradition. For Nietzsche, tragic art displays this recognition in both its *form* (Apollonian images against a Dionysian background) and its *content* (human meanings subjected to terrible limits and loss). Tragic art is therefore a sign of strength in a finite world, as opposed to the weakness that seeks refuge in some secured meaning.

It is a sign of one's *feeling of power and well-being* how far one can acknowledge the terrifying and questionable character of things; and *whether* one needs some sort of "solution" at the end . . . and by all means craves a solution or at least a hope for a solution . . . The *profundity of the tragic artist* lies in this, that he affirms the *large-scale economy* which justifies the *terrifying*, the *evil*, the *questionable* – and more than merely justifies them. (*WP* 852)

The *affirmation* of the tragic-creative character of thought would seem to lend more positive significance to artistic "deception." Indeed, in the passage where Nietzsche depicts all of human thought as a truth-negating "lie," he goes on:

This ability itself, thanks to which he violates reality by means of lies, this artistic ability of man *par excellence* – he has it in common with everything that is. He himself is after all a piece of reality, truth, nature: how should he not also be a piece of *genius in lying*! (*WP* 853)

The "deceptive" character of thought, therefore, is *intrinsic* to nature, it is evident in *any* form of life (recall how will to power and perspectivism include nonhuman life as well). If this is so, then the only measure of "truth" on the other side of deception is no measure at all, only a dissolving limit. If *everything* in life is a lie in this sense, then deception can have no derogatory sense – unless one were to call for a release from deception into, well, nothingness.

In trying to make sense out of Nietzsche's rhetoric of deception, I am trying to make room for some modified sense of *truth* in the midst of this rhetoric. It seems that when Nietzsche wants to emphasize the tragic truth of becoming, he deploys a vocabulary of "lying" to depict forms of meaning. Yet it is also clear that Nietzsche's philosophy displays more positive senses of truth that can still accord with radical becoming (such as perspectivism). To round out this discussion, I want to offer another brief venture into ancient Greek culture, which may help us better understand Nietzsche's rhetorical choices and their meaning.

The Greeks were well aware, from the earliest times, that poetic performances depicted something different from "actual" events. Traveling bards would enthrall audiences with emotionally and musically charged tales about gods and heroes – culturally significant events embellished with heightened language for maximum effect. And such performances were a "pause" set aside from normal life pursuits. What interests us is that a word commonly used to denote this "difference" was *pseudos*, usually translated as "false." Yet the context of this use and the cultural status of poetry would undermine the idea that *pseudos* here denoted "falsehood" as the sheer opposite of truth.[6] In fact *pseudos* was a single word with remarkable flexibility, the different senses of which could only be discerned in different contexts of use. Unlike our language, the Greeks used this same word to connote an "error" and a "lie," that is, a mistaken statement about something and an *intentional* falsehood.

The attribution of "falsehood" to poetry, however, extends the ambiguity of *pseudos* even further. First of all, given the *competitive* nature of Greek poetry (a significant instance of the Greek *agōn*) individual poets would use *pseudos* to target other poets – in this context "false" would mean "inferior" or "ineffective" or "not *my* poetry." More importantly, *pseudos* could refer to what we would call "fiction" as opposed to "fact," yet not in the binary sense that we might expect. The Greek word often translated as "fact" is *ergon*, which had a general meaning of something *done* rather than something merely *said* – a distinction that could apply to the "different" sphere of poetic speech. The poetic sense of *pseudos* would be closer to what we would call verisimilitude, or "fictive truth." In the Greek sense, fictive truth would not only refer to the way in which poetic language could "resemble" reality, but also to its persuasive power to enthrall the audience and absorb it in the *reality* of the poetic fiction (eliciting wonder, joy, fear, etc.). It should be noted that this is precisely one of the basic meanings of the Greek word *mimēsis* – not merely representational likeness, but the psychological *identification*

---

[6] The following remarks are drawn from Louise H. Pratt, *Lying and Poetry from Homer to Pindar* (Ann Arbor: University of Michigan Press, 1993), Ch. 1.

of an audience with a poetic performance (more on this shortly). Nietzsche himself recognized this mimetic power of poetic "appearances" in *The Birth of Tragedy*. Greek tragedy only enhanced mimetic power because it went beyond a bard's mere depiction in speech to actors embodying poetic speech in action – the word *drama* in Greek means something *done*, and so Greek theater showed much less of the difference between "fiction" and "fact," saying and doing, in the Greek sense. In any case, Nietzsche recognized the world-disclosive effects of mimetic poetry in tragedy: He says that poetic images were not "symbolic" because they possessed a living capacity to create their own world (*BT* 8); here dramatic "fiction" was not a departure from reality because it staged powerful scenes of "a world with the same reality and irreducibility that Olympus and its inhabitants possessed for the believing Hellene" (*BT* 7).

If we keep reminding ourselves of the cultural status of poetry in the Greek world, then their attributions of *pseudos* to poetry (even in pre-philosophical periods) cannot be construed as simply critiques or even diminishments of poetic language – but rather, among other things, as a gesture to the "different" sphere of poetry together with its revelatory power. Poetry could not simply be an "entertaining diversion" for the Greeks (akin to our enjoying works of fantasy), because the religious dimension of poetry carried world-disclosive and life-guiding significance. Even the notion of "fictive truth," therefore, might not suffice for capturing the ambiguities surrounding the Greek sense of poetic *pseudos*.

One final historical note on the ambiguity of poetic falsehood: Certain texts tell of the commingling of *pseudos* and truth (*alētheia*) in poetic speech. In Hesiod's *Theogony*, the Muses (who inspire poetry) are said to be capable of both verisimilitude and straightforward truth:

We know how to say many false things (*pseudea*) that seem like true sayings (*legein etumoisin*); but we also know, when we want to, how to speak true things (*alēthea gēurusasthai*). (23–28)

And the *Odyssey* is marked by many alternations between deceptive and true accounts – sometimes mixed together, in the manner of verisimilitude and other senses (see 8.487ff., and 19.203, for example). As we have noted, the *polutropos*-character of Odysseus is a virtue in his precarious wanderings, and the mix of his false and true tellings can be considered contextually appropriate. What is more, as Charles Segal suggests, the many episodes of singing tales in the *Odyssey* show that the poem may be just as much about poetic speech per se – especially with respect to the wandering life of bards – as it is about a hero's homecoming.[7] A remarkable irony is that while wandering is connected with a need to deceive (14.122–127), the Greek word for wanderer is *alētēs*, which is a variant of *alētheia*.

Since Nietzsche was a classical philologist, he was surely aware of the many complex senses in which Greek texts depicted poetry, falsehood, and truth. My hope is that this excursion into Greek material can help us understand the evident ambiguities in Nietzsche's own deployment of falsehood-language in his celebration of art. What I want to explore next is an examination of Greek tragedy, and the tragic in general, in relation to morality, which will enhance our understanding of Nietzsche's charges against morality and also prepare a consideration of whether a tragic conception of *morality* could sustain an ethical sense while still following Nietzsche's critique of traditional morality.

TRAGEDY AND MORALITY

What follows is a continuation of the earlier treatment of tragic values in Greek poetry. My focus is Sophocles' play, *Oedipus the King*. The story of Oedipus can be summarized as follows: An oracle declares that Laius, King of Thebes, will be killed by his son, who will then marry his mother. Dreading such a prophecy, Laius orders that his young child Oedipus be taken from the city by a servant and left to die of exposure. Out of pity the servant instead gives the child to a shepherd, who takes him to his king in Corinth. Oedipus is raised by the king and queen, but upon manhood he hears the prophecy of his fate. Thinking the king and queen to be his real parents, he flees Corinth. On the road Oedipus runs into Laius and kills him in an angry quarrel. Oedipus arrives at Thebes and saves the city from a curse by solving the riddle of the Sphinx. In glory he marries the

---

[7] See Charles Segal, *Singers, Heroes, and Gods in the Odyssey* (Ithaca, NY: Cornell University Press, 1994), Chs. 7–8.

widowed queen Jocasta and rules Thebes as its king. Years later the city becomes victim to a plague, and an oracle declares the need to expiate the guilt of Laius' murder. When the truth is learned, Jocasta kills herself, and Oedipus gouges out his eyes and takes exile from Thebes in disgrace.

Oedipus is a model for the way in which tragic poetry continues, yet alters, the fatal limits of epic heroism. Oedipus' fate looms in the background but without divine personification, and his actions are not prompted by any divine intervention, because they stem from a fully individualized, free agency. Also, Oedipus differs from Achilles and Odysseus because the epic compensations of glory and home life in the face of mortality are now lost in a catastrophe of ruination and disgrace. With Oedipus, the epic values of heroic achievement and the household seem not to be in tension at first because of his successful reign at Thebes. Yet, for Oedipus, both spheres are permeated by a terrible *violation* of these values, a violation that has been ordained by fate and in fact *brought about* by Oedipus' attempt to resist his fate. Indeed, I want to argue that Oedipus' fate is actualized by his *moral* resistance to the awful prospect of patricide and incest, a resistance on behalf of the mix of values sketched above. If this is true, then the Oedipus story is a striking extension of the limit-conditions and ambiguities marking epic poetry: It is no longer simply the limits of epic values of heroism and home life in the midst of finitude; now there are unavoidable limits *in* these values, to the point of being complicit with their violation. With Oedipus, epic ambiguity and an alienating tension between heroism and the home is pushed to its very limit.

I want to highlight those elements of the play that bear most on the issue of morality. In *Oedipus the King* it must be said that no familiar moral notions can be satisfied in this story, not in the sense that there are no human values affirmed in the narrative, but that there can be no overarching moral reading of the text. Human values are shown to be intrinsically checked by what they want to hold off. It is not just that life is limited by death and loss; what is *worthy* in life cannot ultimately be traced to any preserve of its value, even in the older senses of divine immortality or human fame. If this is so, we must reject the idea that the play is any kind of morality tale, or even a warning against impiety. The prophecy that Oedipus will murder his father and marry his mother is surely not the kind of sacred message that would prompt reverence or even resignation. In the face of the oracle, what would "piety" mean for Oedipus' parents? Would it mean that Jocasta wait to knowingly marry her son after he kills his father? We have noted that resistance to the gods is not out of line in the overall economy of Greek religion. Since the prophecy predicts the most awful violation of basic human norms, the original resistance of the parents can be said to stem from moral horror; so too the flight of Oedipus from Corinth when he hears about the oracle there. And the herdsman who spares the child Oedipus from death, by giving him to a Corinthian, does so out of compassion (1178).[8] Yet these acts of *moral* resistance to the fate at hand are in fact what bring its horror to fruition. How could this fate have come about at all if the parents "accepted" it at the start, or if Oedipus accepted it at Corinth? One could say that if they were "pious" from the beginning, the prophecy would *not* have come to pass.

A similar complexity must also apply to Oedipus' character traits, which are often taken to be the cause of his downfall. Well, what are these traits? In almost every way, Oedipus is a model of Greek excellence: strong, brave, intelligent, and a responsible leader. We can find no dismissive criticism of these traits *as such* in the play. Oedipus' mental prowess is distinctive in his heroic posture, especially with his deliverance of Thebes from plague by solving the riddle of the Sphinx, who would devour anyone unable to solve the puzzle (who but a heroic type would want to engage the riddle under these circumstances?). Also worthy is his genuine concern for the welfare of Thebes as its king. At the beginning of the play Oedipus is described as famous and god-like. An elder tells him: "you saved all our lives . . . [you] are our master and greatest power; we are all in your care" (39–41). And none of the benefits of Oedipus' rule would have come to pass apart from his resistance to fate. This is why those moments in the text that speak against Oedipus' "hubris" must be considered carefully.

The choral speech that rebukes Oedipus (863ff.) extols reverence for fate (*moira*), its justice (*dikē*), and the authority of its oracles – this

---

[8] It should be noted again that the child was to die not from direct killing, but from exposure, which was a gesture to fortune as the actual cause of death.

against a man who would arrogantly speak or act contrary to sacred law. An important line (873) is disputed by scholars; it is often translated as "hubris begets a tyrant." Some prefer a corrected text that would read "hubris grows from tyranny." I side with the latter reading because the former lacks sense in the context of the play.[9] First of all, *tyrannos* in Greek does not automatically connote a negative appraisal, but simply kingly power not assigned by law or by inheritance (*basileus*). Moreover, as Oedipus says about his reign: "I never asked for it; it was given to me by the city" (383–384). In this case *tyrannos* was achieved by merit and cannot be the effect of hubris. Yet hubris, as an excess, can be seen as a *potential* effect of *tyrannos*, which lacks the kind of grounding in the other forms of kingship and may rely more on self-effort and its possible excesses.

Nevertheless, the choral complaint about hubris is hard to pin down. The problem cannot be traced simply to kingship, because it was awarded to Oedipus for saving the city. If it is simply Oedipus' traits in general, the city's salvation would then be stained. In the narrative context of this choral speech, hubris is more likely a matter of Oedipus and Jocasta doubting or resisting the oracle's authority. Yet again we face the strange prospect of what "piety" would call for here, because within the overall story the city received great blessings from Oedipus' flight from the prophecy. Moreover, at the moment of this speech in the play, the full details of Oedipus' situation have not yet been revealed. Later on, after everything has been filled out, the chorus speaks in a revised tone about a fatal ambiguity for all concerned (1186ff.). The "high-flying" hubris in the first speech is now the "high-aiming" success of Oedipus' deliverance of Thebes and his glorious rule. The fatal truth is now described as sad and pitiable, and simply a "reversed life." Finally, the chorus sees Oedipus' fate and downfall as not simply his own but indicative of the human condition as such: "O, the generation of mortals. Our lives add up to nothing." Human happiness is thus only apparent, and to Oedipus they say: "You are our model (*paradeigma*), your fate is ours" (1186–1194). This collective notion can also refer specifically to the

---

[9] See *Oedipus Tyrannus*, trans. Peter Meineck and Paul Woodruff (Indianapolis, IN: Hackett, 2000), pp. xxii–xxiv, and 64.

political setting wherein the success of Thebes under Oedipus was likewise caught up in his tragic limits.

I do not think that the text can support any kind of moral judgment of Oedipus. In the *Colonus* play (270ff., 960ff.) Oedipus twice defends himself as morally blameless, since the prophecy preceded his birth, and he actualized the offenses in ignorance of the true identities of Laius and Jocasta; even the unwitting killing of his father was defensive in nature because he was struck first (at a road-crossing involving a typical aristocratic jousting of the "After me! No, after me!" variety). Yet despite Oedipus' moral innocence, he nevertheless takes "responsibility" for his actions and their terrible consequences by accepting disgrace and exile, and by taking out his own eyes, a powerful gesture of shame and self-withdrawal. As he says of this ambiguity: "Apollo! It was Apollo who brought about my miserable sufferings. But it was my own hand that did this [the gouging]" (1329–1332). In this way the early Greek confluence of fate and freedom is pushed to a remarkable limit, with Oedipus taking responsibility and punishment for a terrible offense that both was and was not his own doing. His self-inflicted punishment should actually be seen as a re-affirmation of the moral values that brought about the catastrophe. After all, a more "pious" response could have been: "What I have done was meant to be. My rule came with a terrible price, but let's move on. All praise to the gods!"

Finally, the most notable of Oedipus' traits that brought his transgression to light was his passionate desire for the truth. Even when it is becoming evident that his inquiry will implicate himself, he says to Jocasta: "You will never persuade me not to learn the truth . . . I have to know who I am . . . That is my nature, and I could never be someone else so as not to learn what I was born to be" (1065ff.).

To sum up the masterful tragic structure of Sophocles' play: Oedipus' fate was to enact a horrible transgression of human values. Various actions counter to this fate were morally motivated, yet they wound up bringing this fate to completion. Likewise, Oedipus' estimable qualities and achievements were caught up in this paradox. So we can say that the tragic outcome was caused by normally worthy characteristics: compassion, standing up for family values, heroic rescue, responsible leadership, and a passion for truth.

Moreover, the great achievements and their vital benefit to Thebes would not have come about without this resistance to fate, without this self-contaminating path of life. Such an incredible mix of blessings and curses, with no resolution of its tensions, surely leaves us in breathless suspension, or as the chorus says, "without a foothold" (878). Is it any wonder that the tragic character of Greek poetry incited criticism from later Greek writers? But perhaps we should ask: Isn't it a wonder that epic and tragic poetry were so popular and authoritative in the Greek world? A discussion of Plato's critique of tragic poetry can help crystallize the issues at hand.

PLATO AND GREEK POETRY

To Plato's credit, he fully recognized the tragic sense of life in Greek poetry, and he responded to it authentically by taking to heart its dark themes, moral ambiguities, and what it would mean to call the tragic the last word on life. He wanted to advance a different world-view and set of values that could bring more hope and order to the human condition. The critique of poetry in the *Republic* had nothing to do with "aesthetics" or a censorship of "the arts." Greek poetry was not an "art form" but a world-disclosive source of meaning, and in Plato's day epic and tragic poetry were still primary vehicles for cultural bearings and education. Socrates calls Homer the primary educator of Greece; his poetry has been ordering "our entire lives" (*panta ton autou bion*: 606eff.). Plato's critique had to do with truth, the transmission of cultural values, and pedagogical authority. He was waging a momentous *diaphora*, or contest (607b), against established meanings on behalf of new standards of truth and morality.

Plato's critique of traditional poetry was fundamental because it challenged both the tragic content of the stories and their form, the latter involving the psychic forces at work in poetry's composition, performance, and reception – each of which exceeded conscious control and blocked critical reflection. All together, traditional poetry represented a powerful, ingrained cultural barrier that Plato wanted to overcome in order to clear the ground for two new ideals: rational inquiry and an overarching justice governing the world and the soul (602d–604a; 605a–c).

Epic and tragic poetry presented a world that is unstable, unpredictable, mysterious, and fatally ruinous of human possibilities. Here mortality is the baseline limit of life, and death is portrayed as repulsive in its darkness (*Republic* 386–392). The poets tell "false stories," where heroes come to grief and surrender to powerful emotions, where the gods act immorally, fight each other, cause evil and ruin, punish the innocent, change form, disguise themselves, and lie (377ff.). As I suggested in Chapter 1, although the *Republic* displays a wealth of meanings, I think that the dialogue is essentially an anti-tragic narrative; and we note that in the *Laws* (817b) philosophers are said to be "counter-artists" (*antitechnoi*) to the tragic poets, and thus their "rivals" (*antagōnistai*).

The full course of the dialogue can be called a narrative about the possibility and desirability of a just life in a world that resists justice. The virtue of justice is defended by Socrates against principles of power and self-interest (Books 1–2). The long digression about the *polis* is meant to clarify the picture of a just soul and its advantages, and the digression unfolds to meet the daunting task posed to Socrates in Book 2: Prove not only that the just man is worthy but *happier* than the unjust man, that he will flourish in some way – and this in terms of the toughest case imaginable, pitting the unjust man thought by everyone to be just against the just man thought by everyone to be unjust (361). This task is reiterated as the purpose of the entire conversation in Book 10 (612). And the rectification myth of Er (616–618) performs the climax of Socrates' project. Immortality serves an essential function in overcoming the limits on rationality and justice in earthly life. That the poets and their tragic stories figure prominently at both ends of the dialogue, therefore, cannot be an accident. Traditional myths were fully expressive of the obstacles blocking the path of Socrates' mission. Plato wants to tell a *better* story than the poets, one that can overcome the possible tragedy of a just life. And one cannot help but remember the fate of Socrates, whose death at the hands of Athens *would* be tragic without the kind of rectification suggested in the *Republic*.[10]

---

[10] For an excellent discussion of tragic values and Plato's critique, see Martha C. Nussbaum, *The Fragility of Goodness* (Cambridge: Cambridge University Press, 1986).

The formal element in Plato's critique concerns the psychological structure of poetic production, performance, and reception. The traditional view was that poets were inspired receptacles for the sacred power of the Muses, a "revelation" more than a "creation."[11] This matter of absorption in a force beyond the conscious mind was also implicated in the objections to *mimēsis* in the *Republic*. As noted earlier, *mimēsis* referred not only to representational likeness but also to psychological identification in poetic performance and audience reception, where actors, reciters, and listeners were "taken over" by the poetic imagery and its emotional power.[12] What really mattered to Plato in the *Republic* was not mimetic representation, because the example of painting is described as merely an *analogy* for the genuine matter of concern, mimetic identification with poetic language (603c). And Socrates confesses (605cff.) that even the "best of us" can become enchanted by poetry and swept away by the *pleasure* of empathic union with the sufferings of tragic characters – an effect that ruins the "manly" ideal of silencing and mastering grief (605e). In Books 2 and 3, the censoring of poetry was qualified and seemed restricted to the context of educating children. But later, poetry's power threatens the reflective mental control of sophisticated adults as well, and for this reason *all* mimetic poetry (epic and tragic) is to be banned from the ideal *polis* (595a). What is "false" (*pseudos*) in traditional poetry is not a matter of epistemology, but its effect on souls and how they come to view life. As Socrates puts it, poetry creates falsehood *in* the soul, which is not simply false "words" (*logoi*) or beliefs, but a morally "false life" (382b–c).

Equally important in Plato's critique is the content of tragic poetry, which expresses a way of life and a world-view that are morally problematic.[13] The gods can be responsible for evil outcomes (379a–c, 391d); the repulsive character of Hades (Socrates cites relevant

---

[11] See the Prologue to Hesiod's *Theogony* 98–108.

[12] See Stephen Halliwell, *The Aesthetics of Mimesis* (Princeton: Princeton University Press, 2002), pp. 1–33, and Raymond A. Prier, *Thauma Idesthai* (Gainesville, FL: Florida State University Press, 1989), pp. 169–179. References to *mimēsis* in acting and spoken performance can be found in *Ion* 533ff., and *Sophist* 267. In the *Ion* (533ff.), the power (*dunamis*) of poetry is depicted as a chain of magnetic rings, which transmit a compelling force of attraction from the Muses to poets to rhapsodes to audiences.

[13] See Stephen Halliwell, "Plato's Repudiation of the Tragic," in *Tragedy and the Tragic*, ed. M. S. Silk (Oxford: Oxford University Press, 1996), pp. 332–349.

passages we have treated previously) could dissuade people from noble actions that risk death (386aff.); the death of loved ones is taken as a profound loss that prompts strong lamentation and grief (387dff.); and justice and happiness are often decoupled, so that the unjust prosper and the just come to ruin (392b). This critique comes in the discussion of educating the city's guardians, who in some respects possess characteristics of Homeric heroes. Perhaps times had changed, but surely Homeric heroes had not been dissuaded from noble deeds by the repulsion of death. The darkness of death and the passionate grief over loss did not bring on pessimism, despair, or flinching from risky deeds; rather, mortality tended to magnify the value of life's attractions and define the value of noble action.

In any case, Plato seems to want death and Hades transformed from a repulsive to an attractive prospect for a disembodied soul delivered from earthly limits. The moral context of this proposal is clear in both the *Phaedo* and the *Republic*, in that a belief in an immortal existence tied to one's moral character in life will stand against both the fear of death and the license to indulge any and all carnal desires. In the *Phaedo* Socrates concedes that "most people" believe that the soul is scattered and destroyed when departing from the body at death (80d). Yet he aims for an alternative view that specifically rejects the old picture of Hades. After death, the soul will depart to a place that is "noble, pure, and invisible," which is the "true Hades" (*Adiou hōs alēthōs*), the abode of the "good and wise god" (*ton agathon kai phronemon, theon*) (80d). So little is death now repulsive that the invisible purity of Hades has been the aim of philosophical knowledge all along, and that philosophy has been in fact "the practice of death" (*meletē thanatou*) (80e–81a).

In a similar fashion the myth of Er at the end of the *Republic* offers an alternative to tragic limits with a script of rectification for departed souls that rewards and punishes them based on their past deeds and their own responsibility for having *chosen* the course of their lives. Socrates specifically contrasts this myth with the tale "told to Alkinous," which is a reference to the stories recounted in Books 9–11 of the *Odyssey*, the last of which described Odysseus' journey to Hades. Socrates' tale is told by Er, who is described as a "brave (*alkinou*) man" (614b).

In Homer, Hades was morally neutral, because the human *psuchē* is neither punished nor rewarded for its deeds (only demigods are subject to punishments). With Plato, the after-life is morally informed for human souls, wherein the consequences of injustice and a lack of philosophical wisdom when choosing what life to lead block the soul's happiness.[14] Such a script provides an answer to the task posed to Socrates in Book 2: A life of justice, even if ruined in earthly life, will reap benefits after death (614c–619e). And the reincarnation scheme described in Er's tale has souls choosing the types of lives they will pursue next, and this choice is clearly a break with older conceptions of mixed responsibility in the midst of divine management and fate: "the responsibility is with he who chooses; god is not responsible" (617e).

It cannot be said that Plato's moral reform is equivalent to Nietzsche's account of slave morality in its historical setting. The moral problem for Plato is not the vulnerability of the weak in the face of aristocratic power (Plato was no egalitarian); the problem is the vulnerability of any type of life to tragic limits on its aspirations, with special emphasis on the life of a philosophical hero like Socrates. Yet there are some elements in the Er myth that are similar to Christian rectification when it comes to the shared problem of *moral* tragedy, the possibility that virtue not only can be ruined in life, but perhaps bring on its own ruin (if the crucifixion or hemlock were the last word). Platonic rectification shares with Christianity a certain triumphalist picture: the ultimate victory of the good over its Other. In the Er story unjust souls are beset by "savage men" who bind them, flay them, and lacerate them on thorn bushes before thrusting them into dark Tartarus (615eff.). And in the *Gorgias* (525c), the incurably wicked suffer from their assigned pains for all eternity (*ton aei chronon*).

Of all the revisions of early poetic tropes in the Er myth, the most notable, I think, concerns the soul of Odysseus, the last one to choose a next life in the story. Odysseus is described as deliberately repudiating a heroic existence: since his soul's "memory of its former suffering had relieved it of its love of honor (*philotimias*)," it *gladly*

[14] See Alan E. Bernstein, *The Formation of Hell* (Ithaca, NY: Cornell University Press, 1993), Chs. 1–2.

chose "the life of a quiet, private man who kept to himself away from public struggles" (*bion andros idiōtou apragmonos*) (620c). Was Odysseus spotlighted for revision in this manner because of the troubling fact that in Homer he deliberately chose to reject immortality in favor of a mortal, heroic life? In Socrates' account, Odysseus takes an opposite course that in a way can be paraphrased as a reversal of Achilles' outlook: "I'd rather lead a quiet, ordinary life than be king of Ithaca." And this new Odysseus can stand as a dramatic paradigm of Plato's attempt to reform his poetic tradition.

If the tragic sense of values in Greek poetry is disturbing, it cannot be because certain esteemed moral norms are rejected or doomed to meaninglessness; if that were the case it would be relatively easy to dismiss tragedy as nihilistic or inattentive to important human values. What may actually be disturbing, then, is that Greek poetry does affirm the importance of certain values while simultaneously acknowledging their intrinsic limits – in terms of either irresolvable conflicts between differing values or irredeemable limits on human happiness in a finite world marked by negative forces of fate. In other words, the message behind tragic values is this: Whatever is good in life cannot ultimately be preserved, guaranteed, or immunized from otherness, cannot be tracked all the way down in the nature of things. I think that Nietzsche's philosophy is following this tragic sense of life in many ways – not only the "negative" sense of intrinsic limits, but also the "affirmative" sense that such limits actually figure in the very *meaning* of life-values. It is from this vantage point of tragic "crossing" effects that Nietzsche launches his critique of *binary* valuation in oppositional schemes of good and evil.

We can gain some headway by comparing moral tragedy with a familiar question in Western thought: the "problem of evil." This problem is most notably drawn from the Christian theological tradition: Why would a perfect and good God create a world marked by imperfection and forces of evil? Yet the problem need not be confined to this framework, for the following reason: The problem itself is *created* by an original binary conception of opposite conditions, which from a Nietzschean standpoint is a counter-natural construction that can show itself in any orientation, especially the ascetic truth-ideal. So the significance of the problem of evil touches a wide range of cultural and historical examples.[15] With respect to a moral binary, the problem of evil is not that there is evil in the world, that there are forces antithetical to the good; the problem concerns *why* such forces would exist in a world presumably measured by the *absence* of evil in a binary conception of goodness. The Christian model of a perfect creator concentrates the problem in a stark manner. To be precise, the problem of evil is different from the problem of good people suffering misfortune, which in Christianity is answered by the promise of salvation and rectification. The problem of evil concerns why there is this realm of suffering in the first place, and how it is that terrible conditions in life can be squared with God's perfect attributes.

To its credit, the Christian intellectual tradition met the problem head on and tried to find ways to resolve it. Such were the various attempts to answer the problem of evil that sometimes went by the name of "theodicy," or justifying God's creation of an imperfect world. The contours of the problem can easily be seen to stem from several binary assumptions about the divine: that God is a perfect being, with no limits or deficiencies; thus God has no limits to knowledge, power, or goodness (and so is characterized as omniscient, omnipotent, and omni-benevolent). God *could* have created a perfect world or even a better world (otherwise omnipotence is undermined); God knew in advance every aspect of how the world would turn out (otherwise no omniscience); and God cannot be directly implicated with evil (otherwise no omni-benevolence). Yet there *is* evil in the world (at times to extreme degrees), whether these forces are categorized as *natural* evil (things such as earthquakes that are independent of human choice) or *moral* evil (things such as murder that are caused by human choice). The question is: Why would God create or permit such things?

Of all the questions facing Christian theology, the problem of evil is likely the most difficult to answer, in part because it turns on *internal* conflicts within the full collection of attributes God is said to

[15] See Susan Neiman, *Evil in Modern Thought: An Alternative History of Philosophy* (Princeton: Princeton University Press, 2002). Neiman argues that the problem of evil was at the core of modern philosophy, not simply from a theological standpoint, but in secular, moral, and epistemological concerns about the ability of reason to provide intelligibility in the face of limit-conditions.

possess. And tough cases bring out the problems well: God knew that the Holocaust would happen and could have prevented or curtailed it, but did not do so. Why not? I will leave aside the various attempts to resolve the problem of evil in the Christian tradition, because my purpose is simply to mark it against a tragic conception of life. Compared with the Christian problem of evil, a tragic conception of life – though hard to bear – may exhibit less intellectual vexation, and perhaps even less of a psychological burden than an honest and full engagement with the problem of evil would involve. In Greek tragedy, there *is* no problem of evil, because a binary model of the good is not the operating measure. In early Greek religion, the gods were not marked by "perfection" and they were frequently implicated in undeserved human suffering. How can a tragic outlook be less of a burden compared to Christianity? The impact of suffering can be *magnified* in the face of perfect goodness: there is grief enough in the death of an infant child, but there can be further disturbance in asking why a good God would allow such a thing. There is always the last resort of "God works in mysterious ways," which really amounts to recognizing that the question has no answer. In Greek religion the question would not arise, because the mix of competing deities and fatality amounts to recognizing that human interests are *not* the baseline measure of life, that limits to happiness are in the order of things. For the early Greeks, bad things happening to good people was *not* a mystery, but simply a fact of life.

ETERNAL RECURRENCE AND MORAL TRAGEDY[16]

I think that Nietzsche's inheritance of the Greek tragic tradition follows similar lines in relation to the problem of evil. Nietzsche does not dismiss moral values but rather the standard of *perfection* that creates the problem of evil in the first place, and that can be decoded as a counter-natural path to nihilism, to the nullification of life-values. In this regard I want to pose a question that will lead us to the coming discussion of Nietzsche's relevance for moral and political philosophy: Is it possible that Nietzsche's attack upon traditional measures of the

---

[16] Some of what follows is drawn from *Nietzsche's Life Sentence*, pp. 137ff.

good is actually a defense of a truly "worldly" conception of ethics, that traditional measures are actually a nullification of ethics, a moral nihilism?

To prepare this discussion, it would be useful to consider how Nietzsche's concept of eternal recurrence intensifies a tragic alternative to the problem of evil. Greek tragedy was in place "before good and evil," before binary models came to dominate Western thought. Nietzsche's call to move "beyond good and evil" could be read as a tragic alternative *after* the dominance of a good–evil scheme. Given its *dominance*, a challenge to its precepts must be severe, and eternal recurrence can be viewed in this light, as a dramatic challenge to binary moralism: If the endless repetition of identical conditions of life provides no final consummation of the good over its Other, not even the relief of nothingness, then tragic limits on the good are not only indigenous to life in a general sense but also endlessly repeated in their specific forms.

The challenge of eternal recurrence to morality is fundamental in the following sense: It would seem that the moral point of view in different ways is animated by the belief or hope that what is deemed immoral can be eliminated, overcome, modified, transformed, replaced, or punished. The identical repetition of immoral conditions or acts would seem to render any such moral response ultimately impossible or futile. Western philosophy and religion have issued various projects meant to counter a tragic sense of finitude that dictates intrinsic limits to moral rectification. Yet eternal recurrence apparently adds insult to injury by extending the tragic beyond moral limitation to the affirmation of the exact repetition of all transgressions – from the banal to the monstrous – thus mandating no relief from the material presence of specific offenses.

The charge of moral repugnance is to my mind the most authentic critical response to eternal recurrence, and the one most entitled to repudiate Nietzsche because it squarely engages the core existential significance of cyclic repetition.[17] Moreover, the force of moral

---

[17] Bernd Magnus, in "Self-Consuming Concepts," *International Studies in Philosophy* 21/2 (1989), 63–71, offers a telling and elegant reaction. He claims that eternal recurrence entails affirming each moment unconditionally for its own sake, and that only an *Übermensch* or a god could will such a thing. We should be honest and admit that we cannot help but live

repugnance is inevitable for *any* authentic encounter with eternal recurrence because here we identify its genuine "ethical" significance: not that recurrence can serve as a measure for moral action, but that it crystallizes the existential problem of meaning and value. Repetition dictates that everything I value must include everything that limits, opposes, or negates my values; and this surely can cause me to recoil at the prospect of eternally certifying everything that for me diminishes life. Zarathustra's nausea over the return of the small man is precisely this kind of moral repugnance. It seems to me that finding eternal recurrence morally repellent need not be a sign of life-denial in the manner of overt projects of transcendence, perfection, or annihilation prosecuted by Nietzsche. If moral repugnance were the same as life-denial, there would be nothing to distinguish Zarathustra's resistance from slavish resentment.[18] Can I not affirm life in some kind of Nietzschean way without willing a return of the Holocaust? Would such an omission necessarily indicate a fugitive disposition? Can I not accept and even affirm the existence of an evil without my nose being rubbed in it by endless repetition? Is there any way in which Nietzsche can respond to this critical problem?

I think there is such a way, and it stems from the agonistic structure of will to power and Nietzsche's special sense of life-affirmation. We know that life-affirmation, as distinct from life-enhancement, celebrates the necessity of opposing conditions because of their constitutive and productive role in any meaning-formation. Accordingly, anything of value, absent countervailing forces, would not *be* (or become) a value. Eternal recurrence amounts to an intensive magnification of the agonistic structure of values and it represents, for Nietzsche, the only true "preservation" of worldly value when measured against all other possible models that in one way or another turn away from radical agonistics and thus obviate the very nature of

---

edited lives, cannot help but imagine a life better than what is or has been the case. Who would not will recurrence *minus* extermination camps?

[18] Richard A. Smith suggests that there may be no such distinction, that Nietzsche himself may be guilty of resentment in his attacks upon slave morality: "Nietzsche: Philosopher of *Ressentiment?*," *International Studies in Philosophy* 25/2 (1993), 135–143. See Jonathon Cohen's critical response to Smith in the same volume (145–149).

values as such – thereby positing meaninglessness under the guise of positive constructs.

How can a belief in eternal recurrence respond to the question of moral repugnance? An answer is implied in Zarathustra's own passage *through* such repulsion as a necessary stage in the path of life-affirmation, which for Nietzsche must be understood in agonistic terms. If Zarathustra affirms the recurrence of the small man, this does not mean that he now abandons his opposition to mediocrity and life-denial. The affirmation of a value remains a form of will to power, which must include resistance and opposition; thus any value *requires* countervalues to become what it is – an overcoming. The crucial point is that affirmation does not mean *approving* of everything, but rather affirming the necessity of otherness for the emergence of one's values, which means that affirmation retains *opposition* to countervalues, retains the space of one's Yes and No. Confirmation of this idea can be found in Zarathustra's objection to indiscriminate approval, which he calls *Allgenügsamkeit,* or "omnisatisfaction" (*Z* III, 11, 2). Eternal recurrence, therefore, cannot entail the approval of everything that returns. If I will the return of something I find heinous, I also will the return of my opposition to it. *Amor fati* cannot mean the indiscriminate love of all things but rather the love of the agonistic necessity that intertwines everything I value with otherness (recall how Greek fate included resistance). This does not necessarily dilute or neutralize the moral repulsion that eternal recurrence can generate, but at least there is a way to disarm a charge such as Magnus' that recurrence calls on us to love the extermination camps unconditionally.[19]

Nietzsche's philosophy is all about moral evaluations, in that will to power implies judgments and preferences for living one way over and against other ways. Although perspectivism disallows one's own morality being binding on all, Nietzsche insists that inferring from a plurality of values that no morality is binding or worthy of commitment would be childish (*GS* 345). In the midst of different moral possibilities, what matters is "a brave and rigorous attempt (*Versuche*) to *live* in this or that morality" (*D* 195). Living in such a way requires

[19] Magnus, "Self-Consuming Concepts," 69.

that one contend with other perspectives, that one believe one's own perspective to be the *better* option. This is why something like equanimity would be inappropriate, indeed ruinous, for Nietzsche's agonistic perspectivism, and why eternal recurrence must include one's stance against other perspectives. Notice how an agonistic ethics would differ from both absolutism and relativism, which ironically have something in common: absolutism identifies *one* uncontestable truth, while relativism simply postulates *many* uncontestable truths (each being equally valid for those who hold them and thus immune from external judgment).

Nietzsche believes in the necessity of having "enemies," which distinguishes his unique form of affirmation from traditional projects of the good that aim for the elimination of otherness. Consider this fascinating passage on the "spiritualization of hostility (*Feindschaft*)," which is discussed in both external and internal terms:

> Another triumph is our spiritualization of *hostility*. It consists in the profound appreciation of having enemies: in short it means acting and thinking in the opposite way from that which has become the rule. The church always wanted the destruction of its enemies; we, we immoralists and Antichristians, find our advantage in this, that the church exists. In the political realm too, hostility has become more spiritual . . . Almost every party understands how it is in the interest of its self-preservation that the opposition should not lose all strength . . . Our attitude toward the "internal enemy" is no different: here too we have spiritualized hostility; here too we have come to appreciate its value. The price of fruitfulness is to be rich in internal opposition; one remains young only as long as the soul does not stretch itself and desire peace. (*TI* 5, 3)

The central implication of eternal recurrence is that nothing can be ruled out or wished away when it comes to understanding the significance of any and all human outlooks. Nietzsche specifically connects affirmation with saying Yes even to the presence of priestly decadence (*TI* 5, 5–6). Contrary to exclusionary binaries or alternative worlds, recurrence mandates that *everything is in play*. The *field* of play is the given background of becoming, within which all possibilities of form unfold. None of these possibilities by themselves can be definitive of "reality," to which only the whole field of play can lay claim. Eternal recurrence amounts to the *tangible* presentation of this reality-field – neither an abstract generality of "all forms" nor an (equally abstract) amorphous flux, but the concrete fluid totality of all specific conditions and counter-conditions. The "ethics" of eternal recurrence, therefore, concerns its maximal concentration on the agonistic structure of values. The question we face is whether this orientation can provide a viable moral philosophy.

CHAPTER 7

The Genealogy *and moral philosophy*

Against the background of the previous chapter, I want to explore
further the possibilities of an ethical sense in Nietzsche's philosophy.
To prepare this discussion it would be useful to provide a brief sketch
of familiar models in moral philosophy and to situate Nietzsche in
relation to these traditions.

MODERN MORAL PHILOSOPHY[1]

The modern Scientific Revolution transformed the way nature is
understood. With priority given to objectification, mathematization,
and mechanization, then notions of meaning, value, and purpose
were stripped from the environing world in deference to nature conceived as a set of causal forces and verifiable facts. Whatever space
could be found for moral values or notions of right and wrong would
have to be located in the human subject and not in any objective condition, that is, not in the natural world itself. Usually the turn to the
subject aimed to retain elements of rationality, but in the subject's
practical reason rather than the scientific execution of theoretical
reason.

Modern moral theories in different ways reflected the general intellectual developments in modern thought. The model of a free rational individual took shape in ethics as the promotion of free inquiry
and individual autonomy in determining what is right and wrong,
as opposed to defining norms according to unexamined dictates of

---

[1] Some of what follows is drawn from my *Ethics and Finitude: Heideggerian Contributions to
Moral Philosophy* (Lanham, MD: Rowman & Littlefield, 2000), pp. 51–54.

religion, custom, habit, or various traditional authorities.[2] Modern moral theory turned to the reflective subject as the self-grounding basis of moral inquiry and decision methods.

The modern bifurcation of subject and object, value and fact, prompted various problems for moral philosophy and generated different moral theories to respond to these problems and to secure moral constructs consistent with the contours of modern thought. A significant problem that has endured since the modern period is moral skepticism. Since the subject–object split prompted skepticism even about the possibility of knowledge in general, it was easy for some to claim skepticism about any form of moral knowledge. Since values vary and are not susceptible to objective verification and conformity, it was short work to deny knowledge and truth conditions in the realm of ethics. Although most modern moral theories shared the view that ethical notions cannot measure up to standards of scientific objectivity, several approaches tried to surmount skepticism and articulate reliable principles that could answer decisively the philosophical question of what makes an action right or wrong. In other words, several theories aimed to provide foundational guidance for ethical questions but, in keeping with the modern profile, any such foundation would be subject-based.

Ethical egoism holds that what is right and wrong is based on individual self-interest. The right thing to do is whatever individuals conceive to be in their own self-interest, as opposed to being compelled to act in the interest of others or by way of externally imposed moral constraints. Ethical egoism usually is derived from psychological egoism, which is a theory of human nature arguing that we cannot help but act in our own self-interest: Human beings are atomic, individual organisms that by necessity perceive and interpret everything through the lens of self-interest, of what is beneficial or harmful to each organism. Based on this supposed fact of human nature, ethical egoism argues for a moral theory that is consistent with this fact, and that can prompt honesty in ethical dealings, rather than various poses of altruism that other moral schemes ask us to adopt. Ethical egoism need not be wanton hedonism or narcissism; an egoist can

---

[2] See J. P. Schneewind, *The Invention of Autonomy: A History of Modern Moral Philosophy* (Cambridge: Cambridge University Press, 1998).

delay gratification, help others, and avoid harming others out of a rational analysis of long-term self-interest.

Utilitarianism goes beyond egoism by constructing a socially based normative framework. Utilitarianism is often called consequentialism, in that the right thing to do is what produces the best consequences for the greatest number of people. Utilitarianism is similar to egoism in assuming that human beings are individual subjects moved by self-interest and preferences regarding what brings pleasure and pain, benefit and harm. In its classic form designed by Jeremy Bentham, the good for human beings is happiness, or the utility of what maximizes pleasure and minimizes pain. Yet utilitarianism exceeds egoism by defining moral right as happiness for the greatest number. In considering an action or policy, a utilitarian must weigh the utility for all persons concerned and do what produces more happiness in aggregate than other alternatives. The theory operates by way of quantifying units of utility, and then performing a disinterested calculation of the aggregate that will provide the measure of right and wrong actions. In this way, utilitarianism aims to provide a kind of moral science that offers a precise technique for ethical adjudication. The strengths of the theory include its accommodation of both self-interest and social constraints, its flexibility in adjusting to varying conditions, and its decisiveness in complex cases. In utilitarianism, what is right or wrong is not predetermined or constructed independently of actual outcomes for actual communities.

One of the great legacies of modern thought is the moral philosophy of Immanuel Kant.[3] Kant's ethics is called nonconsequentialist because it critiques both the egoist and the utilitarian emphasis on consequences and happiness, whether in an individual or a collective sense. What brings pleasure and pain, happiness and unhappiness, varies between and within individuals or groups. Moreover, consequences are uncertain in outcome. Basing ethics in happiness and consequences, therefore, produces an unstable, malleable directive that can permit heinous acts or counterintuitive justifications. Not only can egoism permit injurious acts, utilitarianism can permit injury to, or exploitation of, individuals if the calculus produces

[3] See *Critique of Practical Reason*, trans. Lewis White Beck (Indianapolis, IN: Bobbs-Merrill, 1956).

enough utility for the well-being of the community. For Kant, morality should be deontological, or duty-based, independent of good or
bad consequences or the interests of individuals or groups. Just as in
the military, where doing one's duty is independent of, and usually
contrary to, one's normal inclinations, Kant thinks that ethics requires
a principle that can define what is right in a way that commands the
will's compliance, regardless of gains or losses in life.

Kant thinks that the abstract universality characteristic of reason
can supply such a principle and a kind of necessity that can command
the will to act out of duty rather than inclination. Egoism and utilitarianism define what is right on the basis of what individuals or groups
value as good or desirable. Kant turns the tables and insists on the
priority of an abstract principle of right over the good, because of the
variability and inconstancy of conceptions of the good. Kant shapes
a principle of right in the categorical imperative, which dictates that
one act in such a way that one could consistently will one's rule for
action as a universal law. In other words, one should only do what
could universally bind all rational agents. The categorical imperative
is a thought experiment conducted by the rational subject independent of circumstances or particular features of life, and its measure is
rational consistency or inconsistency rather than outcomes or preferences. For instance, false promising is morally wrong not because
it harms our interests but because it cannot be universalized. If every
promise were false, false promising would deconstruct, because no
promise would be believed and yet the aim of a liar is to be believed.

The most influential version of Kant's categorical imperative is the
principle of respect for persons, which can directly intercept possible
injustices in egoism or utilitarianism by dictating that one should
never treat persons solely as a means to one's own ends, but should
allow them the freedom of being ends in themselves. Exploiting persons for one's own purposes violates the baseline freedom of persons
as rational agents, as end-seeking, self-directing beings.

In terms of what actions are right and wrong, Kant's ethics turns out
to be not much different from moral precepts found in the Western
tradition, particularly the Judeo-Christian moral tradition. Kant (and
many other modern moral theorists) did not reject moral tradition
so much as aim to give it a rational grounding and reconstruction. In
this way, the individual subject could truly "own" its moral compass

by discovering its own self-grounded rationale for moral action. For Kant, freedom is not license but *self*-legislation by way of reason. The universality of rational constructs provides a constraint on the will, but as self-generated in the process of rational construction it is autonomous rather than "heteronomous," or directed from external forces or prompted by natural impulses. For Kant, genuine moral worth requires such an autonomous, self-imposed rational ground. For example, helping someone out of sympathy, though laudable, has no moral worth because sympathy is a contingent emotion that, if absent, could not constrain the will or provide a universal ground for right action.

The preceding represents only the barest sketch of some typical modern moral theories, and we can summarize three basic characteristics that mark the philosophical paths outlined above. Modern moral theories are: (1) *foundational*, in claiming to find a unified explanation for what is moral and immoral, and a grounding principle for determining whether an action is right or wrong; (2) *action-guiding*, in that moral philosophy is confined mostly to rules and principles for judging right and wrong actions, rather than broader conceptions such as the nature and quality of persons, forms of life, or comprisals of meaning; and (3) *subject-based*, in that moral analysis is centered in the rational human subject, its faculties, procedures, and decisions.

NIETZSCHE AND MODERN MORAL THEORIES

There are a number of ways in which Nietzsche's approach to morality challenges the modern theories we have sketched. I will not pursue a full discussion of these challenges, but rather focus on a few central topics with each theory, especially with respect to Nietzsche's analysis in the *Genealogy*.[4] Readers should be able to get a provisional sense

---

[4] There are relevant studies that connect Nietzsche with contemporary challenges to moral theory and its rational foundations. Of particular importance is Bernard Williams, *Ethics and the Limits of Philosophy* (Cambridge, MA: Harvard University Press, 1985). See Maudemarie Clark, "On the Rejection of Morality: Williams' Debt to Nietzsche," in Schacht, ed., *Nietzsche's Postmoralism*, pp. 100–122. See also Brian Leiter, "Nietzsche and the Morality Critics," in Richardson and Leiter, eds., *Nietzsche*, pp. 221–254. Those who are analytically inclined will likely appreciate Leiter's book, *Nietzsche on Morality* (New York: Routledge, 2002), which has a separate chapter on the *Genealogy*. This is a careful study with many

of how Nietzsche's philosophy critically engages familiar models of moral philosophy – as distinct from the "historical" emphasis in his genealogical treatment – which can help in assessing the merits of his philosophical project. The topics I will cover concern how modern moral theories exemplify several problems targeted in the *Genealogy*: a universalist refusal of moral diversity and the notion of rank; an uncritical inheritance of slave morality; a reductive rationalism and subjectivism; a counter-natural bad conscience; and an alliance with the ascetic truth-ideal.

One general Nietzschean criticism of modern moral theories – particularly the utilitarian and Kantian models – would stem from their own admission (implicitly or explicitly) that their theories are not reinventing the ethical wheel, but rather offering a rational *reconstruction* of familiar values, so as to sidestep mere custom and religious allegiance and provide a reflective model that can strengthen and secure these values with a universal rational consensus. Utilitarianism provided a reconstruction of familiar notions of happiness and the balancing of different goods. Kant offered a reconstruction of familiar notions of freedom, responsibility, and unconditional value. As the *Genealogy* makes clear, Nietzsche does not rule out such values, but he does dispute the uncritical stipulation that these values exhaust the sphere of morality. Therefore Nietzsche questions the exclusive status of both traditional values and their rational reconstruction. Of moral philosophers he says:

They wanted to supply a *rational foundation* for morality . . . Morality itself, however, was accepted as "given." . . . What was lacking was any suspicion that there was something problematic here. What the philosophers . . . tried to supply was, seen in the right light, merely a scholarly form of the common *faith* in the prevalent morality, a new means of *expression* for this faith. (*BGE* 186)

insights, especially his challenge to non-elitist and non-fatalistic readings of Nietzsche. Yet the analytic framework is a significant distortion of Nietzsche's texts in many ways. Leiter also assumes that Nietzsche's naturalism is of the scientific kind, which is questionable, despite the useful distinction between "methodological" and "substantive" naturalism. Leiter claims that the issue of creativity is not a part of Nietzsche's naturalistic account of values (p. 11). Yet this is precisely why Nietzsche's naturalism is more expansive than scientific naturalism, because creativity is also an essential force in nature, in how values emerge in the first place, a dynamic that is not susceptible to rational explanation.

Compared with utilitarian and Kantian morality, one thinks that Nietzsche would find favor with moral egoism, especially given its proposed liberation of individual selves from larger constraints. Moreover, both of the other theories would perceive a reduction to individual self-interest as threatening the very basis of morality. Seen in this light, there are indeed elements of egoism that could appeal to Nietzsche, and he has sometimes been read as a moral egoist. Nevertheless, we must exercise caution (as usual) in aligning Nietzsche with typical moral theories, including egoism.

The theory of moral egoism has usually been cast as a universal model for all selves, in order to avoid the unacceptable notion that the self-interest of one self could trump the interest of another self (which would be more like a moral solipsism). In addition, the theory has generally been framed in terms of *rational* self-interest, to avoid an overly wide definition of self-interest that could haunt the theory. What could recommend moral egoism if it could sanction a sincere wanton hedonism or the machinations of a power advocate? The suggestion is that one's *long-term* interests would not be served by such behaviors (which seems right whenever we regret a behavior that we once thought was in our interest). Yet, as indicated earlier, the theory seems to have no resources in the face of someone who simply charges ahead, ignoring a warning about future regret – or worse, *not* expressing regret after a bad outcome. In other words, although egoism might dispute its susceptibility to utilitarian and Kantian critiques, it is hard to see how it could hold off these challenges on its own terms.

Nietzsche's particular problem with egoism, however, rests primarily on its universal application, which offends his insistence on different levels of worth among human types.

The natural value of egoism. – The value of selfishness is equivalent to the value of the one who has it: its value can be very great or it can be worthless and contemptible. All individuals can be viewed in terms of whether they represent the ascending or descending line of life. Once we have settled this question, we have a criterion for the value of their selfishness. (*TI* 9, 33)

The passage continues with a repudiation of the underlying philosophical commitment of egoism, that there *is* such a thing as an ego, an individual "self." This rebuke follows from two features of Nietzsche's thinking that we have encountered: (1) there is no fixed "being" that can identify a "self"; and (2) the human self is subordinated to a larger economy of life. If individuals are of the ascending type, "their value is in fact extraordinary," and they deserve special consideration – not for their own sake but "for the sake of life as a whole, which through them takes a step *further*." Nietzsche favors *exceptional* individuals (creator types), but even here there is no discrete "individual" framework apart from larger life forces.

> After all, the single one, the "individual," as understood by the masses and the philosopher up to now, is an error: The individual is nothing in himself, not an atom, not a "link in the chain," no mere bequest from former times – the individual is the entire single human lineage leading up to him. (*TI* 9, 33)

Nietzsche's objection to universal egoism (on behalf of rank) compares with objections from other quarters about the dangers of excess in egoistic liberation (but not for the same reasons).

> Excess is a reproach only against those with no right to it; and almost all the passions have been brought into ill repute on account of those who were not sufficiently strong to employ them. (*WP* 788)

Nietzsche claims that, without "spiritual greatness, independence ought not to be allowed, it causes mischief" (*WP* 984). Unlike other counter-egoistic theories, therefore, a certain kind of liberation from constraint *is* valuable in Nietzsche's outlook, but only for the higher prospect of culture-creation. Nietzsche advocates freedom *for* creative work and not simply freedom *from* constraint or an unbridled satisfaction of desires (*Z* I, 17). That is why the restraints of normalization are affirmed by Nietzsche for the masses: To repeat a passage we cited earlier: "My philosophy aims at an ordering of rank: not an individualistic morality. The ideas of the herd should rule in the herd – but not reach out beyond it" (*WP* 287).

Once we are in the sphere of Nietzsche's select group of creative types it seems that a select model of egoism might apply. And yet there is one final caution in this regard, which touches on Nietzsche's attribution of the ascetic truth-ideal even to the phenomenon of "free spirits" in modern culture. Even a binary of free-spirit*ism* (and so even a select egoism) falls short of Nietzsche's vision, especially if it perceives normalcy as its Other, as something to be disdained and attacked for its conventional ways.

> It would be completely unworthy of a more profound spirit to find medi-
> ocrity in itself objectionable. In fact, it is the very *first* necessity if there are to
> be exceptions: a higher culture depends on it. When the exceptional human
> being treats the mediocre more tenderly than himself and his peers, this is
> not mere politeness of heart – it is simply his *duty*. (*A* 57)

In an 1887 note (*WP* 891), Nietzsche decries an "absurd and con-temptible form of idealism" that becomes *indignant* over mediocrity, rather than simply taking delight in an agonistic sense of overcoming ("a sense of triumph at a state of exceptionalness"). Even creativity can become a binary opposition that finds otherness to be a stain. As Nietzsche puts it in this note: "*Chief viewpoint*: establish *distances*, but *create no antitheses*."

With regard to utilitarianism, we have already encountered some of Nietzsche's objections in the initial stages of the *Genealogy*, in his analysis of "English psychologists," which has clear associations with utilitarianism. While Nietzsche appreciates its more worldly approach to natural human relations and dispositions – and thus a deflation of "pure" conceptions of the good – he nevertheless rebukes the notion that morality can be sufficiently explained in terms of happiness and the beneficial consequences of self-restrictions. What is missing is the historical awareness of an earlier aristocratic morality and its different senses of value. In this context Nietzsche can say that utilitarianism is simply the formalization of slave morality and its modern version of herd morality.

Nietzsche specifically draws this connection in *Beyond Good and Evil* 228: The "happiness of the greatest number" is not only a mea-sure of herd interests, from within that perspective it *is* truly useful and should even be *encouraged*. The problem, again, is an exclusive, universal conception of the good in these terms, which would be "detrimental for higher men." More pointedly, in Section 225 of this text, Nietzsche takes aim at the fundamental principle of utilitarian-ism: He declares that happiness (whether individual or collective) – conceived as the maximization of pleasure or well-being and the minimization of pain or ill-being – is antithetical to the exercise of creative power. The same holds for a generalized motive to alleviate suffering in life. There can be a place for such measures, but the very phenomenon of creative moves in life would seem to require the displacement of such norms. Since creativity is disruptive of the existing order and risky for the innovator, it would not likely get off the ground if happiness were the criterion – indeed creative possibilities *are* often thwarted when innovative types *retreat* for fear of disturbing the peace.

What is interesting here is that Nietzsche's challenge to utilitarianism can even be framed in terms internal to the theory itself. It seems that human creativity has produced many beneficial consequences for life, and thus it has contributed to human happiness. Yet from a Nietzschean standpoint, the utilitarian recognition of this fact would likely only be in *retrospect*: Creative moves – in their *own time* – are usually marked by disruptions to happiness and might readily be resisted because any future benefit is not yet evident, and a benefit may indeed *not* come to pass; so the preservation of current happiness would undermine the possibility of a new kind of happiness in the future. Nietzsche can highlight this stress in utilitarian theory, not to discount it outright but to challenge its universal application and its temporal myopia, even on its own terms.

When it comes to Kant's moral theory, we have already encountered intimations of Nietzsche's critical response. His most fundamental criticism takes aim at Kant's model of an autonomous rational agent, which I think is a notable example of the sovereign individual targeted in the *Genealogy*. On my reading, the sovereign individual is a compressed internalization of moral cruelty and the ascetic ideal. When Nietzsche said that Kant's categorical imperative "smells of cruelty" (*GM* II, 6), we might now have a better sense of what he meant. Since moral worth, for Kant, can never be grounded in natural inclinations, since moral duty can only be recognized when natural impulses run against it, and since natural forces are yet intrinsic to human life – then genuine moral worth, for Kant, always runs counter to natural human life in some basic way, and so it requires a disciplined stand "against ourselves" in this sense. Accordingly, genuine morality in Kant cannot become settled in the self as a natural expression of desire that could even be experienced as pleasurable (this would be Aristotle's ideal, as we will see). Such a self-inflicted struggle against nature is precisely what Nietzsche called ascetic cruelty, and so Kant can fit the bill. In an earlier text, Nietzsche specifically addresses this point in the following way:

> When duty ceases to be a burden but, after long practice, becomes a pleasurable inclination and a need, the rights of others to whom our duties, now our inclinations, refer become something different: namely occasions of pleasing sentiments for us . . . We are now seeking *pleasure* when we recognize and sustain the sphere of [another's] power . . . To require that duty must *always* be something of a burden – as Kant does – means to demand that it never become habit and custom: in this demand there is concealed a remnant of ascetic cruelty. (*D* 339)

Nietzsche's charge of asceticism highlights both the psychological and intellectual demands of Kant's moral philosophy, in that universality is purchased at the expense of natural conditions of life; indeed the binary opposition between duty and lived experience guarantees that a reconciliation of the two spheres can never be attained. In Kant's defense, from a comparative standpoint his promotion of an abstract universal right can stand against possible abuses in egoism and utilitarianism in principle; and the inviolable dignity of persons that commands respect is given a powerful voice in ethics to stand against injustices of all kinds. Universal consistency provides an effective tactic in ruling out injustice without appeal to human dispositions. Respect for persons on *rational* grounds is well illustrated in the example of slavery, which easily fails the categorical imperative test: I cannot will the universal enslavement of human beings because that would rule out the very institution of slavery; if everyone were a slave then no one could be master – note that this has nothing to do with the suffering and abuses experienced by slaves; Kant's principle would not even sanction voluntary enslavement.

Nietzsche's *Genealogy*, of course, tries to intercept such an argument in his analysis of master and slave morality. Master morality *ruled out* any universal standpoint or attribution of value, and it justified subjugation by actual outcomes of power over others. The tactic of positing universal enslavement would be met with bemusement. Nietzsche would not deny the power that universalization has achieved in history, but he would deny the universality of universalization. Rational moral principles are an inheritance of *one kind* of moral perspective, which was built from dissatisfaction with another moral perspective animated by natural hierarchies.

It seems that any moral viewpoint would involve some kind of expanded horizon beyond brute immediacy. Nietzsche's question would be: Why does an expanded horizon have to achieve universality to be truly moral? Why is moral particularity unacceptable?

Even apart from the value of such claims as "there is a categorical imperative in us," one can still always ask: What does such a claim tell us about the man who makes it? (*BGE* 187)

The urge toward universality, for Nietzsche, is akin to slave morality's need for relief from a natural economy of differing forces. And like slave morality, moral universalism is a redirected will to power, especially with Kant's belief that rational consistency is a *power* that commands the will. And to whatever extent rational consistency is recognized and affirmed in a culture, something like Kant's theory can have enormous force and appeal. And yet Nietzsche would insist on recognizing here a *particular* perspective that might not suffice for ethical thinking.

There is a special sense in which Kant's moral theory is subject to Nietzsche's critique. Kant's overall philosophy in its own way recognized what Nietzsche called the death of God. For Kant, the science of nature and its epistemological provisions rendered impotent any knowledge of metaphysical realities such as God, immortality, and freedom. Since freedom is essential for morality, Kant's strategy was to limit scientific reason to appearances, so that the *possibility* of a noumenal freedom could be preserved. Such a possibility is enhanced when Kant distinguishes between theoretical reason (in science) and practical reason in ethics. Since Kant maintains that we could not practice morality without a sense of freedom, then the latter can be secured as a *presumption* of moral practice. Such a presumption is not the same as a proof, but it is stronger than a mere hypothetical possibility because it amounts to a *necessary* precondition for moral action – necessary, for Kant, because without it we would have to conclude that morality is impossible.

Beyond this defense of practical reason in ethics, I think it can be said that Kant also recognized the existential trauma emphasized by Nietzsche in his account of the death of God. Even though Kant aimed to justify moral principles for human life, he was well aware that a moral life restricted to *natural* existence faced a tragic limit, akin to Plato's confrontation with moral tragedy. Kant's solution differed only to the extent of employing Christian theological concepts. Kant was honest and attentive enough to realize that *absent* the existence of God and the promise of immortality, morality would face a cold truth: Natural life not only runs counter to the demands of moral duty, it also exhibits the ruination of moral ideals when good people fare poorly and bad people fare well – and in the end an earthly grave collapses both outcomes into a neutral rot. In other words, like Plato, Kant knew that the natural order does not guarantee a conjunction of virtue and happiness, of moral ideals and a consummation of human aspirations. Accordingly, Kant proposed the existence of God and the promise of salvation as an essential extension of the very *meaning* of moral ideals and their *disjunctive* relation to natural life.[5] As in the case of freedom, although God and immortality are not demonstrable by theoretical reason, they are preconditions for a robust commitment to moral practice. Modern moral philosophers did not always follow Kant in this way, but from a Nietzschean standpoint it has to be said that Kant was authentically responding to the full implications of the eclipse of God in modern thought. Of course Nietzsche considers the Kantian reliance on God and immortality to be one more version of an anti-natural asceticism that cannot tolerate the tragic limits of life.[6]

As a transition to the next section, I want to emphasize the sense of the tragic that I believe is essential for comprehending Nietzsche's approach to morality. Tragic limits can be understood in both an intellectual and an existential manner: that there are intrinsic limits on what we can know and what we can be. In *The Birth of Tragedy*, Nietzsche addressed each condition: the philosophical limits on knowledge gleaned from Kant and Schopenhauer, and the tragic stories of life depicted in Greek drama. Nietzsche's aim was to blend these conditions into a tragic *philosophy* of life. From

[5] See *Critique of Practical Reason*, p. 118.
[6] Given that Nietzsche's concept of eternal recurrence, as I read it, presses an acute form of tragic limits on moral life, I should note that a number of writers (Karl Jaspers, Georg Simmel, and Gilles Deleuze, among others) have depicted eternal recurrence as a kind of ethical imperative that presents a Nietzschean spin on the Kantian categorical imperative. See my discussion and critical response in *Nietzsche's Life Sentence*, pp. 120–122.

this perspective, *moral* philosophy has been an enterprise that pursues intellectual *security* in existential matters – by constructing a rational foundation for values that give meaning in life. Nietzsche's critique of moral philosophy can be termed an attempt to bring intellectual and existential limits to bear on moral thinking. His critique is nothing like a refutation or rejection, but rather a relentless psychological probe into the *natural* environment of moral philosophy – to uncover the suppressed ambiguities and tensions in this environment, especially the simultaneous benefits and costs that mark all human enterprises. A "naturalized" ethics would have to surrender the security of any foundational scheme when it comes to values.

The *Genealogy* issues the following general charge against moral philosophy: It is always thinking *about* (and rethinking) moral values, but it has not questioned the *value* of moral values. The kind of questioning Nietzsche explores can be tied to the idea of tragic limits: Can our very thinking about moral values itself be questionable, or limited in prospect? Nietzsche is continually probing cherished values to uncover the danger of their concealed antipathy toward the finite conditions of life. Such antipathy in fact is an overt or covert *recognition* of tragic limits in the lived world (albeit with the hope of resolving them). In general terms I think that Nietzsche's genealogical analysis of morality can be summed up as a *prosecution* of traditional moral systems that cannot come to terms with intellectual and existential finitude, and at the same time as a *defense* of a tragic conception of ethical life. Against this background, in what follows I want to expand upon the possibilities for ethics in Nietzsche's thought by considering the question of virtue ethics, which I think can provide some interesting avenues for thinking about morality in the face of intellectual and existential limits.

VIRTUE ETHICS[7]

For much of the twentieth century, moral philosophy was primarily engaged in debates between deontological and consequentialist theories. Then what has come to be called virtue ethics came on the

---

[7] Some of the following is taken from my *Ethics and Finitude*, Ch. 4.

scene, in part as a revival of an Aristotelian orientation.[8] Virtue ethics is not restricted to human actions, the consequences of actions, or rules and principles to guide actions; it focuses on character traits and dispositions at the heart of human actions, capacities that are needed to lead a good life and to act appropriately in ethical situations. Virtue ethics gives voice to the way in which we assess persons and not just actions. When we admire a benevolent person, for instance, we extol more than simply benevolent acts. Someone who performs a helping act, but simply with an eye toward reciprocation or reward, would not be considered a benevolent person. When we think of a benevolent person, we think of certain dispositions, such as a genuine interest in the well-being of others. Virtues, then, involve existential capacities, motivations, aims, and bearings that mark *how* one lives ethically; and a virtue model allows for a self-directed ethical life as opposed to merely following rules or avoiding penalties.

If any moral tradition can fit well with Nietzsche's approach it would be virtue ethics, which has been widely recognized in the literature.[9] There are several reasons: the emphasis in virtue ethics on self-development, on character traits rather than mere social configurations and consequences; and especially the de-emphasis on formal principles and demonstrative reason in favor of a self-manifesting moral compass that would not require external constraints (whether legal or logical) in order to lead a good life.[10]

Nietzsche's overall preference for "noble" over "slavish" traits can come to bear on this question. Consider the following aristocratic slant on virtue:

[8] A key work in this development was Alasdair MacIntyre, *After Virtue* (South Bend, IN: University of Notre Dame Press, 1981). Significant earlier works were G. E. M. Anscombe, "Modern Moral Philosophy," *Philosophy* 33 (1958), 1–19, and Iris Murdoch, *The Sovereignty of Good* (New York: Schocken Books, 1970). A good representative collection is Roger Crisp and Michael Slote, eds., *Virtue Ethics* (Oxford: Oxford University Press, 1997).
[9] See Lester H. Hunt, *Nietzsche and the Origin of Virtue* (London: Routledge, 1991), Michael Slote, "Nietzsche and Virtue Ethics," *International Studies in Philosophy* 30/3 (1998), 23–27, and, in the same volume, Christine Swanton, "Outline of a Nietzschean Virtue Ethics," 29–38. See also Robert C. Solomon, "Nietzsche's Virtues: A Personal Inquiry," in Schacht, ed., *Nietzsche's Postmoralism*, pp. 123–148, and, in the same volume, Alan White, "The Youngest Virtue" (pp. 63–78), which is an excellent account of honesty (*Redlichkeit*) as a facing up to the hard truths of life that limit rational truth.
[10] Many have taken the sovereign individual in the *Genealogy* to fit this kind of self-constitution in ethics (yet my reading would cast doubt on this).

One should defend virtue from the preachers of virtue: they are its worst enemies. For they teach virtue as an ideal *for everyone*; they take from virtue the charm of rareness, inimitableness, exceptionalness and unaverageness – its aristocratic magic... Virtue has all the instincts of the average man against it: it is unprofitable, imprudent, it isolates; it is related to passion and not very accessible to reason; it spoils the character, the head, the mind – according to the standards of mediocre men. (*WP* 317)

Most notably, Nietzsche on occasion specifically affirms certain virtues that clearly apply to ethics. In *Daybreak* he names "the good four":

Honest toward ourselves and whoever *else* is a friend to us; *brave* toward the enemy; *magnanimous* toward the defeated; *courteous* – always: this is what the four cardinal virtues want us to be. (*D* 556)

In *Beyond Good and Evil* 284, he names another set of virtues: courage, insight, solitude, and sympathy. The last of these is interesting given Nietzsche's critique of pity (*Mitleid*). Yet the word here is *Mitgefühl*, which can connote simply a general capacity to "feel-with" others, to sense their affective condition – a better translation would be "empathy," which can capture both positive and negative feelings; and we note where Nietzsche says that friendship involves "fellow-rejoicing (*Mitfreude*), not *Mitleiden*" (*HAH* 499).

Virtue ethics is often connected with "perfectionism" (especially in Aristotle), which means a process of self-development toward estimable traits or capacities that fill out the purposes of human life. A number of scholars have interpreted Nietzsche as a kind of perfectionist, and such discussions have wrestled with traditional questions in this model – whether self-development should be understood consequentially (for the sake of outcomes) or intrinsically (for its own sake). In my view, the attempt to situate Nietzsche within standard models and categories can be a distraction, especially given the complexities of Nietzsche's thinking we have witnessed. However, a perfectionist reading of Nietzsche can have some merit, particularly when cast in terms of the development of excellence.[11] The most

---

[11] See especially James Conant, "Nietzsche's Perfectionism: A Reading of *Schopenhauer as Educator*," in Schacht, ed., *Nietzsche's Postmoralism*, pp. 181–257. This is an impressive and extensive attempt to counter elitist readings of Nietzsche, yet I find it selective and reliant on an early work that would seem to be challenged by later developments.

cogent discussions recognize that, in light of Nietzsche's philosophy of radical becoming and his critique of final purposes, a Nietzschean perfectionism cannot be posed as a development toward some completed condition that drives human activity as its "goal."[12] This is right, but then I wonder why the idea of "perfection" has any use in understanding Nietzsche's ethical sense.[13]

In general I think that virtue ethics is the most appropriate traditional model applicable to Nietzsche, but some hesitation is still called for. In *Beyond Good and Evil* 214, Nietzsche connects "believing in one's own virtue" with "good conscience," which seems to be an endorsement. Indeed he says that this kind of individuated virtue far outshines that old-fashioned sense of "simple-minded and four-square virtues." And yet, he says that this form of good conscience is still a remnant of the old tradition. In Section 216 he warns against the attribution of familiar moral words to the new values and possibilities he is promoting. These new horizons require "a modesty and concealed goodness that forbid the mouth solemn words and virtue formulas." In Section 230 he says the same about "moral word-tinsels" such as honesty, love of truth, love of wisdom, and even the "heroism" of truth-seeking. This is the section where Nietzsche directly names his naturalistic project: "to translate man back into nature." And nature does not support the elevation of humanity to some special higher status. That is why Nietzsche is suspicious of high-flown moral words, because such "verbal pomp" is too much "human vanity" (recall the counsel for modesty in Section 216). With a clear reference to tragedy, Nietzsche declares that nature presses a limit on human self-estimation, which demands that we regard our nature with "fearless Oedipus eyes."

NIETZSCHE AND ARISTOTLE

The question of Nietzsche and virtue ethics is a rich and wide-ranging topic. I want to concentrate the discussion, however, by focusing on

---

[12] Especially good here is David Owen, "Equality, Democracy, and Self-Respect," cited in Ch. 4.
[13] In *Beyond Good and Evil* 227, Nietzsche does say that free spirits "should not become weary of 'perfecting' ourselves in *our* virtue," which involves a mix of honesty, courage, and a "most spiritual will to power" that challenges established values. Yet "perfecting" is written with quotation marks, which should prompt caution.

the ethics of Aristotle, which serves my purpose in the following way: First, Aristotle's ethics is the classic rendition of the virtue model, and a comparison with Nietzsche can be illuminating for the question at hand. Second, I believe that Aristotle's ethics implies some disquieting elements, not only for traditional moral theories of the modern kind, but also for common forms of virtue ethics. Nietzsche's ethical thinking is at odds with Aristotle in a number of ways, as we will see. I would suggest that Nietzsche advances a radicalization and destabilization of Aristotle's virtue model. Yet I also think that Aristotle's ethics is not as stable as commonly thought, even by Nietzsche. In particular I mean that Aristotle seemed to recognize a tragic limit in moral life. If a classic model of virtue ethics can display some proximity with Nietzsche's outlook (more than he realized), then a link with a presumably esteemed historical source can add some weight to the philosophical relevance of Nietzsche's thinking on ethics.

In Aristotle's philosophy, the being of the human soul is the active capacity to lead a life. And the capacity (*dunamis*) that moves human life is desire (*On the Soul*, 433b1), understood as a striving toward conditions in the world affecting the actualization of potential. Desire involves the experience of an absence with respect to a desired condition (*orekton*), which then opens up the structure of striving toward a desired end (*telos*), as well as modes of deliberation regarding ways of actualizing such a potential end. Ethics, for Aristotle (in the *Nicomachean Ethics*), begins with the recognition that "good" indicates a desired end (*NE* 1094a1–5), and that goodness takes a plurality of forms (1096a24–25). Living well amounts to an organization of a plurality of desires in various practical milieus, in such a way as to allow the development of human potential.

The unifying term for the good life, for Aristotle, is *eudaimonia*. The usual translation of "happiness" does not sufficiently capture Aristotle's meaning, which is better rendered as human flourishing, living well, the active realization of human potentials and attainment of various natural goods. Beginning with the phenomenology of desire, ethics is the consideration of various orderings and judgments concerning better and worse choices. *Eudaimonia* will require the exercise of virtue (*aretē*), which is better rendered as excellence, or a mode of high-level functioning. In other words, virtues are the character traits, habits, and dispositions that disclose appropriate choices and judgments regarding the ordering of desires, all for the sake of living well.

Aristotle's ethics is specifically counterposed to Platonic tendencies toward a rationalistic, universal, perfected ethics. The good must be a *human* good, reflecting the finite condition of a desiring being experiencing lacks and limits, and so it should not be measured by divine perfection (1096b30–35, 1178a5–15). The good is also pluralized, not uniform (1096a24–25), particular, not universal (1109b22–23), contingent, not necessary (1139b7–10), temporal, not eternal (1096b4), immanent, not transcendent (1196b30–35), inexact, not precise (1094b20–25), and difficult to achieve, not easy (1106b30–35). Finally, the good life and *eudaimonia* cannot be taken as conditions of the single individual, because it must include the larger order of social and political environments (1094a27ff., 1097b8ff.).

The good has a decidedly performative meaning for Aristotle, since it is identified with activity and *ergon*, which means function, task, or work (1097b24ff.). *Eudaimonia* is called the activity of the soul in accordance with virtue, or moral excellence (1098a15–17). We should think of virtue here in the sense of "virtuosity," as excellence of performance, as effective, successful action in social life. *Eudaimonia* is measured by the fulfillment and achievement of various goods that are naturally beneficial for human beings: goods of the environment, the body, and the soul (1098b13ff.). The virtues are the capacities, dispositions, and habits that enable a person to orchestrate all the various possible goods, measured by the successful performance of a well-rounded life. In this regard, Aristotle insists on the importance of good upbringing prior to mature reflection on the good life. Aristotle seems quite pessimistic about the prospects for an ethical life without the cultivation of good habits and dispositions from early on in life (1095b4ff., 1103b21–25). He says that virtues arise mostly through teaching and learning, and they require time and the accumulation of experience to develop (1103a14ff.). This is why Aristotle points to the limits of rational argument in ethics (1179b1ff.). There is just so much you can say to a person inclined to vice, and people open up to ethical matters in ways other than strict analysis of beliefs and their rational justification (1179b5ff.).

Virtues are defined as the capacity to discover a mean (*mesotēs*) between extreme conditions of excess and defect, of too much and too little (1104a25ff.). For instance, the virtue of moderation in pleasure-seeking is a mean between over-indulgence and ascetic denial or insensitivity. Acting well according to virtue, however, is a performance that does not operate on the basis of theoretical formulas or rules to guide action. Virtuous activity is inexact and can only be executed by a competent person in the context of a particular *kairos*, a particular situation at a particular time (1104a5ff.). Virtuous action can only be rendered at the specific time and situation of a particular agent (1109a24ff.). To be sure, ethics can involve generalizations presented in an unqualified (*haplōs*) form (e.g., it is good to be generous), but ethical practice will always have to confront qualifications in experience (1134a25ff.).

In Aristotle, a virtue becomes a mode of the soul's being, a *hexis*, or "having" (*NE* 1106a13), a capacity to make appropriate choices in various ethical contexts. A *hexis* does not arise in the soul automatically, it requires prior training, cultivation, and repetition until it becomes habit, or second nature (see 1152a31–34). Just as one becomes skilled in playing a musical instrument by training and practice, one becomes courageous and understands courage by performing courageous actions (1103b1–2). An ethical habit, for Aristotle, is not some mechanical operation or instinctive drive, but an acquired capacity to act well that eventually can become relatively unforced and natural. Aristotle seems to be saying that a truly virtuous person will do the right thing without much analysis or difficulty.

How does Nietzsche's approach to ethics compare with Aristotle's? The general features of a virtue model that can fit Nietzsche's thinking are well exemplified in Aristotle. We should also recall Nietzsche's point about overcoming the "burden" of duty in the direction of habit, which compares with Aristotle's idea of second nature (more on this shortly). And in the *Genealogy* Nietzsche cites the Greek phrase *eu prattein*, or living well, as a designation of aristocratic values (I, 10) – the same phrase that Aristotle associates with happiness (*NE* 1095a14ff.). Nevertheless there are several elements in Aristotle that Nietzsche would find problematic.[14] First and foremost

---

[14] A helpful treatment of these issues can be found in Christine Daigle, "Nietzsche: Virtue Ethics ... Virtue Politics?," *Journal of Nietzsche Studies* 32 (Autumn 2006), 1–21. For a classic critical account on behalf of a more Aristotelian approach see MacIntyre, *After Virtue*.

would be Aristotle's primary measure of happiness, understood as the successful development of intrinsic human goods and capacities, a well-rounded fulfillment of a definable human nature. An associated problem would seem to be the central role that reason plays in ethical development. Yet it is not clear that "reason" in Aristotle's ethics is anything like the standards of modern rationality that Nietzsche questions.

For Aristotle, the ability to discover the mean is based in the intellectual virtue of *phronēsis* (1107a1–2), which is different from *epistēmē*, or deductive reason (1140a33ff.). Rather than the performance of some kind of rational inference, *phronēsis* is the discovery of an appropriate path in the midst of conflicting forces (the vices at each extreme). When the mean is associated with *orthos logos* (1138b20–25), usually translated as "correct reason," the phrase is connected with aiming at a target and with a tightening and relaxing that suggests either a bow string or tuning a lyre string; at another point (1109b24–27) Aristotle says that finding the mean is facilitated by tending toward the excess and defect, again suggesting a "tuning." Since *orthos* can mean the successful accomplishment of an aim, *orthos logos* can mean successful action in a practical milieu, accomplished by an attunement of the soul with its milieu, something very different from "correct reason." *Phronēsis* could be called a capacity for practical discernment, a cultivated aptitude to uncover the appropriate balancing and ordering of practical possibilities. Aristotle specifically says that *phronēsis* is not mere knowledge, it must include action (1152a8–9). Discovering the mean is relative to a particular person's situation (1106b1), and it demands an *experience* of particulars, which is neither exact nor universal (1109b22ff.). Consequently, Aristotle's ethics does not involve moral axioms or formulas that can transcend and govern the specificity of experience.

Such qualifications aside, surely it seems that the account of ethical life in the *Nicomachean Ethics* presents a rather unvexed tone of description within a well-ordered recipe for human happiness measured by a well-tempered mean. Nietzsche specifically objects to this kind of measure, claiming that Aristotle promotes a life of satisfaction achieved through a "tuning down of the affects to a harmless mean" (*BGE* 198). Moreover, Aristotle seems too conservative in simply clarifying and organizing inherited values, in simply articulating their implications, measures, and task-ways. With Nietzsche's emphasis on creativity, there is always the need for exceeding a cultural inheritance, a movement requiring certain "extremes" that disturb a culture and alienate an innovator. This represents a clear difference in Nietzsche's outlook, and yet we must keep in mind that creativity, for Nietzsche, is culture-creation, which itself is meant to settle into *new* forms of culture (rather than unhinged or indiscriminate anomalies). In fact, Nietzsche himself offered a notion of "second nature," which could be called a radicalization of Aristotle's concept, in the sense of achieving settlement *after* having disrupted a given "first nature" – and then *itself* having to face disruption after its own settlement. Recognizing the risk in undoing an inheritance, Nietzsche says:

It is always a dangerous process, especially so for life itself: and men and ages that serve life by judging and destroying a past are always dangerous and endangered men and ages. For since we are the outcome of earlier generations, we are also the outcome of their aberrations, passions, and errors, and indeed of their crimes; it is not possible to wholly free oneself from this chain. If we condemn these aberrations and regard ourselves as free of them, this does not alter the fact that we originate in them. The best we can do is confront our inherited nature with our knowledge of it, and through a new, stern discipline combat out inborn heritage and implant in ourselves a new habit, a new instinct, a second nature, so that our first nature withers away . . . – always a dangerous experiment because it is so hard to find a limit in the denial of the past, and because second natures are usually weaker than first natures . . . Yet here and there a victory is nonetheless achieved, and for the combatants, for those who employ critical history for the sake of life, there is even a noteworthy consolation: that of knowing that this first nature was once a second nature and that every victorious second nature will become a first nature. (*UM: UDH* 3)[15]

What makes Nietzsche's position different from Aristotle's is that Aristotle holds second nature to be an intrinsic *potential* in first nature, and so second nature is an actualization of that potential – thus

---

[15] For helpful treatments of this idea, see Alexander Nehamas, "The Genealogy of Genealogy," in Acampora, ed., *Nietzsche's* On the Genealogy of Morals, pp. 57–65, and, in the same volume, Tracy B. Strong, "Genealogy, the Will to Power, and the Problem of the Past" (pp. 93–106).

a process of "completion." For Nietzsche, first nature in the passage above is simply a settled traditional inheritance that can be challenged, and in the midst of this movement there is a shift from first to second nature, where the latter becomes a first nature subject to subsequent challenge, and so on. Within the sphere of culture, for Nietzsche, there is no original first nature that serves to guide development. What is truly "first nature" is the brute realm of natural will to power, out of which cultural forms emerge – as modifications of will to power that are *not* "actualizations" of intrinsic potentials in nature, but rather tensional conflicts between nature and culture that do not resolve into one side or the other (any such resolution, for Nietzsche, would entail a loss of meaning in hyper-natural or hyper-cultural extremes). In Aristotle we are *meant* to be virtuous and to achieve happiness; whereas for Nietzsche we are not "meant to be" anything, but we can and do create *meaning* in the midst of natural limits.

ARISTOTLE AND MORAL TRAGEDY

I want to close the historical portion of this chapter by considering the most interesting aspect of a Nietzsche–Aristotle comparison – the question of moral tragedy. Virtue and vice, for Aristotle, are in our power and constitute the realm of voluntary action (*NE* 1113b4ff.). In connecting virtue with *eudaimonia*, Aristotle clearly alters the older notion of *eu-daimonia*: good fortune granted by a sacred power (*daimon*). Aristotle does recognize, however, elements of fortune that contribute to *eudaimonia* (1099b1ff., 1153b17), and one can see an analogy to the older notion in Aristotle's insistence on the necessity of good upbringing. Aristotle also exhibits resonances of the Greek sense of the tragic when he recognizes the possibility of bad fortune limiting or even ruining *eudaimonia* (1100b23ff.). Even though a noble person can endure bad fortune well and not succumb to misery, if misfortunes are many and great enough, happiness and even noble bearing can come to ruin. In other words, the good is not necessarily inscribed in the human condition. It is possible for a fully virtuous person to come to grief in life, without any transcendent rectification or compensation (as in Platonism or Christianity). So it is possible for a good person to not flourish, to not experience *eudaimonia* (1153b14–25). Aristotle seems to acknowledge that the good life and human aspirations can run up against irredeemable limits.[16] Nevertheless, *eudaimonia* can still serve as a measure for life, and a good upbringing and the practice of virtue can certainly enhance the prospects of its attainment to whatever extent possible.

What is remarkable about the *Nicomachean Ethics* is that the great bulk of the work is a detailed recipe for human happiness and all its ingredients. Then there occur those remarks reporting that it could all come to naught, and these comments are few and rather parenthetical in nature – said simply in passing and reverting to the main discussion. These almost casual insertions are striking when we recall that Plato dedicated ten books in the *Republic* to countering such a possible ruination of virtue and happiness. Was ethical ruin simply too rare a thing to bother Aristotle? Perhaps. Yet Aristotle's differences with Plato in this regard *are* given a more developed treatment, I think, in another of Aristotle's works, the *Poetics*.

Aristotle's *Poetics* has great renown for being the first truly formal analysis of art, particularly the art of tragic poetry. And it is surely that: with all the attention to definition, classification, formal structure, style, quality, and so on. Yet Aristotle also provides much reflection on the *content* of tragic poetry, on the meaning of the dramas. Unlike Nietzsche, Aristotle suppresses whatever religious significance tragedy may have had; but he does focus on the ethical significance of the plays. He considers *Oedipus the King* to be a model tragedy, and perhaps our previous discussion of that work can provide some entry to the ethical element of tragic poetry in Aristotle's analysis. The *Poetics* has often been deemed Aristotle's defense of art in response to Plato's critique in the *Republic*. If we only focus on formal or cognitive questions about art, however, we miss what I think occupies *both* thinkers' primary concern about *tragic* art – the question of tragic limits in *moral* life. Aristotle defends poetry against Plato in several ways, of course, but most especially I think that the *Poetics* is a *filling out* of what were only parenthetical remarks in the *Nicomachean Ethics*. The *Poetics*, therefore, is in some respects an extension of Aristotle's ethics, and in this sense it also challenges some central *moral* provisions in the *Republic*.

---

[16] For a rich discussion of the intrinsic limits of ethical life in Aristotle, see Martha Nussbaum, *The Fragility of Goodness*, Ch. 11.

In his text[17] Aristotle classifies tragic poetry as a form of *mimēsis*, specifically that of actors who imitate by "performing deeds and being in activity" (Ch. 3) – which I think fits the sense of *mimēsis* as "personification." Moreover, tragic actors imitate "people of serious moral stature." Aristotle's famous definition of tragedy includes the following: the imitation of "a complete action of serious stature," and "accomplishing by means of pity and fear the cleansing (*katharsis*) of these states of feeling" (1449b23ff.). There is an important sense in which Aristotle's treatment of poetry challenges Plato's critique of artistic imitation. For Aristotle, imitation is a natural capacity in humans, which is responsible for our ability to *learn*, a process that begins in childhood (Ch. 4). Poetic imitation continues this process and has a high status for Aristotle. He claims that poetry differs from history in teaching us counter-factual meanings that go beyond a mere recording of events. Accordingly, "poetry is a more philosophical and more serious thing than history, since poetry speaks more of things that are universal, and history of things that are particular" (1451b5–8).

What kind of universal significance do we learn from tragedy? In the main, it has to do with moral limits. In Chapter 13 Aristotle concentrates on the emotions of pity and fear that figure centrally in his definition of tragedy. An exemplary tragedy must involve a person of high repute and success who suffers undeserved misfortune, which is brought about "not through badness of character but a great mistake (*hamartia*)" – and so *not* a "moral flaw" in the character (a common mistranslation of *hamartia*). Oedipus is directly mentioned as an example (the mistake was his unwitting killing of his father). The performance of such a story evokes pity and fear in the audience – pity for the undeserved downfall, and fear because of the character being someone "like ourselves" (1453a2–6). What is required for these effects is *to philanthrōpon*, a love of humanity or fellow-feeling (1452b38). It is clear that pity must be a kind of moral emotion that responds to "bad things happening to good people." It is not entirely clear what fear means, however. It could be another sympathetic emotion in that we fear *for* the character (who is like us). Yet I think this would not capture a stronger "universal" element in tragedy, which would

[17] I refer to the following translation: *Aristotle/Poetics*, trans. Joe Sachs (Newburyport, MA: Focus Publishing, 2006).

reach further than the individual character's unfortunate plight. The fear evoked by tragedy could involve the prospect that some kind of undeserved misfortune could befall *us* as well (since the character is someone "like us"). This question has no decisive answer, but I think that the second option is more consonant with Aristotle's high estimation of tragedy for teaching us something universal about the human condition – and we noticed something along these lines in the Oedipus story, when the chorus came to see Oedipus as "a model for us all." It seems that tragedy, for Aristotle, confronts us with vexing themes about the possible limits of morality and happiness in human life.

In this regard, Aristotle offers a remark that is quite intriguing for a comparison with Nietzsche. When it comes to the structure of the story, an exemplary tragedy must be "single rather than double, as some people claim" (1453a12–13). The meaning of this odd remark becomes clear as pertaining to moral rectification. A double-structure story is one that "ends in opposite ways for good and bad people" (1452a32–33), which means that good people suffering misfortune and bad people enjoying good fortune wind up in a *reversal* of these morally troubling circumstances. We all know how satisfying it is when such reversals occur, especially when the powerful "bad guy" gets his comeuppance in the end. Yet Aristotle says that such reversal stories are "second best" compared to a proper tragedy – which has a *single* structure in *not* having a moral reversal, in depicting a good and noble person suffering an undeserved misfortune, period. Why are double-stories thought by some to be the best kind? Aristotle's answer (1453a33): because of the *weakness* of audiences! Poets who deploy such story lines are pandering to the wishes of (weak) audiences. And weakness here can only mean a preference for morally satisfying endings! To appreciate and learn from tragic (single) stories is a more worthy experience, and it seems to demand a certain strength in bearing unresolvable limits on morality and happiness. Could it be that Aristotle's critical reply to Plato's critique of tragedy can be gathered around the idea that the *Republic* itself is a double-story? Does not Aristotle's account resonate with Nietzsche in a significant way?

Nietzsche did not seem to recognize any such resonance, most likely owing to the formal elements of Aristotle's analysis and his emphasis on ethical questions. In fact, Nietzsche poses his own life-affirming interpretation of tragedy against Aristotle's concept of *katharsis*, which Nietzsche took to mean a purging of supposedly dangerous emotions that he insists are implicated with a Dionysian embrace of suffering. The following passage from *Twilight of the Idols* addresses this point, and it also offers testimony for the enduring role that the tragic played throughout Nietzsche's philosophy:

> The psychology of the orgiastic as an overflowing feeling of life and strength, where even pain still has the effect of a stimulus, gave me the key to the concept of *tragic* feeling, which had been misunderstood both by Aristotle and, quite especially, by our modern pessimists . . . Saying Yes to life even in its strangest and hardest problems, the will to life rejoicing over its own inexhaustibility even in the sacrifice of its highest types – *that* is what I called Dionysian, *that* is what I guessed to be the bridge to the psychology of the tragic poet. *Not* in order to be liberated from terror and pity, not in order to purge oneself of a dangerous affect by its vehement discharge – Aristotle understood it that way – but in order to be *oneself* the eternal joy of becoming, beyond all terror and pity – that joy which included even joy in destroying. And herewith I again touch that point from which I once went forth: *The Birth of Tragedy* was my first revaluation of all values. (*TI* 10, 5)

Of course Nietzsche's interest in tragedy greatly exceeds the scope of Aristotle's treatment. Yet my focus here pertains to ethics, and I want to stay within that sphere while still paying attention to Nietzsche's complaint about *katharsis* in the *Poetics*. There is much debate about how to understand this word in Aristotle's definition of tragedy.[18] In Greek usage, *katharsis* could carry a number of meanings: a medical sense of physical purges and discharges; religious senses of purging pollution or ecstatic transformation; a general sense of a healing power; and metaphorical senses drawn from all of these, especially the idea of "clarification" (an analogy from the cleansing of a soiled object to let show its true appearance). The question seems to gather around whether Aristotle's use of *katharsis* means the *purging* or the *clarification* of pity and fear in tragedy. Since Aristotle offered no explicit articulation of the word's meaning in the *Poetics*, the question may be impossible to resolve.

[18] For a helpful discussion, see Halliwell, *The Aesthetics of Mimesis*, Ch. 6.

In any case, Nietzsche seems to take *katharsis* as a purgation, as a discharge of harmful emotions, which has been a widely held interpretation. Yet it seems wrong to say that Aristotle believes pity and fear to be harmful emotions that have to be discharged for psychic health, as though tragedy would simply *release* us from suffering these emotions – similar to the way that venting anger can make us feel better. How would an audience feel *better* simply by experiencing pity and fear over the fate of Oedipus? Surely the *causes* of these emotions in the story are not overcome in the play. A mere "ventilation" theory would not do justice to the cultural status of tragic stories in the Greek world, or to the "universal" significance of tragic stories in Aristotle's treatment. It seems that the surest path for "purging" an audience of pity and fear would come from double-stories, from rectifying reversals that *remove* pity over undeserved misfortune and fear of the same in us.

Accordingly, I think that *katharsis* is more likely a form of "clarification" in Aristotle's usage, but not in the narrow sense of mere cognitive understanding. What universal notion is clarified in tragedy? In a dramatic way, the stories bring us face to face with something we may already sense in a vague manner – that goodness and happiness can still be ruined in life, without rectification. In this way we *learn* something through pity and fear, and these emotions are not purged but clarified in their significance – and presumably they *remain* with us in our sensitivity to moral limits, which may enhance our *philanthrōpon* in the light of these limits.

Nevertheless, Aristotle's ethical thinking does not elevate the tragic to the central role it plays in Nietzsche's philosophy. Perhaps extreme cases of tragic ruin are too rare to be worrisome for Aristotle; or perhaps the tragic simply represents the *marginal* limits of ethical life that must be acknowledged but without too much disturbance. Although Aristotle did not share Plato's transcendent hopes for human souls, he did retain a sense of divine transcendence that could provide some element of comfort for the mind. The ultimate nature of god, for Aristotle, was a realm of pure thought apart from material bodies. Aristotle's god is not even a creator *of* the world but simply an eternal dimension co-present with the world as its ultimate reference point for knowledge. The divine is so disengaged from the world that it doesn't even think *about* the world: "its thinking is a thinking on thinking" (*Metaphysics* 1074b34). Divine *theoria* is a perfectly self-sufficient, self-referential condition disengaged from the material movements of natural life.

In Book 10 of the *Nicomachean Ethics*, Aristotle concludes that, for human beings, intellectual contemplation (*theoria*) provides the highest degree of happiness. Even though we are mortal, we can approximate divine self-sufficiency in philosophical contemplation, by engaging in thought for its own sake, not for the sake of practical circumstances in life (ah, the happiness of philosophy as a thinking about thinking!). In a state of contemplation, the human mind becomes "most self-sufficient" (*NE* 1177b) by being least hindered by desires, external needs, even other people.

As a transition to discussing ethics in Nietzsche's thought, I retrieve what was said in the previous chapter about the "ethics" of eternal recurrence, in terms of its acute concentration on the agonistic structure of values. As an *ethical* structure it can be understood by contrasting it with the counter-ideal of self-sufficiency that has been pervasive in the Western tradition. In Aristotle's discussion of *theoria* there is an interesting moment that can clarify the question at hand. For Aristotle, human ethical life is marked by limits, lacks, and needs, which is why virtue involves the balancing act of *phronēsis*, the negotiation between competing forces at work in the desires of fragile, embodied beings. Accordingly, Aristotle denies that the gods exhibit moral virtue, since they are completely self-sufficient, and thus they need or lack nothing (1178b10–16). The life and activity of the gods are identified with *theoria*, which is completely self-sustaining and needs nothing outside itself (1178b20ff.). An illuminating gloss on Aristotle is provided by Plotinus (*Enneads* VI.8.5): No truly virtuous person would *want* to have the opportunity to act courageously or generously (which presuppose the existence of danger and need). If these virtues were *essential* to well-being and fulfillment, we should *wish* that there be things like war and poverty.

What is useful here from a Nietzschean standpoint is the clarification of a certain self-consuming character in traditional ethical conceptions: that virtue is intrinsically related to finitude and that a preference for the "divine" perfection of self-sufficiency implies the deconstruction of finite ethical life. Nietzsche's question resounds: What would the affirmation of life truly entail? For Nietzsche, it would have to reject any project of overcoming the limits of finitude. Is there not a certain nihilistic implication in the aforementioned position on virtue in relation to divine perfection? Would it not also explain why Christian writers found such Greek philosophical models congenial? Put it this way: Given the analysis of Aristotle and Plotinus, what would be left in human life if the ideal of self-sufficiency were to be fully realized, if limits on desire, knowledge, and achievement were actually lifted? With regard to life as we know it, *nothing* would be left.

Here is where an interesting thought emerges: Measured against the "nihilating" implications of an ethics measured by perfection or completion – where the good is framed in binary opposition to otherness – it could be that Nietzsche's ideal of life-affirmation prompted by eternal recurrence – an affirmation of *agonistic* opposition – can suggest a *defense* of an immanent ethics of finite life, a tragic refusal of moral perfection that precludes the nihilistic implications of a perfect measure. The connection between tragedy, eternal recurrence, and a possible ethics can be noted in the passage from *Twilight of the Idols* cited earlier. After declaring the life-affirming understanding of the tragic that marks his thought, Nietzsche says he has extended this understanding in his teaching of eternal recurrence. And since the tragic is caught up in his "revaluation of all values," we need to keep in mind that revaluation is still valuation, that a tragic sense of life-affirmation is a *new* valuation that can open up a new ethics.

ETHICS AND NIETZSCHE'S THOUGHT[19]

Although he occasionally calls himself an "immoralist" and suggests an overcoming of "morality," it is a *particular* moral system that is being challenged in these maneuvers. If morality refers to values that assess human actions and attitudes in terms of better and worse ways of living, then Nietzsche is certainly recommending a kind of morality, and so thinking about ethics in general in the light of Nietzsche's thought is quite appropriate.[20] A nihilistic denial of

---

[19] What follows is drawn in part from *A Nietzschean Defense of Democracy*, Ch. 6.
[20] See Maudemarie Clark, "Nietzsche's Immoralism and the Concept of Morality," in Schacht, ed., *Nietzsche, Genealogy, Morality*, pp. 15–34, which is a helpful treatment of the debate over whether "immoralism" is a rejection of all or only some versions of morality. See also

values would be the farthest possibility in a thinker who champions the affirmation of life and who proclaims the human condition to be that of *der Schätzende*, the esteemer, the creator of values (*Z* I, 15). As we have noted, Nietzsche's recommendation to surpass the distinction between good and evil does not mean a refusal to distinguish between good and bad (*GM* I, 17). A note appended to that section in the *Genealogy* reiterates Nietzsche's intention to advocate a *reordering* of values, an "order of rank among values" (*Rankordnung der Werte*), rather than an abandonment of values. Herd morality is only one type of morality among others. It is the *reduction* of "the good" to herd morality that Nietzsche opposes.

Morality in Europe today is herd animal morality – in other words, as we understand it, merely *one* type of human morality beside which, before which, and after which many other types, above all *higher* moralities, are, or ought to be, possible. But this morality resists such a "possibility," such an "ought" with all its power: it says stubbornly and inexorably, "I am morality itself, and nothing besides is morality." (*BGE* 202)

Drawing on life-affirming features implicated in master morality, Nietzsche wants to displace a transcendent, anti-natural morality with a naturalized morality that serves, and is measured by, life instincts:

I bring a principle to formula. Every naturalism in morality – that is, every healthy morality – is ruled by an instinct of life; some command of life is fulfilled by a determinate canon of "should" and "should not"; some inhibition and hostile element on the path of life is thus removed. *Anti-natural* morality – that is, almost every morality that has so far been taught, revered, and preached – turns, conversely, *against* the instincts of life. (*TI* 5, 4)

Continuing in this text, Nietzsche reiterates his life-centered philosophy, wherein a *larger* order of life is served by, and therefore not exclusively based in, human life:

When we speak of values, we speak under inspiration, under the perspective of life: life itself forces us to posit values; life itself values through us when we posit values. (*TI* 4, 5)

Richard Schacht, "Nietzschean Normativity," in Schacht, ed., *Nietzsche's Postmoralism*, pp. 149–180, which is an impressive attempt to draw from Nietzsche a viable moral philosophy.

What follows from this, he says – echoing a point in the *Genealogy* – is that even an anti-natural morality is "a value judgment of life," but one that serves only a particular kind of life, a weakened, declining form of life, summed up by Schopenhauer's recognition of morality as "negation of the will to life." And in the next section of the text, Nietzsche connects the idea of "immoralism" with a counter-counter-natural form of affirmation, which is open to all forces in natural life, even counter-natural forces:

We others, we immoralists, have conversely made room in our hearts for every kind of understanding, comprehending, and *approving* (*Gutheissen*). We do not negate easily; we make it a point of honor to be *affirmers* (*Bejahende*). More and more our eyes have opened to that economy which needs and knows how to employ everything that is rejected by the holy witlessness of the priest, of the *diseased* reason in the priest – that economy in the law of life which finds an advantage even in the repugnant species of the hypocrites, the priests, the virtuous.

Given such complexity in Nietzsche's affirmative posture, we should not oversimplify or polarize his approach to herd morality. The kinds of moral values that are so problematic for Nietzsche still find a place in his world-view, and they might even be revamped and rehabilitated in the light of his criticisms. First of all, part of Nietzsche's point is that herd values such as harmony and peacefulness are not entirely misguided, but rather harmful when extended to all contexts and all human types – creativity, for example, is a context in which such values can be detrimental. In certain contexts and for certain types, then, herd values can be appropriate. Consequently Nietzsche's attack upon certain moral systems is not meant to erase them or to promote a mere reversal of their values by promoting opposite actions or forms of life. As Nietzsche puts it in the context of religion, refuting God does not mean we are left with the devil (*BGE* 37). Simply recommending what a moral system finds wrong, its Other, would be still to be caught up in the measure of that system. To put this in concrete terms, it would be a mistake to interpret Nietzsche's texts as a call for suspending traditional moral prescriptions against killing, stealing, lying, abuse, violence, and so on; nowhere can we find blanket recommendations for such behaviors. Rather, Nietzsche wants to contextualize and problematize traditional moral values so as to undermine their transcendent isolation from earthly conditions of finitude, their pretense of purity, universality, and stability.

It goes without saying that I do not deny – unless I am a fool – that many actions called unethical (*unsittlich*) ought to be avoided and resisted, or that many called ethical (*sittlich*) ought to be done and encouraged – but I think they should be encouraged and avoided *for reasons other than hitherto*. We have to *learn to think differently* (*umzulernen*) – in order at last, perhaps very late on, to achieve even more: *to feel differently* (*umzufühlen*). (*D* 103)

Nietzsche's destabilization of traditional moral *belief systems* may not imply a renunciation of certain *values* that operate in those systems. Indeed there may be hidden resources in Nietzsche's critique that can open up these values in a more existentially meaningful way. There are passages in Nietzsche's texts that suggest as much – that one might uncover concealed insights and a deeper sense of morality by denying it and unsettling its unambiguous presumptions and comfortable acceptance (see *GS* 292).

Nietzsche's moral criticisms might therefore be called internal in a sense, and this would fit in with the complex meaning of "overcoming" that animates his thought. Just as one must overcome the sedimented fixations of one's culture, one must also overcome the polar *opposition* to one's culture that marks the initial gesture of independence.

If one would like to see our European morality for once as it looks from a distance, and if one would like to measure it against other moralities, past and future, then one has to proceed like a wanderer who wants to know how high the towers in a town are: he *leaves* the town. "Thoughts about moral prejudices," if they are not meant to be prejudices about prejudices, presuppose a position *outside* morality, some point beyond good and evil . . . a freedom from everything "European," by which I mean the sum of imperious value judgments that have become part of our flesh and blood . . . One must have liberated oneself from many things that oppress, inhibit, hold down, and make heavy precisely us Europeans today. The human being of such a beyond who wants to behold the supreme measures of value of his time must first of all "overcome" this time in himself – this is the test of his strength – and then not only his time but also his prior aversion and contradiction *against* this time (*seiner bisherigen Widerwillen und Widerspruch gegen diese Zeit*), his suffering from this time . . . (*GS* 380)

Therefore we need not segregate certain moral notions that Nietzsche identifies with the "herd" from the rest of his reflections on value and meaning. We need not rest with clear delineations between "Nietzschean" values on the one hand and "traditional" values on the other. We might be able to give a Nietzschean interpretation of familiar moral themes that can *revise* our understanding of ethics, rather than overcome, supersede, or marginalize perennial normative concerns.

Nietzsche's deconstruction of "good and evil" is not concerned with denying normative judgments, but rather supplanting the polar opposition of the good and the nongood. Such categorical segregation generates a number of mistakes and distortions in moral understanding. First of all, it encourages a hyper-confidence in the rectitude of one's sense of the good and in the malignancy of the Other – which can instigate exclusion, oppression, or worse. Second, it ignores or conceals the essential *ambiguity* in values, that no value is "pure" or separable from otherness or immune from complicity with harmful effects. Human existence is enormously complex, and no moral category can be clean enough to sufficiently cover the normative field or to avoid discrepancies, ironies, and unintended detriment in its own operation. In many contexts it is no mystery to recognize the harm in something like murder and violence, or the benefit in something like nurturance and kindness. Nietzsche's contribution lies in alerting us to the margins – to contexts in which familiar moral juxtapositions become unsettled. What is called "kind" and "cruel" is not always "good" and "evil." Sometimes what is meant to be kind can be overprotective and inhibiting, and what is perceived as cruel can be a proper challenge to break a debilitating fixation. The "dangerous" is often productive of good results, and the "safe" is often productive of bad results. Any apparently positive value contains an intrinsic capacity for negative effects, and vice versa.

Finally, with whatever is called good, *becoming* good will involve a continual contest with otherness, without which the existential sense of developing and living out the value would evaporate. Without a capacity to be cruel, "being kind" would not have any moral meaning; recommending kindness would be like recommending aging. So becoming kind in an authentic sense would have to involve an existential confrontation with our capacity for cruelty, with an eye toward cultivating its Other. Consequently the existential *field* of kindness includes cruelty, and without such a field-concept, the nature of kindness is distorted or even lost. The moral polarization of kindness and cruelty would attempt to insulate us from our cruelty and view it with disdain, but a moral developmentalism would require that we acknowledge, examine, and orchestrate the tensions between kindness and cruelty in our nature. What is more, polarization can encourage a *repression* of propensities toward cruelty, and we know well that repression can produce pathological effects and even terrible outbursts of cruelty when the force of subliminal drives becomes too great. In these ways, then, the polarization of values into "good" and "evil" can subvert an existential appropriation of cherished values, and can even nourish the fermentation of the most vicious forces that such values are presumably meant to prevent. Becoming good, therefore, must include an engagement with contrary forces: "Of all evil I deem you capable: therefore I want the good from you. Verily, I have often laughed at the weaklings who thought themselves good because they had no claws" (*Z* II, 13). One other effect of binary polarization that Nietzsche stresses again and again is the tendency toward a nihilistic psychology of self-consumption. An ideal of "love" divorced from "hate" conjures up a notion of *perfect* love that eventually leads to self-hatred, since finite existence can never measure up to such an ideal. Self-loathing (embodied in bad conscience and the ascetic ideal) is for Nietzsche an endemic danger in, and a frequent consequence of, traditional moral systems that trade on perfection and unambiguous virtues.

If we take a lead from Nietzsche's preference for the good–bad distinction over the good–evil distinction, we can conclude that moral distinctions and judgments regarding good and bad are possible in the light of Nietzsche's thinking, and are preferable to the traps and distortions that follow from isolating the good from its Other in the manner of good and evil. One and the same action can be called either "evil" or "bad." In both cases there is a moral judgment, but the second term is favored from a Nietzschean perspective, since it allows for the ambiguities and correlations that adhere to normative judgments. With an alteric structure of goodness, there can be no overarching principle of unambiguous moral purity, or judgments without remainder or regret, or hopes for the complete rectification of tensions within the moral field. What is lost here? Is it certain values that are lost or simply a certain way of interpreting these values?

It seems to me that we can distinguish Nietzsche's critique of the slave/herd mentality from certain traditional moral values and not assume that his critique exhausts what can be said of those values. How is it that feeding the hungry is a sign of slavish weakness and life-denial? Or preventing violence and abuse? Or aiming for honesty in human relations? Or treating people with kindness and respect? I have no trouble saying that all these actions are worthy of moral praise and are worth recommending, and I see nothing of weakness or denial in them as such. Nietzsche is surely right when he targets a revulsion against suffering and finite life conditions that spawns resentment, exclusions, unhealthy dispositions, and perfectionist hopes. He is mistaken, however, if he means to suggest that moral prescriptions against violence, let's say, arose only and exclusively by way of a slave mentality. The issue concerns a certain *attitude toward life* that can be implicated in such values, not necessarily the values themselves. I prefer to say that such values can be healthy and life-affirming, but that they are complex and always in danger of inciting or valorizing life-denying attitudes and practices.

We can make some headway here by distinguishing the following: (1) existential moral commitments, decisions, and judgments that indicate particular estimations of better and worse ways of living, that reflect particular decisions about a normative affirmation or denial – choosing one's Yes or No in a certain ethical context; (2) moral theories, formulas, and metaphysical foundations that have served to ground and guarantee moral judgments, which in effect decide the issue *for* us – we only have to conform our decisions to such measures in order to be in the right; (3) moral universalism and perfectionism, which suggest some transformed condition wherein normative differences and conflicts can be resolved or overcome in the light of a secure concept of the good; and (4) moral judgments that involve a condemnation or vilification of the Other, of that which stands on the other side of the good – which tends toward practices of exclusion or demonization. I think that items 2, 3, and 4 – which can interconnect – are proper targets of a Nietzschean critique; but the first item can be sustained, indeed it can be called an ethical version of the agonistic perspectivism championed by Nietzsche, by allowing for existential moral decisions without guarantees, without suppression of conflict, and without casting the Other into oblivion, invisibility, or silence.

Any moral value or virtue, in its emergent conditions and existential environment, is constituted by a contest with counter-forces. When we make a moral decision or act out a moral commitment, when we take a moral stand and are willing to judge better and worse ways of living, we are engaged in specific instances of overcoming, the creation of meaning in the midst of opposition – which is what Nietzsche means by will to power. Indeed moral practice in this sense seems to embody central Nietzschean motifs such as challenge, strife, differentiation, rank, and risk. Moreover, we cannot reduce morality to the herd mentality, since it is often conformist and group forces that work against and inhibit certain moral behaviors – honesty, for example, is often the last thing most people want to hear. In the midst of convention and established power interests, moral action will often require a "pathos of distance." It is in this sense that egalitarian aversions to harm, offense, difference, and rank that have marked traditional moral rhetoric deconstruct themselves when we consider contexts of moral enactment – *being* moral often entails disruption, conflict, and gradation.

Applying Nietzsche's agonistic perspectivism to ethics would certainly disallow any absolute foundation for morality, but we can also intercept a crude intellectual pessimism or facile relativism by recalling that perspectivism, for Nietzsche, is not equivalent to radical skepticism or to the notion that differing viewpoints are equally valid. Although Nietzsche considers all knowledge and value to be perspectival, he advocates *commitment* to one perspective over others; a detached condition or an absence of resolve or a skeptical reserve are diagnosed by Nietzsche as forms of weakness.

A phenomenology of commitment and decision would help distinguish a nonfoundationalist ethics from a crude moral relativism, which tends to mean that different moral beliefs simply hold true for those who hold them, that the different beliefs are no better or worse in comparison with each other, simply different. Although some normative areas might properly be called relativistic in this sense, certain moral decisions and commitments would not make existential sense in the light of such thinking. If I believe that political imprisonment and torture are wrong, for example, and I join Amnesty International to make appeals to governments that practice such things, it would seem strange if I were to claim that these governments' "perspectives" on the matter are right "for them" or simply "different" from my perspective. I can be a moral perspectivist who denies the possibility of a global foundation and still commit to my position – which in this instance would have to mean that I think these governments are *wrong* and that my position is *better* than theirs. Such decision and commitment fit in well, I think, with what Nietzsche means by willing in the midst of opposition. From an existential, lived standpoint, one cannot equally affirm one's own values and opposing values; that would make morality so arbitrary as to be blind and meaningless. One must *contend* with other perspectives, both practically and intellectually, and this entails that one argue and work *against* other perspectives and *for* one's own, that one think one's own perspective to be the *better* option – all of which would make an attitude of equanimity inappropriate. An agonistic perspectivism simply stipulates that one's commitments cannot be backed up by some decisive "truth," and that a complete resolution or adjudication of differential strife will not be forthcoming. We must simply see the ethical field *as* agonistic and *decide* how to live – without allowing *global* undecidability to demoralize us or debilitate our capacity to make local commitments. Nietzsche claims that the *desire* for certainty is a remnant of religion and that certainty "is not *needed* at all . . . in order to lead a full and excellent human life" (*WS* 16).

The absence of a ground for moral action will strike some as a threat to moral commitment, but Nietzsche would diagnose this worry as a weakness in the face of the only possible condition for any kind of commitment: a willingness to stand for something that is *not* guaranteed. The search for a decisive ground in ethics can be understood as an attempt to *escape* the existential demands of contention and commitment. Moral "decisions" and the sense of "responsibility" for decisions may in fact be constituted by the global *undecidability* of ethical questions. In cognitively decidable areas we do not talk of human choice or responsibility: I do not "decide" that $2 + 2 = 4$. The absence of a warrant need not prevent, and has not prevented, people from fighting for beliefs in the midst of opposition. In fact, I think that one of the most profound elements in Nietzsche's conception of agonistic will to power can be stated as follows: To act in the world cannot help but be action in the face of obstacles and resistances. To dream of action without agonistic difference is actually an unwitting annulment of action. Any assertion of a stable, essential "being" would be "the expression of a world *without* action and reaction" (*WP* 567). To affirm otherness as constitutive of one's action is to affirm action *as* action, that is to say, an actual move in life amidst actual resistances. An agonistic model of action is advanced by Nietzsche to counter the fantasy of self-sufficient, fully free, uncontested movement born in Western conceptions of divine perfection and sustained in various philosophical models of demonstrative certainty, theoretical governance, and self-originating agency.

With all the different characteristics of Western culture challenged by Nietzsche, I think one central common thread can be located in the course of ancient, medieval, and modern thought: the ideal of *self-sufficiency*. In different ways and registers, the notion of unimpeded, unneedful, independent, unencumbered, self-causing agency and power can be found in Plato and Aristotle's conversion of early Greek religion (from poetic narratives of gods engaged with the world toward self-sufficient transcendence), in medieval conceptions of divine omniscience and omnipotence, and in the modern paradigm of the rational subject (which grounds epistemological warrants in the certainty of self-posited methods and principles, and moral warrants in the freedom of self-directed agency). The advantage of Nietzsche's agonistic model of action is twofold: First, rather than inhibiting action it can spur it toward the existential environment of its enactment (as opposed to the passivity of waiting for warrants or deferring to external governance); second, it can avoid the latent tyranny of closed models of agency, wherein presumed standards of regulated action can underwrite the exclusion, silencing, or destruction of agents that stray from or contest the proper form of life.

CHAPTER 8

The Genealogy *and political philosophy*

At the close of the *Nicomachean Ethics* (1179a34ff.), Aristotle deals with a question that is often posed against virtue ethics: If goodness is a matter of self-manifesting virtue, what if people are not developed in virtue and prone to vice? Aristotle's answer is not that they need adherence to some moral principle (why would a vicious person commit to any rational principle?), but that this is where the sphere of ethics requires the sphere of politics and law. Politics differs from ethics in providing external forms of coercion that punish bad behavior or help motivate people with under-developed virtue. Aristotle says that the immediate effect of law is to motivate people by fear rather than reason or ethical education. Political and legal institutions reflect in one way or another the norms and values of a society, but with the addition of tangible and coercive penalties in response to transgressions. Such institutions could be said to embody the limits of virtue, of a self-motivated ethical life. Public regulations represent an external force governing the self, but the issue of virtue could still be a central concern in addressing how human beings exist ethically in a lived sense. Aristotle actually saw the ethical and political spheres to be a unified social domain; he even describes his ethics as a part of political philosophy (1094a27ff.). In any case, the question of politics will always involve matters of coercive force in social life. Our task is to explore how Nietzsche's *Genealogy* opens up his approach to political philosophy, and how this approach compares with traditional models. It would be helpful to begin with the classic social contract theory.

THE SOCIAL CONTRACT THEORY

The contract theory of government was a guiding model in early modern thought, most notably in Hobbes and Locke. The force of the theory was its role in reflecting new political ideals that challenged traditional warrants grounded in divine or natural principles, which were barriers to emerging Enlightenment principles of individual freedom and rational self-determination. The old idea that social and political norms were founded in some intrinsic "nature" was countered by the idea that social institutions are not "natural" but rather "conventional" constructions devised by human agreements. This is why the "state of nature" hypothesis was so important for contract theories. In Hobbes, the state of nature prior to the formation of government possesses no intrinsic social norms; it is a continual "state of war" between free, solitary, self-interested individuals who exist in a perpetual condition of conflict and fear. The social sphere first emerges when individuals, realizing the futility and limiting character of the state of nature, agree to limit their natural freedom (the absence of restraint) in a reciprocal contract that will leave each individual to his own interests, free from incursions. The contract, however, only begins as a mutual *promise* to comply, and so as insurance against a broken promise the parties further agree to sanction a third party that will punish transgression. Hence the parties will "author" their own punishment if they break their promise. In this way a government of law and punishment is set up as a "sovereign" inviolable power that will convert the *natural* sovereignty of free individuals into self-imposed subordination to a sovereign state; yet such subordination will at least guarantee as much individual freedom as the reciprocal contract will allow, and so agreeing to the social contract is a function of calculated self-interest.

Because modern political philosophy begins with the baseline notion of a free, individual human self, the collective and coercive nature of the state requires justification, and the contract theory aims to provide this by basing the political order in the free consent of rational individuals to submit themselves to legal constraints that will bring peace and order to the original strife in the state of nature. It is not hard to see how Nietzsche's philosophy could represent various challenges to the contract theory of government, especially given his critique of collective norms and his celebration of power, creative individuals, and free spirits. Yet I think there are interesting complications in this scenario. First of all, in the *Genealogy* (II, 17) Nietzsche says that he rejects the idea of a contract as the origin of the "state." Yet in Sections 4 and 9 of the Second Essay he uses the idea of a contract to account for the force of social norms. We may have an inconsistency here but I think that there is a difference between his own uses of the term and the way it has been deployed in classic contract theories. His uses are in the context of early conceptions of justice having to do with creditor–debtor relations, whereas the classic contract had to do with the formation of modern political forms of government.

In any case, a main difference reflects the baseline role of individual selfhood in modern contract theories. In Nietzsche's philosophy, social forces are primal, though not exhaustive of the human condition. This is another reason why the "sovereign individual" would be problematic for Nietzsche as a primary human ideal. Yet even if Nietzsche's "free spirit" is different from the sovereign individual, many would read the former notion as antithetical to political philosophy, as an ideal that would subvert political institutions. Indeed Nietzsche has been read as an anti-political thinker, in that the force of social institutions would be a slavish domination of creative spirits. We will see, however, that this assumption may not hold up, especially given Nietzsche's positive account of law in the *Genealogy*. Moreover, if it is true that Nietzsche does not subscribe to a baseline individualism, then the burden of "justification" occupying classic contract theories of government would not have the same hold on Nietzsche's political thinking. Indeed Nietzsche may be able to present a concept of governmental *power* that is more primal, even more "natural," than contractarian conventionalism would have it. More on this in due course.

NIETZSCHE AND MODERN POLITICS[1]

For the sake of economy, I will limit the discussion of politics to modern liberal democratic theory and Nietzsche's critique of this tradition. In the wake of the death of God, Nietzsche assails democracy

---

[1] Much of what follows relies on selected material from *A Nietzschean Defense of Democracy*.

as a secular, political extension of traditional religious and philosophical frameworks that are now suspect, that have already lost their central role in culture. The Enlightenment did represent a break with religious authority and with political authority that claimed a religious warrant (e.g., the divine right of kings), but most thinkers who were forging new political principles did not display a complete break with religious tradition, since their arguments reflected a blend of scientific rationalism and Judeo-Christian paradigms of morality and theology.[2] Nietzsche claims that many modern political ideals are rooted in the Christian notion of "the equality of souls before God" (*A* 62); for Nietzsche, "the democratic movement is the heir of the Christian movement" (*BGE* 202). If democratic political principles are descendants of transcendent constructs that can no longer be sustained in a turn to the natural world, then Nietzsche sees no reason to believe in democracy, and he insists on revising in naturalistic terms the script of democracy's development.

Nietzsche's primary political target is egalitarianism, which, like slave morality, gives the appearance of something positive but is in fact a reactive negation. The promotion of political equality is unmasked as the weak majority grabbing power to incapacitate the strong few.[3] Democracy is different from slave morality in one very important respect: Democracy repairs the lack of agency that constituted the slave mentality, because slave values have now been redirected from the more internal realms of religious imagination and moral ideals to the external public realm of political power and cultural institutions (*WP* 215). In democratic politics, the herd instinct actually rules and legislates against hierarchical domination. For Nietzsche, the unfortunate consequence is the dominance and promulgation of mediocrity and a vapid conformism, which obviates creativity and excellence

---

[2] For a discussion of Hobbes and Rousseau in this regard, see William E. Connolly, *Political Theory and Modernity* (London: Blackwell, 1988), Chs. 2 and 3. For a full discussion, see Joshua Mitchell, *Not by Reason Alone: Religion, History and Identity in Early Modern Political Thought* (Chicago: University of Chicago Press, 1993). See also A. S. P. Woodhouse, *Puritanism and Liberty* (Chicago: University of Chicago Press, 1938).

[3] Hobbes mentions that a "confederacy" of the weak can overpower the strong, but it is odd that he would use such a scenario in defense of the notion that humans are "by nature equal" (*Leviathan* I, Ch. 13). The need for a confederacy is prompted by a natural *inequality* of strength.

and portends the aimless contentment, the happy nihilism of the "last man," who makes everything comfortable, small, and trivial (*Z* P, 5). On behalf of excellence and high aspirations, Nietzsche challenges democracy by promoting rank, distance, and domination. The doctrine of human equality is diagnosed as weakness and decadence, a poison that destroys the natural justice of differentiation. Nietzsche sees equality as a blending that washes out differences, something that offends his constant affirmation of *distinctions*, which requires a demarcational hold against an Other.

> The doctrine of equality! There is no more poisonous poison anywhere: for it seems to be preached by justice itself, whereas it really is the termination of justice. "Equal to the equal, unequal to the unequal" – *that* would be the true slogan of justice; and also its corollary: "Never make equal what is unequal." (*TI* 9, 48)

Nietzsche is at odds with most modern political formats (see *HAH* I, 438–482), but he is most particularly a challenge to liberal democratic theories born out of Enlightenment paradigms. It is no wonder that Nietzsche was preoccupied with liberal thought because its assumptions about human nature, human relations, and citizen–state relations have dominated democratic theory, and the philosophical structures targeted by Nietzsche have been given their most extensive and focused political expression in liberalism. Throughout most of his writings, Nietzsche attacks liberal notions of egalitarianism, individualism, rationalism, optimism, emancipation, and human rights: The vaunted French Revolution is called a "horrible farce" (*BGE* 38) and is traced to resentment (*GM* I, 16); humanitarianism is repudiated (*GS* 377); progressivism is associated with fear of suffering and an incapacity to punish (*BGE* 201); a "free society" is deemed the "degeneration and diminution of man into the perfect herd animal" (*BGE* 203); "equal rights" are diagnosed as a "war on all that is rare, strange, privileged, the higher man" (*BGE* 212; *A* 43); "autonomy" is decoded as the prerequisite for moral responsibility and thus for social control (*GM* II, 2); modern political theories and constitutions are judged to be consequences of decadence (*TI* 9, 37); universal suffrage is designated as a system whereby inferior types "prescribe themselves as laws for the higher" (*WP* 861–862).

...there are no worse and no more thorough injurers of freedom than liberal institutions. Their effects are known well enough: they undermine the will to power; they level mountain and valley, and call that morality; Liberalism: in other words, herd-animalization. (*TI* 9, 38)

There are a number of deep currents in Nietzsche's objections to liberalism, which mainly concern the central modernist categories of equality, freedom, subjectivity, and agency. In liberal theory, equality and freedom seem to have a comfortable association, but a socio-psychological doctrine of equality is ruinous for Nietzsche's peculiar version of freedom, which reflects the *disequilibrium* of a struggle against an opposing force, of a creative overcoming that achieves something in and through this strife.

The free man is a *warrior*. How is freedom measured in individuals and peoples? According to the resistance which must be overcome, according to the exertion required, to remain on top. The highest type of free men should be sought where the highest resistance is constantly overcome. (*TI* 9, 38)

Liberalism conceives freedom politically as state-guaranteed liberty to pursue individual self-interest. The state is born in a contract meant to prevent individuals from thwarting one another's interests. Philosophical justifications for political freedom have flowed from a modernist picture of human nature: All human beings share a com-mon general structure as individual subjects grounded in reflective consciousness; each individual has a definable nature, a unified order of needs and faculties that can be discovered by rational examina-tion and actualized by individual powers of agency. The individual subject is a discrete "substance," the unified foundation for attributes and faculties, the site of identity, and the causal source of action.

As we have discovered, Nietzsche rejects this modernist model of an individual, unified, substantive, autonomous, rationally ordered human nature. Nietzsche's challenge to liberalism's commerce with this model of selfhood is another angle on his anti-egalitarianism. The idea of an enduring self grounding its attributes opened up a space for equality by supplying a site that could be distinguished from con-tingent characteristics and performances (talent, skill, success, fail-ure, etc.). In Nietzsche's outlook, there is no substantive self behind or even distinct from performance: "There is no 'being' behind doing, effecting, becoming; 'the doer' is merely a fiction added to the deed – the deed is everything" (*GM* I, 13). Consequently the variations of achievement are irreducible, which subverts egalitarianism in favor of an economy of differences.

Much of Nietzsche's political language suggests an aristocratic, authoritarian political arrangement. The historical precedent of the master–slave relation coupled with the notion of will to power as the fuel of human activities leads easily to an apparent approval of political domination and exploitation (*BGE* 259). Democratic movements are traced to a kind of "misarchism," a hatred of everything that dominates and wants to rule (*GM* II, 12). As we have seen, Nietzsche insists that cultural excellence is the result of conquest and hierarchical rule (*BGE* 257; *GM* II, 17). The masses are valuable only as a necessary support system for the production of excellence, as the broad base upon which and over which higher individuals can stand (*BGE* 258; *A* 57). Nietzsche's naturalistic bent often dresses his hierarchism in provocative references to biology and race (*GM* I, 5; *BGE* 224, 251). The development of higher types and races is sometimes discussed in the context of "breeding" (*BGE* 262; *WP* 960). There are also chilling references to letting the failures, the sick, and the weak perish or die out in the interests of life (*A* 2; *TI* 9, 36; *EH* III, BT, 4).[4] Finally, there are cryptic remarks about a future "great politics" woven with images of impending warfare (*EH* IV, 1).

Such pronouncements make it very difficult indeed to sustain the profile of a "kinder and gentler Nietzsche" who is only interested in individual self-creation. In any case, to whatever extent these aristocratic motifs were meant to assume a concrete political form, it is clear that in the main Nietzsche rejected the guiding criteria of traditional political theory – which conceived the purpose of politics and the state variously as the promotion of prosperity, happiness, human rights, justice, public security, harmony, unity, or emancipation – in favor of a politics dedicated to cultivating and furthering the highest cultural individuals and achievements.[5] It seems clear that Nietzsche

---

[4] Although Nietzsche's language can easily seem to prefigure the Nazi movement, most scholars agree such a connection is dubious at best, especially given his pronouncements against nationalism and anti-Semitism. An excellent collection examining this question is *Nietzsche, Godfather of Fascism? On the Uses and Abuses of a Philosophy*, eds. Jacob Golomb and Robert S. Wistrich (Princeton: Princeton University Press, 2002).

[5] Perhaps, as Bruce Detwiler has remarked, it is this dissociation from traditional politics that clarifies Nietzsche's claim to being "anti-political" (*EH* I, 13), which would not have

saw democracy and liberalism as forms of cultural decadence and obstacles to a higher politics.

IS DEMOCRACY INCONSISTENT WITH NIETZSCHE'S PHILOSOPHY?

A number of writers (myself included) have attempted to appropriate Nietzsche's thought, or significant elements of it, for democratic politics.[6] Needless to say, such attempts are surprising given his apparent opposition to liberal democracy. In a nutshell, these projects have suggested that Nietzsche's emancipatory critique of Western foundationalism, essentialism, and rationalism can help correct supposed blind spots and exclusions haunting modern political ideals born of the Enlightenment. Nietzsche's celebration of perspectivism, the openness of identity, and agonistic dynamism can prepare a "postmodern" vision of democratic life that is more vibrant, inclusive, creative, and life-affirming than that of modern political theories grounded in the rational subject.

Of course such ventures have met criticism, and this in the spirit of resistance to the embrace of Nietzsche in much of continental thought. Jürgen Habermas has been in the forefront of this resistance in Germany.[7] And a collection of essays from France, *Why We Are Not Nietzscheans*,[8] has reproached so-called French Nietzscheans such as Derrida, Foucault, and Deleuze for not owning up to the political dangers of Nietzsche's thought.[9] In America, Fredrick Appel has

---

to mean being apolitical or against the political sphere as such, but rather being against existing political models, the idolization of the state (as in Hegelianism), and the notion that culture should be subservient to the state. For his discussion see *Nietzsche and the Politics of Aristocratic Radicalism* (Chicago: University of Chicago Press, 1990), pp. 54–64.

[6] In addition to my own book, *A Nietzschean Defense of Democracy*, significant works include Warren, *Nietzsche and Political Thought*, William E. Connolly, *Identity/Difference: Democratic Negotiations of Political Paradox* (Ithaca, NY: Cornell University Press, 1991), Honig, *Political Theory and the Displacement of Politics*, and David Owen, *Nietzsche, Politics, and Modernity* (London: Sage, 1995).

[7] See *The Philosophical Discourse of Modernity*.

[8] *Why We Are Not Nietzscheans*, eds. Luc Ferry and Alain Renaut, trans. Robert de Loaiza (Chicago: University of Chicago Press, 1997).

[9] For an excellent overview of the issues involving the French reception of Nietzsche, see Alan D. Schrift, *Nietzsche's French Legacy: A Genealogy of Poststructuralism* (New York: Routledge, 1995).

offered a vigorous criticism of attempts to employ Nietzsche for democratic purposes, particularly with respect to agonistics.[10] In response to these challenges I do not argue that Nietzsche was an overt or covert democrat, but that in the spirit of his own thought he could have or should have been an advocate for democracy, but not in terms of traditional political theories. For example, I agree that Nietzsche's thought is indeed anti-egalitarian, but I also argue that egalitarianism may not be the *sine qua non* of democratic politics, and that many elements of democratic practice and performance are more Nietzschean than he suspected (or we have suspected). In particular, a Nietzschean sense of agonistics has been advanced by some as applicable to democracy, yet there is a problem rarely faced in such appropriations of Nietzsche: An agon, for Nietzsche, is a selective activity restricted to an elite and not extended to the public as a whole, which surely clashes with democratic provisions. Moreover, a radical agonistics all the way down in political life could easily threaten important democratic principles of justice, equality, and universal human rights born in the modern Enlightenment. This is indeed a pressing question that many postmodern writers have not addressed adequately. Yet many critics of postmodernism simply assume the truth and necessity of these traditional democratic notions, without much articulation of how agonistics threatens these notions, and without any defense of the viability of these notions in the wake of Nietzschean genealogical challenges. Such challenges can reveal how modern principles cannot help being caught up in what they presume to overcome – namely regimes of power – and consequently cannot help producing exclusionary effects and constraints that belie the modern rhetoric of universal emancipation.

Nietzsche's philosophy has helped shape the now familiar critiques of the "dark side" of the Enlightenment and modernity. We have become alert to ways in which self-definition has historically required an "Other" for its articulation and social placement. Modern philosophy was not only concerned with epistemology and metaphysics, there was also a concomitant interest in the science of "anthropology," especially in Descartes, Hume, and Kant. Why was there a central concern with the nature of the "human"? The purported

[10] Fredrick Appel, *Nietzsche Contra Democracy* (Ithaca, NY: Cornell University Press, 1999).

"universality" of human nature was a construct that did more than satisfy a perennial philosophical interest in rational principles and essences; it was inseparable, I think, from the historical context of the European discovery of the New World, which spawned a combination of schemes for exploitation, and anxieties over manifest divergences from European cultural forms. This perspective helps explain not only the pervasive interest in anthropology among modern philosophers, but also the manifest racism in thinkers such as Hume, Kant, and Hegel.[11]

If we retrieve the contract theory of government, we can consider another sense in which a Nietzschean genealogy can uncover disguised forms of power in modern ideals of emancipation. The state-of-nature stories in modern political thought emerged in a historical setting that can show them in a different light. These stories picture the formation of political society as an act of will on the part of rational individuals to replace the state of nature, rather than the ancient idea that the state emerges out of a natural social condition. The "artificial" construction of the state accorded with and bolstered the ideal of individual autonomy; it could also help make sense out of the apparent contingency of political forms in the face of encountering new lands in the Age of Discovery. Political "naturalism" could be haunted by contingency when familiar formats were not evident in Asia, Africa, and America. The state as a willed artifice would not suffer from the same difficulty. Yet another consequence of the contractarian alternative was its implicit, if not explicit, complicity with colonialism. The artificial willful construction of the political order could underwrite the willful *imposition* of European models upon the supposed pre-political, "natural" condition of native peoples, especially when their forms of life were deemed "backward," not to mention exploitable.[12]

---

[11] See Emmanuel Chukwudi Eze, *Achieving Our Humanity: The Idea of the Postracial Future* (New York: Routledge, 2001).

[12] A glance at Locke can be illuminating here. In his *Second Treatise* (V.24–43), Locke framed the social contract in terms of property rights. Each individual is rightfully its own "property," its own self-possession (i.e., a sovereign individual). When through artifice individuals mix their labor with nature, they are entitled to the product as their own property. Locke connects this idea with the divine command to subdue and cultivate the earth, and modern forms of production seem to be the highest expression of following this command. Locke at times mentions American Indians and their primitive production in the midst of vast stretches

The dark side of the Enlightenment may also give us bearings for decoding the promotion of equality and its decidedly non-ideal history. Universal egalitarianism has been rare in practice and indeed absent until recent periods. Political equality was not universalized in Greek democracy, of course, given the non-status of slaves, women, and resident aliens. And the modern conception of the "universal rights of man" was dishonest and myopic owing to a host of exclusions and the subordination of "barbaric" peoples in the name of political progress. It seems that the professed confidence in egalitarian ideals was originally based on in-group allegiance (e.g., white male property owners). *Actual* universal equality was absent and even resisted when proposed. Why? Not simply due to an interest in protecting power and privilege, because a "positive" sense of equality may not have been conceivable apart from differentiating a "we" from a "they" – "We are all equal" translates as "We are equally not *them.*" I suggest that traditional egalitarianism was structurally "alteric" in simultaneously *bringing*-down an aristocratic elite and *keeping*-down existing "others" (women, the poor, savages). The Nietzschean spin here is that the force of this alteric structure was the fuel for actual egalitarian movements emerging in history. And if traditional egalitarianism was fueled by power relations, then equality-talk can be unmasked and shown the dangers of exclusionary effects inimical to its professed rhetoric. Is it possible that an agonistic deconstruction of equality is actually more inclusive and healthier for politics? And can a Nietzschean agonistics be viably democratic?

Few writers who celebrate difference and democratic openness in Nietzsche's name have embraced his elitism and affirmation of cultural excellence. Excellence is a form of difference that implies gradations and judgments concerning superior and inferior, better and worse performances. Many have embraced a Nietzschean openness

of uncultivated land. He says that even the smallest parcel of cultivated land in England is superior in value to the largest area of untapped land in America. Revealingly, Locke calls this uncultivated land "waste." Who could fail to notice here the hints of colonialist rhetoric, in the sense that the "state of nature" in discovered lands not only lacks proper political conditions that can be imposed, it also lacks legally protected property that can *by right* be claimed by productive settlers because nature is *wasted* by the natives (besides, as Eddie Izzard puts it, the natives had no "flags")? Certainly one advantage of Nietzsche's genealogy is its capacity to put a critical spotlight on such philosophical moments in the contract theory that otherwise might be only dimly seen, if at all.

to difference on behalf of a generalized liberation of diverse life-styles and modes of self-creation. Such a generalized emancipation, however, would repulse Nietzsche. He was interested in fostering special individuals and high achievements. I wonder whether certain postmodern celebrations of difference conceal a kind of egalitarianism in their avoidance or suppression of Nietzsche's clear comfort with social stratification. And it is important, in my view, to sustain a sense of excellence that is vital for both democratic politics and cultural production. Excellence and democracy are compatible as long as excellence is understood in a contextual and performative sense, rather than a substantive sense of permanent, pervasive, or essential superiority.

In this regard we can consider a meritocratic sense of apportional justice modeled on Aristotle's conception of justice in the *Politics* (1280a10–15), which in fact matches Nietzsche's formula of "equal to the equal, unequal to the unequal" (*TI* 9, 48). What is usually missed in Aristotle's formulation is that sometimes it is just to treat people unequally, if they are unequal in a certain attribute relevant to a certain context. For example, it is just to deny children the right to vote since they do not have the maturity to engage in political practice. Similarly, we can grant praise, status, even privilege to certain performances in social and political life as long as they exhibit appropriate levels of distinction that fit the circumstances. We can still be "democratic" in opening opportunity to all to prove themselves, without assuming fixed or protected locations of excellence. Yet we can be "aristocratic" in apportioning appropriate judgments of superiority and inferiority, depending on the context, and thus we can avoid what Nietzsche took to be the most insidious feature of egalitarianism, resentment in the face of excellence. We can also borrow from Nietzsche's denial of a substantial self on behalf of a pluralized sphere of actions in order to keep the contextual apportionment of excellence open both between and within selves, so as not to slip into any essentialistic aristocratic confidences about superior selves per se.

What is helpful to democratic political philosophy in appropriating a Nietzschean comfort with stratification is that we are no longer bedeviled by puzzles surrounding so-called "democratic elitism." Whenever democratic practice has exhibited unequal distributions of power, authority, function, or influence, it has seemed to be incompatible with democratic ideals because equality has usually been the baseline principle defining democratic life. But as long as opportunities are open in a democratic society, a meritocratic, contextual apportionment of different roles and performances need not seem undemocratic. Such phenomena as representative government, executive and judicial powers, opinion leaders, and expertise can be understood as appropriate arrangements in political practice. One way to ascertain this is to realize that the only way to guarantee purely egalitarian practices would be to have all political decisions produced by direct tally of all citizens, or to have political offices distributed by lot. Any reservations about such prospects will open space for a non-oxymoronic conception of democratic elitism.

Democratic politics can avoid many of the difficulties attached to egalitarian assumptions by trading the notion of "equal respect" for "agonistic respect." I believe that the latter notion can capture all of the practical features of egalitarianism without the theoretical puzzles concerning how and in what sense human beings are "equal." Nietzsche had a strong case that traditional egalitarian ideals were animated and prepared by transcendent warrants that are no longer philosophically viable. He thought that such a critique would doom democracy and open the way for an aristocracy of artist-tyrants, whose selective agon would create cultural and political values that would guide humanity and be liberated from metaphysical fictions. Any democratic appropriation of Nietzsche must face the question of how and whether the agon can be extended to the body politic and still be viably democratic and Nietzschean in significant senses.

My contention is that Nietzsche's aristocratic, artistic agon applied to politics is either unworkable or itself susceptible to a Nietzschean suspicion (or both). We need a distinction between (1) the aristocracy–democracy encounter in the *cultural* sphere pertaining to matters of creativity and normalcy, excellence and mediocrity, and (2) the aristocracy–democracy encounter in the *political* sphere pertaining to the formation of institutions, actual political practices, the justification of coercion, and the extent of sovereignty. I maintain that Nietzsche's aristocraticism is defensible regarding the first encounter but not so regarding the second.

Perhaps one could argue for a coexistence of a Nietzschean cultural elite and a democratic egalitarian politics. Some of Nietzsche's own remarks suggest as much (see *HAH* I, 438 and *KSA* 10, p. 244). One passage seems to imply that a fortified democratic egalitarianism would spur even higher forms of creativity (*BGE* 242), which would be consistent with Nietzsche's overall agonistics, in the sense that part of creativity is a resistance to the established norm. Nietzschean cultural creators could simply coexist with a democratic polity, even be given some honor, yet not be given unchecked political power. Such an interpretive outcome might be satisfying, but I would not want to establish it by *separating* the cultural and political spheres, as some would be happy to do in order to either preserve democratic ideals from Nietzsche's critique or rescue Nietzsche from reprobation by sidestepping his frightful political remarks or decoding them as simply metaphors for self-creation. I think that Nietzsche's attack on democracy ought to be challenged; not by reasserting democratic traditions, but by showing that much of Nietzsche's cultural and philosophical outlook is compatible with, even constitutive of, much of democratic politics and life.

I believe that a Nietzschean promotion of agonistics and non-foundational openness can go a long way toward articulating and defending democratic practices without the problems attaching to traditional principles of equality. My earlier suggestion that traditional equality was alterically structured can account for the fact that contemporary egalitarianism generally operates with non-substantive conceptions of equal treatment or procedural equality. The reason for this may be that the greater inclusiveness of contemporary politics inevitably chipped away at substantive conceptions so that equality would no longer have much descriptive force or would be harder and harder to identify. The now vague and questionable character of equality may be due to the *loss* of its alteric structure owing to genuine inclusiveness. Traditional "substantive" equality was a differentiated "we" who are equally not "them." With no alteric "Other" in inclusive politics, the equal "we" loses its specific, positive contours. Agonistic "equality" can include an alteric structure and need no longer make excuses for the dissipation of substantive equality.

If political respect implies inclusiveness and an open regard for the rightful participation of others, an agonistic model of politics can underwrite respect without the need for substantive conceptions of equality or even something like "equal regard." Moreover, the structure of an agon conceived as a contest can readily underwrite political principles of fairness. Not only do I need an Other to prompt my own achievement, but the significance of any "victory" I might achieve demands an able opponent. As in athletics, defeating an incapable or incapacitated competitor winds up being meaningless. So I should not only will the presence of others in an agon, I should also want that they be able adversaries, that they have opportunities and capacities to succeed in the contest. And I should be able to honor the winner of a fair contest. Such is the logic of competition that contains a host of normative features, which might even include active provisions for helping people in political contests become more able participants.

In addition, agonistic respect need not be associated with something like positive regard or equal worth, a dissociation that can go further in facing up to actual political conditions and problematic connotations that can attach to liberal dispositions. Democratic respect forbids exclusion, it demands inclusion; but respect for the Other *as* other can avoid a vapid sense of "tolerance," a sloppy "relativism," or a misplaced spirit of "neutrality." Agonistic respect allows us to simultaneously affirm our beliefs and affirm our opponents as worthy competitors in public discourse. Here we can speak of respect without ignoring the fact that politics involves perpetual disagreement, and we have an adequate answer to the question, "Why should I respect a view that I do not agree with?" Political respect in this sense entails giving all beliefs a hearing, refusing any belief an ultimate warrant, and perceiving one's own viewpoint as agonistically implicated with opposing viewpoints.

NIETZSCHE AS A POLITICAL THINKER

We have noted that Nietzsche's social philosophy undermines the central elements of selfhood that underwrite the liberal contract theory of government (elements of individual sovereignty, equality, and rationality).[13] Yet Nietzsche's challenge does not amount to a complete repudiation of social norms and political institutions. Nietzsche

---

[13] For an extensive discussion of a Nietzschean critique of liberalism, see Owen, *Nietzsche, Politics, and Modernity.*

is not an anti-political thinker in a strict sense.[14] I want to argue that from a Nietzschean standpoint the state is neither "artificial" nor "natural" in the usual connotations of these terms, because "nature" and "culture" are not incommensurate spheres for Nietzsche; rather, culture arises out of, and modifies, natural forces. We can gain entry into this question by reconsidering Nietzsche's interest in the Greek *agōn*. We have established that in *Homer's Contest* Nietzsche holds that culture for the Greeks was not something separate from nature but a modulation of more vicious natural drives into agonistic contests predicated on victory and defeat rather than annihilation. Cultural contests represented a sublimation of brute cruelty in the direction of a managed struggle with competitors for excellence and recognition. Nietzsche did in fact recognize the political purpose of the *agōn* (*KSA* 1, p. 789), but he took it to be an aristocratic activity, where the few talented types would compete for cultural and political status. He did not seem to recognize a connection between an agonistic spirit and the emergence and practice of Greek democracy. The philosophical development of a questioning spirit and challenges to traditional warrants helped nurture practices of open debate and public contests of speeches that came to characterize democratic procedures.[15]

Before exploring these questions, it is important to set the stage by considering the matter of institutions, without which political philosophy could not get off the ground. Modern societies, at least, cannot function without institutions and the coercive force of law. Appel, like many interpreters, construes Nietzsche's "political" thought as advancing more an "aesthetic" activity than institutional governance.[16] Supposedly Nietzsche envisions an elite who compete

---

[14] For studies of Nietzsche and political thought, see Tracy B. Strong, *Friedrich Nietzsche and the Politics of Transfiguration*, expanded edition (Urbana: University of Illinois Press, 2000), Keith Ansell-Pearson, *An Introduction to Nietzsche as a Political Thinker* (Cambridge: Cambridge University Press, 1994), and Daniel W. Conway, *Nietzsche and the Political* (New York: Routledge, 1997).

[15] For a discussion of the connections between Greek democracy and contests, see Jean-Pierre Vernant, *Myth and Society in Ancient Greece*, trans. Janet Lloyd (Sussex: Harvester Press, 1980), pp. 19–44. On the open atmosphere of uncertainty and interrogation see Cornelius Castoriadis, "The Greek *Polis* and the Creation of Democracy," in *Philosophy, Politics, Autonomy: Essays in Political Philosophy*, ed. David Ames Curtis (New York: Oxford University Press, 1991), Ch. 5.

[16] Appel, *Nietzsche Contra Democracy*, pp. 160ff.

with each other for creative results in isolation from the mass public; indeed the elite simply use the masses as material for their creative work, without regard for the fate or welfare of the general citizenry. Appel maintains that such a political aesthetics is problematic because it is incompatible with the maintenance of stable institutions. And Nietzsche is also supposed to eschew the rule of law in favor of the hubris of self-policing. If this were true, one would be hard pressed to find Nietzsche relevant for any political philosophy, much less a democratic one.

It is a mistake, however, to read Nietzsche in simple terms as being against institutions and the rule of law on behalf of self-creation. Those who take Nietzsche to be an anti-institutional transgressor and creator should take heed of a passage from *Twilight of the Idols*, where Nietzsche clearly diagnoses a repudiation of institutions as a form of decadence. Because of our modern faith in a foundational individual freedom, we no longer have the instincts for forming and sustaining the traditions and modes of authority that healthy institutions require.

The whole of the West no longer possesses the instincts out of which institutions grow, out of which a *future* grows: perhaps nothing antagonizes its "modern spirit" so much . . . That which makes an institution an institution is despised, hated, repudiated: one fears the danger of a new slavery the moment the word "authority" is even spoken out loud. That is how far decadence has advanced in the value-instincts of our politicians, of our political parties. (*TI* 9, 39)

In the light of these remarks, a Nietzschean emphasis on power and agonistics offers significant advantages for political philosophy. In some respects we are freed from the modern project of "justifying" the force of social institutions owing to a stipulated freedom from constraint in the "state of nature." With a primal conception of power(s), we can retrieve an Aristotelian take on social institutions as fitting and productive of human existence. Forces of law need not be seen as alien to the self, but as modulations of a ubiquitous array of forces *within which* human beings can locate relative spheres of freedom. And an agonistic conception of political activity need not be taken as a corruption or degradation of an idealized order of political principles or social virtues.

With respect to democracy, however, it seems that Nietzsche's analysis of justice and law insists on their aristocratic origins; it also seems evident that his own political vision sustains an elitist character and that he would designate democracy as a cultural inheritor of slave morality. Yet I believe it is possible to identify elements of democratic *practice* (not necessarily traditional democratic *theory*) that might disrupt Nietzsche's assumptions about democracy, particularly by considering agonistic elements in democratic politics.

AGONISTIC DEMOCRACY

How can we begin to apply the notion of agonistics to politics in general and democracy in particular? First of all, contestation and competition can be seen as fundamental to self-development and as an intrinsically social phenomenon. Agonistics helps us articulate the social and political ramifications of Nietzsche's concept of will to power. As we have seen, since power can only manifest itself in the midst of resistance, then one's power to overcome is essentially related to a counter-power. Without one's counter-power, one's power would no longer *be* power. Power, therefore, is not simply an individual possession or a goal of action; it is more a global, interactive conception. For Nietzsche, every advance in life is an overcoming of some obstacle or counter-force, so that conflict is a mutual co-constitution of contending forces. Opposition generates development. This indicates another sense in which the modern conception of an autonomous, "sovereign individual" is displaced in Nietzsche's philosophy. The human self is not formed in some internal sphere and then secondarily exposed to external relations and conflicts. The self is formed in and through what it opposes and what opposes it; in other words, the self is formed through agonistic relations. Therefore, any annulment of one's Other would be an annulment of one's self in this sense. Competition can be understood as a shared activity for the sake of fostering high achievement and self-development, and therefore as an intrinsically social activity. It is interesting to note that the etymology of the word "compete" is "to seek together."

In Nietzsche's appropriation of the two forms of strife in *Homer's Contest*, we have noticed the distinction between agonistic conflict and sheer violence, and also the implication that a radical agonistics rules out violence, because violence is actually an impulse to *eliminate* conflict by annihilating or incapacitating an opponent, bringing the agon to an end. In his discussion of the "spiritualization of hostility" – wherein one must affirm both the presence and the power of one's opponents as implicated in one's own posture (*TI* 5, 3) – Nietzsche specifically applies such a notion to the political realm. What this implies is that the category of the social need not be confined to something like peace or harmony. Agonistic relations, therefore, do not connote a deterioration of a social disposition and can thus be extended to political relations.

Democracy in general terms can be understood as agonistic in the following manner: Political judgments are not preordained or dictated; outcomes depend upon a contest of speeches where one view *wins* and other views *lose* in a tabulation of votes; since the results are binding and backed by the coercive power of the government, democratic elections and procedures establish temporary control and subordination – which, however, can always be altered or reversed because of the succession of periodic political contests. Democratic elections allow for, and depend upon, peaceful exchanges and transitions of power. Language is the weapon in democratic contests. The binding results, however, produce tangible effects of gain and loss that make political exchanges more than just talk or a game. The urgency of such political contests is that losers must yield to, and live under, the policies of the winner; we notice, therefore, specific configurations of power, of *domination and submission* in democratic politics.

The agonistics of democracy shows itself at every level of political practice, from local formats (which can operate in a direct manner, as in town meetings) to state and national formats (which tend to require direct election of representative bodies). In all cases the contestation of different perspectives seems to be a necessary (if not sufficient) condition for democratic procedures. The open invitation to all perspectives and the employment of vote tabulations to provide periodic settlement of contested issues seem to *presume* that politics is an arena of differences that cannot be resolved by a globally decisive truth. Accordingly, all the seemingly fractious features of democratic practice – from local debates to election campaigns to legislative disputations to judicial arguments – are in fact simply the orchestrated

rituals of political life, without which democracy would evaporate.
Democracy should not recoil from the disorder and friction of political dispute; something like sheer harmony or unanimity would spell
the end of politics or perhaps amount to nothing more than the
silhouette of coercion, suppression, or erasure.

LEGAL AGONISTICS

With respect to the law, Nietzsche's treatment in the *Genealogy* (II,
11) has received very little attention, if any, in the literature.[17] This
may be due to the assumption that Nietzsche is an anti-political
thinker who is always aiming to protect creative types from (slavish)
forces of constraint. Yet his positive account of the law betrays that
assumption. And his espousal of an agonistic conception of law may
help uncover elements of democratic legal and political practice that
can be understood in a more Nietzschean light.

There are many parallels between political agonistics and a democratic legal system, at least in the Anglo-American common law
tradition. That tradition is often called an adversarial system, to distinguish it from the so-called inquisitorial system that operates in
France and Germany, for example. An adversarial model pits two
procedurally equal parties against each other in open court, each
competing to persuade a jury of the guilt or innocence of a defendant. Most of the procedural rules and the presumptions about the
posture of lawyers are built around the notion that each party in a
trial is entitled to have its best possible case presented in court and to
vigorously challenge the other side's case; the judge in most respects
serves as an impartial, procedural referee; the contest is then decided
by the deliberations of a jury. An inquisitorial system is different to
the extent that a judge is given much more deliberative and evidentiary power. Proceedings are not restricted to aggressive advocacy of
competing parties; the court is responsible for presenting the arguments and is not confined to the parties' presentations; a judge does
most of the questioning of witnesses and can guide the course of a

---

[17] A good collection examining the general question of Nietzsche and law is *Nietzsche and
Legal Theory: Half-Written Laws*, eds. Peter Goodrich and Mariana Valverde (New York:
Routledge, 2005). Nevertheless, there is not much attention to *GM* II, 11.

case in ways that are impermissible in an adversarial system.[18] One
attraction of the inquisitorial system is that it is simpler, less restricted
by procedural rules, and much relieved of the various lawyerly tactics,
probings, and challenges that often frustrate observers of the adversarial system, and that often acquit a seemingly guilty defendant on
a technicality or because of evidentiary exclusions.

Despite its difficulties, the agonistics of an adversary system can at
least be better understood in the context of our discussion of democracy (and it can be noted that in Greek democracy trials were called
agones and litigants *agonistai*). An inquisitorial system puts much
more trust in the performance, integrity, and impartiality of judges
and the judicial system. An adversarial system in many ways is animated by suspicions about the competence and possible motives of
the government and judicial officials. Adversarial procedures, then,
are intended to give competing parties every appropriate means of
challenging or subverting possibly unfair, deceptive, fallacious, or dis-
criminatory practices. Cognitive and ethical suspicion are operating
here, and this is often forgotten in complaints about legal machinations that clog proceedings or block the government's case against an
apparently guilty party. We should at least remember that procedural
rules and the so-called presumption of innocence are meant to *contest*
the government, to protect citizens from abuses of power – and not,
as is often supposed, to express "sympathy" for the interests of criminals.[19] Accordingly, we should be *willing* to trade the acquittal of
guilty persons for protections against the presumably more heinous
outcome of convicting innocent persons. Acquitting a guilty person
may be morally repugnant, but it upholds the legal *system*, because
each case also concerns *any* case that can come before the system.
Since the power of government is contested in the system, acquitting

[18] For an overview of the differences between the two systems see David Luban, *Lawyers and
Justice: An Ethical Study* (Princeton: Princeton University Press, 1988), Ch. 5, "Why Have
an Adversary System?"
[19] We might spotlight the dangers of foregoing a more adversarial system by considering the
case of Japan: In the Japanese legal system a suspect can be interrogated without a lawyer
for up to 23 days. The confession rate of suspects is 92%. Of those suspects brought to trial,
the conviction rate is 99.9% (*Harper's*, July 2007, p. 15). We could admire such a system
only if the actual rate of guilt and innocence roughly matched these percentages. Yet even a
God's-eye view of actual guilt or innocence would have to be surprised at the success rate in
the Japanese system.

a guilty person simply means that the government has failed to prove its case, that the defendant is *legally* not guilty, rather than proven innocent. At a systematic level, the government should affirm such defeats, because the presumption of innocence and the legal tactics afforded the defense constitute the government's own self-imposed *test* of its strength.

In this way, an adversarial legal system mirrors the separation of powers that marks the American form of government; legal and political structures are organized around the contestation of power sites, rather than the termination of conflict (and this can accord with Nietzsche's formulation that a legal order is "a means in the conflict between power-complexes," rather than a means of preventing conflict (*GM* II, 11)). James Madison (in *Federalist* 51) argued that the division and separation of powers in government provides an internal structure that prevents tyranny by simply *multiplying* the number of potentially tyrannical units and permitting them to check each other by mutual "ambition" and distrust. A main reason why I think Nietzsche's philosophy is important for democracy is this: An agonistic framework is not a "new theory" for democratic political thought but a genealogical critique of traditional political *theories*. In inception and practice, democracy has *always been* agonistic, and political philosophy has tended to suppress or resist this agonistic structure because its radically tensional character disturbs certain principles presumed to be the bedrock foundation of democracy.

DEMOCRACY AND TRAGEDY

An important question facing a Nietzschean approach to democratic politics is this: Does not a radical agonistics undermine any warrant for democratic governance, however conceived? In my work I have tried to face this question and suggest a "tragic" model of democratic openness, to borrow from Nietzsche's interest in tragedy. Many democratic theorists insist that politics must be grounded in secure principles, which themselves are incontestable, so as to rule out anti-democratic voices from having their day and possibly undermining democratic procedures or results. A radically agonistic, open conception of democracy that simply invites any and all parties to compete for favor seems utterly decisionist, with no justification beyond its contingent enactment. But from a historical perspective, despite metaphysical pretenses in some quarters, democratic foundings have in fact emerged out of the "abyss" of conventions and decisional moments. And with the prospect of a constitutional convention in our system, it is evident from a performative standpoint that any results *are* actually possible in a democracy, even anti-democratic outcomes (not likely, but surely possible). The "tragedy" is that democracy could die at its own hands. Foundationalists would call such an outcome contradictory, but a tragic conception would see it as a possibility intrinsic to the openness of democratic practice.

Can there be more than simply a negative register in such a tragic conception? I think so. Just as, for Nietzsche, the tragic allows us to be sensitized and energized for the fragile meanings of existence, thus enhancing life, a tragic politics could wean us from false comforts in foundations and open us to the urgent finite conditions of political life in an enhanced way. And even if one conceded the existence of foundational self-evident political principles, would the force of such principles by themselves necessarily be able to prevent non-democratic outcomes? If not, the force of such principles would be restricted to the solace of intellectual rectitude that can comfort theorists while the walls are coming down. The nonexistence of foundational guarantees surely does not prevent one from living and fighting for democratic ideals. What is to be said of someone who, in the absence of a guarantee, would hesitate to act or be obstructed from acting or see action as tainted or less than authentic? Nietzsche would take this as weakness. As we have seen, Nietzsche claims that action in the world is always action in the midst of otherness, of resistances and obstacles. Hence to dream of action without otherness is to annul action. The irony of a tragically open, agonistic politics is that it need not "infect" political life but in fact *spur* it toward the existential environment of its *enactment*. And as radically open, an agonistic politics has the virtue of precluding the silencing of any voice, something especially important when even purportedly democratic dispositions are comfortable with exclusions (frustrated by citizens who will not come around to being impartial enough, rational enough, secular enough, deliberative enough, communal enough, virtuous enough, and so on), thereby becoming susceptible to the most ironic and insidious form of tyranny done in democracy's name.

POLITICS AND COMMUNITY

There is a significant problem facing an appropriation of Nietzsche for social thought. An agonistic pluralism is significantly "negative" in its depiction of human nature and human relations – arguing against universality, sameness, and harmony in favor of differences and conflict. Ethical and political theorists might well ask whether something like love, compassion, or concern for others would find a place – indeed whether such things are even possible, or might be discouraged – in an agonistic social dynamic. Would not ethical and political life need some sense of *positive* regard in human relations, where people care for and about each other? I want to engage this question and answer Yes with respect to ethics and a qualified No with respect to politics.

Nietzsche's deconstruction of atomistic individualism and subjectivity opens up an intrinsically social and interactive sense of selfhood. The emphasis, however, is on an agonistic interaction, ruling out any baseline sense of social unity, harmony, or collectivity. Nietzsche's texts do indeed emphasize strife, challenge, and distance, with less attention to "positive" experiences of love and beneficence. In fact love and compassion are in some instances reduced to egotistical and possessive instincts (*GS* 14; *WP* 777). Neighbor-love is counterposed to a sense of solitude (*Z* I, 16) and to a kind of friendship that thrives on challenge rather than support and nurturance: "In a friend one should have one's best enemy. You should be closest to him in your heart when you resist him" (*Z* I, 14). We do find positive remarks about love – at one point it is associated with going beyond good and evil (*BGE* 153) – and we recall his promotion of sympathy (*BGE* 284). Nonetheless there is much more "distance" in a Nietzschean relation, and this would seem problematical in ethical and political relations. Do we not need a stronger sense of *recognition* of others and *concern* for them, at least as a counter-movement to our capacity for hatred, violence, and abuse?

Although I have suggested a kind of agonistic recognition that can generate a sense of civic respect, such a notion indeed does not require any positive feeling about or toward others, and one might wonder whether stressing a Nietzschean agonistics would only encourage or instigate elements of hatred and abuse that are all too ready to assert themselves. It is true that a positive regard for others does not often show itself in Nietzsche's texts, but we should give him his due in his diagnosis of hatred and violence. An openness to becoming and strife is ambiguous; for Nietzsche, it is something that is connected with creativity and human development; it can, however, serve the instincts of those who simply hate and want to destroy.

The desire for destruction, change, becoming *can* be the expression of an overfull power pregnant with the future (my term for this, as is known, is the word "Dionysian"); but it can also be the hatred of the ill-constituted, disinherited, underprivileged, which destroys, *has* to destroy, because what exists, indeed existence itself, all being itself, enrages and provokes it. (*WP* 846)

In fact Nietzsche suggests that human abuse does not stem from a wanton exercise of power; rather, hurting people "is a sign that we are still lacking power, or it shows a sense of frustration in the face of this poverty" (*GS* 13). It is the blockage of self-development that may lie behind abusive behavior, since "whoever is dissatisfied (*unzufrieden*) with himself is continually ready for revenge, and we others will be his victims" (*GS* 290). Consequently, one route to diminishing maltreatment is not to call for more love toward others, but to encourage and foster a sense of empowerment that stems from striving to overcome obstacles and enact one's projects. Self-development is an avenue toward human joy, and "if we learn better to experience joy (*uns freuen*), we learn best not to hurt others or to devise hurts for them" (*Z* II, 3).[20]

Nevertheless, it is right to worry that ethics would at least be greatly diminished without some sense of positive regard *toward* others, especially some affective regard – if not love, then at least compassion for human suffering. Some philosophers have made compassion the centerpiece of their ethics (Hume and Schopenhauer, for example), as the existential fuel that animates the moral life, rather than mere

[20] An excellent examination of love in relation to affirmation in Nietzsche's thought is Robert B. Pippin, "Morality as Psychology, Psychology as Morality: Nietzsche, Eros, and Clumsy Lovers," in Schacht, ed., *Nietzsche's Postmoralism*, pp. 79–99.

rules, formulas, or commands. What is interesting here is that such an ethical openness to the pain of others is generated not by some positive condition but by an openness to the *negativity* of finitude. Accordingly, we might diagnose moral indifference as a flight from finitude, as a psychological strategy to *minimize* one's exposure to the pains of life. Despite all this, we would have to heed Nietzsche's warnings about the dangers in our moral sentiments. The danger in compassion, as we have seen, is that it can prompt a life-denying attitude, or tend toward an insidious benevolence that controls people, debilitates them, or covers up the life lessons that arise from confronting pains and losses. Ethical compassion should involve a delicate oscillation between responding *to* suffering and letting people learn *from* suffering.

Although ethics and politics will always overlap, nevertheless certain ethical intimations about positive regard and our attitudes toward each other can only go so far in politics and might even be misplaced. A Nietzschean agonistic perspectivism serves us well when we recognize that politics involves a perpetual *conflict* of perspectives, which renders an interest in positive dispositional bearings limited at best, and potentially oppressive at worst.

The problem addressed here can be traced to proposals or hopes for a political "community." To a certain extent I am siding with liberalism in its debate with communitarianism.[21] A community suggests a group of people held together by certain common values, interests, projects, or identities. Defining a *political* community in a pluralistic society, however, runs into the problem of suppressing or washing out differences, particularly in the light of coercive institutional power that marks the political sphere. If community is meant to designate a unified "whole" in any sense, or reflect some kind of universal category, then the status of different particulars is automatically diminished. If it refers to particular groups or some sort of integrated harmony of different sub-groups, we run into several problems. What groupings will we select to emphasize? People can be grouped into multifarious associations: religion, race, ethnicity, gender, sex, economic class, age, language, geographical region, social

---

[21] A good collection of sources is *Communitarianism: A New Public Ethics*, ed. Markate Daly (Belmont, CA: Wadsworth, 1994).

role, occupation, and so on. Moreover, differences both between and within these groupings are more than differences; they manifest an array of *tensions* that render the idea of an organized harmony suspect. Moreover, we should be suspicious about any nostalgia for a lost sense of community that has become ruined in our fractious times, because any such "harmony" in the past was due more to *exclusions* of certain groups from political participation, or to mutual *seclusions* of different cultural groups within their own enclaves. If we could go back in time and institute complete political inclusiveness, and introduce modern forces of mobility and interpenetration that disrupt group identities, I daresay that "harmony" would directly give way to the kind of turmoil we know today.

The point is that past experiences of a cohesive community were *selective* and therefore defined by identities that were *not* really holistic. Once we have genuine political inclusiveness, all *differing* identities are permitted to assert themselves, and we are faced with the dissensus familiar to contemporary politics. It would seem that the only truly "inclusive community" would be one that did not define itself according to any particular *content*. Reflections on a democratic political order should avoid incorporating larger meditations on human relations that connote or imply conditions of meaning, purpose, or attitude, since such things do not lend themselves to communal convergence. Democracy *is* communal in the sense of a political "gathering," but only to orchestrate a conflicted field of meanings toward contingent decisions.

DEMOCRACY AND MODESTY

If a restriction of political justice to competitive fairness and a confinement of a civic attitude to agonistic respect seem inadequate, too narrow, or disheartening, let me suggest how such criticisms might be intercepted. Ethical concerns and larger narratives about meaning, purpose, dispositions, and human relations are not banished from politics in an agonistic model; they are *contestants* in the political agon. Such narratives, however, should not be folded into an overall political design as necessary conditions for civic justice. One advantage here is that any perspective has the opportunity to win political support and temporary power, but it cannot claim to have "democracy" on its side, or "the people," or the "common good," or "justice," and so on; it can only claim a temporary victory in an ungrounded field of political conflict over what the public good ought to be. A socialist redistribution of wealth, for example, can result from democratic procedures, but neither it nor competing perspectives can claim any normative or political warrants that would render opponents less democratic or less just. This kind of political "modesty" can work against the tendency of social factions to wittingly or unwittingly deny rights and freedoms to people on the other side of "the good." Again, the political elements of coercion and institutional power make possible the dangers that can befall us at the hands of *immodest* narratives. An agonistic model of politics will certainly not deliver everything one might want regarding human relations, but it may suffice for *political* relations.

The Nietzschean lesson here is that the most well-meaning conception of the good will become tyrannical if it attains control in the midst of finite conditions of existence that will inevitably include *resistances* to the perceived good.

Mistrust all who talk much of their justice! Verily, their souls lack more than honey. And when they call themselves the good and the just, do not forget that they would be pharisees, if only they had – power. (*Z* II, 7)

Agonistic democracy is the preferable arrangement for devising political rule, since as such it has no overarching conception of the good, and the sites of power that do unfold in democracy will always be unstable and susceptible to challenges from other power sites. In this respect a general conception of democracy should steer clear of visions that propose some *transformation* of the life-world, and limit itself to less grandiose concerns of orchestrating the tensions and conflicts that mark the continual *formation* of political life.

What is most interesting about Nietzsche's philosophy is the implicit modesty of his agonistic model of life; to be sure, not the kind of modesty that shrinks from assertion, but rather one that refuses ideological purity or the certainty of being in the right – any form of which, for Nietzsche, is an echo or shadow of the "old faith" in a transcendent truth. In addition, Nietzsche's historical analysis is more relevant than ever, given various "faith-based" conceptions of politics and violence on the world stage today. To the consternation of most secularists, it seems that God is not actually dead; he has been on life support and has been revived in many quarters. Nietzsche's writings are unsurpassed in probing into how such things can happen, and what they mean, and what responding to them would have to mean. And lest some democratic secularists think of Nietzsche as an ally here, they should take heed of his complicated account of the ascetic ideal – where the shadows of God can be detected in any viewpoint, even a confident atheism. Moreover, any secularist (or anyone for that matter) who has not flinched when hearing exhortations about "freedom on the march," or "the spread of democracy" around the world, or "the end of history" in the victory of liberal democracy should be ashamed; they should confess their sins and read Nietzsche over and over again.

ACTIVE FORGETTING AND DEMOCRACY

When we hear of spreading freedom and democracy around the world, the question arises of how suited other cultures are for appropriating the kind of democratic politics with which we are familiar. Certainly the idea of exporting or imposing democracy elsewhere has to face the historical fact of how long it took Western democracies to develop the forms we now extol and how much turmoil was involved in such developments. I have argued that Nietzsche's philosophy can uncover elements of democratic practice that help us better understand how democracies operate and thus how they might or might not fare well. A central element I advance is agonistic practice coupled with at least a deferral on the question of decisive truth. If one believes in a foundational truth, one is less inclined to submit political matters to an open contest of ideas or to accept the victory of a position that falls outside the truth. Another related Nietzschean concept I would like to highlight in closing is the idea of active forgetting that appears in the *Genealogy*.

My reading of active forgetting distinguishes it from sheer forgetting and stresses the notion of forgetting the moral offense taken at past abuses, of moving on with life without the need for an ultimate rectification of harms. Nietzsche associates this kind of disposition with strong natures who can cultivate a sense of justice that lets go of vengeful impulses for the sake of future possibilities. A "reactive" memory cannot let go in such a manner and becomes poisoned by a fixation on the past that blocks a healthy impulse toward the future. Active forgetting is an important counterweight to moralistic offense that can affect any area of life. Such offense stems from the refusal of a tragic sense of life, an incapacity to tolerate negative outcomes, which must be repaired in some way if life is to remain meaningful.

I want to focus on how active forgetting is implicated in dispositions and formats that make democracy possible. Ancient Greek democracy grew in part out of indigenous forces spotlighted by Nietzsche: particularly agonistic modifications of natural violence into rituals of competition. In Greek democracy, voting was expressed as *diaphora*, meaning to divide up or disagree. The outcome of a vote was often described as a "victory" (*nikē*), but in the sphere of speech rather than violence.[22] It became clear to the Greeks that civil war was the ultimate danger to the *polis*, the turn to violence in the face of disputes that could destroy the political order from within. After the Peloponnesian and civil wars, the restoration of democracy was predicated in part on a conception of "amnesty," on swearing an oath "not to recall past misfortunes" (*mēmnēsikakein*). Such amnesty required a kind of active "amnesia" that would let go past passions and violence in favor of accepting the "victories of speech" in democratic debate, which could always be revisited because the force of language would supplant the terminating force of violence. Consequently, the acceptance of democratic outcomes demanded a capacity to willingly accept defeat, to live under results that could "offend" one's interests. Such offense must be "forgotten" in accepting political defeat.

The capacity to accept defeat in democratic contests is less likely when secure conceptions of the good are in place and when historical memory rules over the ability to suspend offense at past wrongs. The cultivation of intellectual and moral "suspension" is a background force in the development of democratic formats and cannot therefore be guaranteed simply by implementing such formats. Often the conflicts between peoples or groups are irresolvable and prone to

---

[22] See Nicole Loraux, *The Divided City: On Memory and Forgetting in Ancient Athens*, trans. Corrine Pache (New York: Zone Books, 2001), Ch. 1. I am indebted to this work for the historical points under discussion.

violence owing to competing memories held fast in a delusional zero-sum game of vengeance or rectification. This is a political version of what Nietzsche calls "revenge against time and its 'it was'" (*Z* II, 20). Active forgetting can make political coexistence more likely, but it need not involve dismissing the past, nor would it require reconciliation or forgiveness. Historical memory is essential to human life, but an agonistic conception of will to power can exchange a vengeful memory for an incorporation of the past that overcomes offense on behalf of a new future. Nietzsche's challenge to our moral tradition can certainly seem rough and disturbing, and perhaps his charge of life-denial is too sweeping. Yet his diagnosis of reactive memory is an important contribution to moral and political philosophy; it not only shows how a binary fixation on the good and its violations can be a symptom of life-aversion, it also alerts us to a stagnation that traps the present and the future in the past. Moralistic memory understands movement as a rectifying rewind of the past, but this may be less like actual movement and more like the indefinite continuance of a law suit. A tragic sensibility may be less a demoralizing lament and more an active forgetting of offense that frees us to create something new.

References

Acampora, Christa Davis. "Of Dangerous Games and Dastardly Deeds: A Typology of Nietzsche's Contests." *International Studies in Philosophy* 34/3 (Fall 2002), 135–151.

Acampora, Christa Davis, ed. *Nietzsche's* On the Genealogy of Morals: *Critical Essays*. Lanham, MD: Rowman & Littlefield, 2006.

Allison, David B. *Reading the New Nietzsche*. Lanham, MD: Rowman & Littlefield, 2001.

Anscombe, G. E. M. "Modern Moral Philosophy." *Philosophy* 33 (1958), 1–19.

Ansell-Pearson, Keith. "Nietzsche: A Radical Challenge to Political Theory?" *Radical Philosophy* 54 (Spring 1990), 10–18.

An Introduction to Nietzsche as a Political Thinker. Cambridge: Cambridge University Press, 1994.

Appel, Fredrick. *Nietzsche Contra Democracy*. Ithaca, NY: Cornell University Press, 1999.

Aristotle. *Poetics*. Trans. Joe Sachs. Newburyport, MA: Focus Publishing, 2006.

Ascheim, Steven E. *The Nietzsche Legacy in Germany, 1890–1990*. Berkeley: University of California Press, 1992.

Babich, Babette. "A Note on *Chaos Sive Natura*: On Theogony, Genesis, and Playing Stars." *New Nietzsche Studies* 5, 3/4 and 6, 1/2 (Winter 2003/Spring 2004), 48–70.

Bernstein, Alan E. *The Formation of Hell*. Ithaca, NY: Cornell University Press, 1993.

Binion, Rudolph. *Frau Lou: Nietzsche's Wayward Disciple*. Princeton: Princeton University Press, 1974.

Burkert, Walter. *Greek Religion*. Trans. John Raffan. Cambridge, MA: Harvard University Press, 1985.

Chukwudi Eze, Emmanuel. *Achieving Our Humanity: The Idea of the Postracial Future*. New York: Routledge, 2001.

Clark, Maudemarie. *Nietzsche on Truth and Philosophy*. Cambridge: Cambridge University Press, 1990.

Claus, David B. *Toward the Soul: An Inquiry into the Meaning of* Psuchē *Before Plato*. New Haven: Yale University Press, 1981.

Connolly, William E. *Political Theory and Modernity*. London: Blackwell, 1988.

Identity/Difference: Democratic Negotiations of Political Paradox. Ithaca, NY: Cornell University Press, 1991.

Conway, Daniel W. *Nietzsche and the Political*. New York: Routledge, 1997.

"*Wir Erkennenden*: Self-Referentiality in the Preface to *Zur Genealogie der Moral*." *Journal of Nietzsche Studies* 22 (Fall 2001), 116–132.

Cox, Christoph. *Nietzsche: Naturalism and Interpretation*. Berkeley: University of California Press, 1999.

Crisp, Roger, and Michael Slote, eds. *Virtue Ethics*. Oxford: Oxford University Press, 1997.

Curtis, David Ames, ed. *Philosophy, Politics, Autonomy: Essays in Political Philosophy*. New York: Oxford University Press, 1991.

Daigle, Christine. "Nietzsche: Virtue Ethics... Virtue Politics?" *Journal of Nietzsche Studies* 32 (Autumn 2006), 1–21.

Daly, Markate, ed. *Communitarianism: A New Public Ethics*. Belmont, CA: Wadsworth, 1994.

Detwiler, Bruce. *Nietzsche and the Politics of Aristocratic Radicalism*. Chicago: University of Chicago Press, 1990.

Dodds, E. R. *The Greeks and the Irrational*. Berkeley: University of California Press, 1968.

Ferry, Luc, and Alain Renaut, eds. *Why We Are Not Nietzscheans*. Trans. Robert de Loaiza. Chicago: University of Chicago Press, 1997.

Golomb, Jacob, and Robert S. Wistrich, eds. *Nietzsche, Godfather of Fascism? On the Uses and Abuses of a Philosophy*. Princeton: Princeton University Press, 2002.

Goodrich, Peter, and Mariana Valverde, eds. *Nietzsche and Legal Theory: Half-Written Laws*. New York: Routledge, 2005.

Griffen, Jasper. *Homer on Life and Death*. Oxford: Oxford University Press, 1980.

Habermas, Jürgen. "The Entwinement of Myth and Enlightenment: Rereading *Dialectic of Enlightenment*." *New German Critique* 26 (1982), 13–30.

The Philosophical Discourse of Modernity. Trans. Frederick G. Lawrence. Cambridge, MA: MIT Press, 1987.

Halliwell, Stephen. *The Aesthetics of Mimesis*. Princeton: Princeton University Press, 2002.

Hatab, Lawrence J. *Myth and Philosophy: A Contest of Truths*. Chicago: Open Court, 1990.

A Nietzschean Defense of Democracy: An Experiment in Postmodern Politics. Chicago: Open Court, 1995.

Ethics and Finitude: Heideggerian Contributions to Moral Philosophy. Lanham, MD: Rowman & Littlefield, 2000.

Nietzsche's Life Sentence: Coming to Terms with Eternal Recurrence. New York: Routledge, 2005.

Hayman, Ronald. *Nietzsche: A Critical Life.* Oxford: Oxford University Press, 1980.

Hollingdale, R. J. *Nietzsche: The Man and His Philosophy.* Second edn. Cambridge: Cambridge University Press, 1999.

Honig, Bonnie. *Political Theory and the Displacement of Politics.* Ithaca, NY: Cornell University Press, 1993.

Hunt, Lester H. *Nietzsche and the Origin of Virtue.* London: Routledge, 1991.

Kant, Immanuel. *Critique of Practical Reason.* Trans. Lewis White Beck. Indianapolis, IN: Bobbs-Merrill, 1956.

Critique of Judgment. Trans. Werner Pluhar. Indianapolis, IN: Hackett Publishing, 1987.

Kemal, S. "Some Problems of Genealogy." *Nietzsche Studien* 19 (1990), 30–42.

Leiter, Brian. *Nietzsche on Morality.* New York: Routledge, 2002.

Loraux, Nicole. *The Divided City: On Memory and Forgetting in Ancient Athens.* Trans. Corrine Pache. New York: Zone Books, 2001.

Luban, David. *Lawyers and Justice: An Ethical Study.* Princeton: Princeton University Press, 1988.

MacIntyre, Alasdair. *After Virtue.* South Bend, IN: University of Notre Dame Press, 1981.

Magnus, Bernd. "Nietzsche's Philosophy in 1888: *The Will to Power* and the *Übermensch.*" *Journal of the History of Philosophy* 24/1 (January 1986), 79–98.

"Self-Consuming Concepts." *International Studies in Philosophy* 21/2 (1989), 63–71.

May, Simon. *Nietzsche's Ethics and His War on Morality.* Oxford: Clarendon Press, 1999.

Mitchell, Joshua. *Not by Reason Alone: Religion, History and Identity in Early Modern Political Thought.* Chicago: University of Chicago Press, 1993.

Murdoch, Iris. *The Sovereignty of Good.* New York: Schocken Books, 1970.

Nehamas, Alexander. *Nietzsche: Life as Literature.* Cambridge, MA: Harvard University Press, 1985.

Neiman, Susan. *Evil in Modern Thought: An Alternative History of Philosophy.* Princeton: Princeton University Press, 2002.

Nussbaum, Martha C. *The Fragility of Goodness.* Cambridge: Cambridge University Press, 1986.

Owen, David. *Nietzsche, Politics, and Modernity.* London: Sage, 1995.

"Equality, Democracy, and Self-Respect: Reflections on Nietzsche's Agonal Perfectionism." *Journal of Nietzsche Studies* 24 (Fall 2002), 113–131.

Peters, H. F. *Zarathustra's Sister: The Case of Elisabeth and Friedrich Nietzsche.* New York: Markus Wiener, 1985.

Pratt, Louise H. *Lying and Poetry from Homer to Pindar.* Ann Arbor: University of Michigan Press, 1993.

Prier, Raymond A. *Thauma Idesthai.* Gainesville, FL: Florida State University Press, 1989.

Redfield, J. M. *Nature and Culture in the* Iliad. Chicago: University of Chicago Press, 1975.

Reginster, Bernard. "Nihilism and the Affirmation of Life." *International Studies in Philosophy* 34/3 (2002), 55–68.

Richardson, John, and Brian Leiter, eds. *Nietzsche.* Oxford: Oxford University Press, 2001.

Ridley, Aaron. *Nietzsche's Conscience: Six Character Studies from the "Genealogy."* Ithaca, NY: Cornell University Press, 1998.

Risse, Mathias. "The Second Treatise in *On the Genealogy of Morality*: Nietzsche on the Origin of the Bad Conscience." *European Journal of Philosophy* 9/1 (2001), 55–81.

Safranski, Rüdiger. *Nietzsche: A Philosophical Biography.* Trans. Shelley Frisch. New York: Norton, 2002.

Sallis, John. *Crossings: Nietzsche and the Space of Tragedy.* Chicago: University of Chicago Press, 1991.

Santaniello, Weaver, ed. *Nietzsche and the Gods.* Albany, NY: SUNY Press, 2001.

Schacht, Richard, ed. *Nietzsche, Genealogy, Morality: Essays on Nietzsche's* On the Genealogy of Morals. Berkeley: University of California Press, 1994.

Nietzsche's Postmoralism: Essays on Nietzsche's Prelude to Philosophy's Future. Cambridge: Cambridge University Press, 2001.

Schneewind, J. P. *The Invention of Autonomy: A History of Modern Moral Philosophy.* Cambridge: Cambridge University Press, 1998.

Schopenhauer, Arthur. *The World as Will and Representation.* Vol. I. Trans. E. F. J. Payne. New York: Dover Publications, 1958.

Schrift, Alan D. *Nietzsche and the Question of Interpretation: Between Hermeneutics and Deconstruction.* New York: Routledge, 1990.

Nietzsche's French Legacy: A Genealogy of Poststructuralism. New York: Routledge, 1995.

Schrift, Alan D., ed. *Why Nietzsche Still? Reflections on Drama, Culture, and Politics.* Berkeley: University of California Press, 2000.

Segal, Charles. *Singers, Heroes, and Gods in the Odyssey.* Ithaca, NY: Cornell University Press, 1994.

Siemens, H. W. "Agonal Communities of Taste: Law and Community in Nietzsche's Philosophy of Transvaluation." *Journal of Nietzsche Studies* 24 (Fall 2002), 83–112.

Silk, M. S., ed. *Tragedy and the Tragic*. Oxford: Oxford University Press, 1996.

Silk, M. S., and J. P. Stern. *Nietzsche on Tragedy*. Cambridge: Cambridge University Press, 1981.

Slote, Michael. "Nietzsche and Virtue Ethics." *International Studies in Philosophy* 30/3 (1998), 23–27.

Small, Robin, ed. *Paul Rée: Basic Writings*. Urbana: University of Illinois Press, 2003.

Smith, Richard A. "Nietzsche: Philosopher of *Ressentiment?*" *International Studies in Philosophy* 25/2 (1993), 135–143.

Soll, Ivan. "Attitudes Toward Life: Nietzsche's Existentialist Project." *International Studies in Philosophy* 34/3 (Fall 2002), 69–81.

Solomon, Robert, ed. *Nietzsche: A Collection of Critical Essays*. Garden City, NY: Anchor Books, 1973.

Sophocles. *Oedipus Tyrannus*. Trans. Peter Meineck and Paul Woodruff. Indianapolis, IN: Hackett, 2000.

Strong, Tracy B. *Friedrich Nietzsche and the Politics of Transfiguration*. Expanded edition. Urbana: University of Illinois Press, 2000.

Swanton, Christine. "Outline of a Nietzschean Virtue Ethics." *International Studies in Philosophy* 30/3 (1998), 29–38.

Ure, Michael. "The Irony of Pity: Nietzsche Contra Schopenhauer and Rousseau." *Journal of Nietzsche Studies* 31 (Autumn 2006), 68–91.

van Tongeren, Paul. "Nietzsche's Greek Measure." *Journal of Nietzsche Studies* 24 (Fall 2002), 5–24.

Vernant, Jean-Pierre. *Myth and Society in Ancient Greece*. Trans. Janet Lloyd. Sussex: Harvester Press, 1980.

Warren, Mark. *Nietzsche and Political Thought*. Cambridge, MA: MIT Press, 1988.

White, Richard. *Nietzsche and the Problem of Sovereignty*. Urbana: University of Illinois Press, 1997.

Wilcox, John T. "That Exegesis of an Aphorism in *Genealogy* III: Reflections on the Scholarship." *Nietzsche Studien* 27 (1998), 448–462.

Williams, Bernard. *Ethics and the Limits of Philosophy*. Cambridge, MA: Harvard University Press, 1985.

 Shame and Necessity. Berkeley: University of California Press, 1993.

Woodhouse, A. S. P. *Puritanism and Liberty*. Chicago: University of Chicago Press, 1938.

Zeitlin, Froma, ed. *Mortals and Immortals*. Princeton: Princeton University Press, 1991.

Index

Acampora, Christa Davis 6n.4, 14n.7, 76n.2,
    114
Achilles 53
active forgetting 70
    and democracy 271–273
agonistics 13–14, 97–98, 258
    contra violence 261
    and democratic practice 251, 256–257,
        260–262, 265, 268
    and life-affirmation 142–143, 201, 233
    and selfhood 266–267
Allison, David B. 4n.3
amnesty 272
Anscombe, G. E. M. 218n.8
Ansell-Pearson, Keith 76n.2, 258n.14
Apollo/the Apollonian 18–20, 177
appearance 131–133, 181
Appel, Fredrick 250, 258n.16
Aquinas, Thomas 64
aristocraticism 249, 260
    cultural vs. political 255–256
Aristotle
    compared with Nietzsche 223–226
    on ethics 220–227
    on justice 254
    and katharsis 230–231
    and moral tragedy 226–231, 233
    the Poetics 227–229
    and theoria 232
art 116–117
    and the ascetic ideal 115–121, 179–181
    and deception 181–186
    and truth 133–134
ascetic ideal 114–115, 119, 164–171
    as a force for life 125–127, 139, 140,
        145–146, 149–151, 169–170
    as life-denying 146–148
    in the modern world 147, 151–152

naturalistic account of 164–165
and philosophy 117–121, 122–125, 128–129,
    176
and science 153–164
self-overcoming of 166–169
and truth 128–130, 155–159, 165–168
as will to power 127–128
asceticism 83–85, 114
    naturalistic account of 121–122
atheism 165–167

Babich, Babette 10n.3
bad conscience 85, 100–104, 140
    and Christian theology 103–104
    and creative cruelty 101–102, 105–110
    self-overcoming of 104–107, 108–109
being and becoming 8–9, 135
Bernstein, Alan E. 195n.14
blond beast 48–49
Burkert, Walter 18n.12, 52n.9, 55

Castoriadis, Cornelius 258n.15
Christianity 152–153
Clark, Maudemarie 130n.7, 135n.11, 208n.4,
    233n.20
Claus, David B. 52n.10
Cohen, Jonathon 200n.18
community 92–93
    and politics 268–269
competition 257, 260
Conant, James 219n.11
concepts, history of 99, 100–104
Connolly, William E. 246n.2, 250n.6
conscience, see also bad conscience 83–84
consciousness 84
Conway, Daniel W. 49n.7, 59n.20, 134n.9,
    258n.14
Cox, Christoph 10n.3

creative individual/type 46–48, 80, 134, 142,
    148, 211
creativity 213, 225, 256
cruelty 86–89, 213
    spiritualization of 87–89
culture, *see* nature

Daigle, Christine 223n.14
death of God 10–11, 109–110, 157, 160
    and Kant's moral philosophy
        215–216
    and politics 271
deception 181–184
    in Greek poetry 184–186
degeneration and creativity 46–47, 124
democracy 152–153
    agonistic 260–262, 264, 269–270
    ancient Greek 272
    attempt to reconcile with Nietzsche
        250–257
    and modesty 270–271
    Nietzsche's critique of 246–249
    and tragedy 264–266
Descartes, René 84
Detwiler, Bruce 249n.5
Dionysus/the Dionysian 18–20, 117, 119, 178,
    179, 230

egalitarianism 246–249, 251
egoism 205
    Nietzsche's challenge to 210–212
elitism
    democratic 254–255
    in Nietzsche 253–254
Enlightenment, the 251
    disguised forms of power in 251–253
equality
    agonistic 256
    exclusionary history of 253
    unnecessary for democratic politics
        251–257
eternal recurrence 137
    and ethics 216n.6, 232–233
    and moral tragedy 198–203
ethics in Nietzsche's thought 233–242
evil, the problem of 196–198
experimentalism 135
Eze, Emmanuel Chukwudi 252n.11

forgetting, *see* memory
free spirits 155–156
free will

Nietzsche's critique of 62–63, 77
    and responsibility 63, 66
freedom
    in modern politics 244–245
    in Nietzsche 79–81, 248

Gemes, Ken 130n.7
genealogy/genealogical method 29–30, 35,
    96–98, 142
    in relation to time and history 110–111
Genealogy, the
    how to read 3–7
    Nietzsche's development toward 28–29,
        35–36
    overview 172–176
    relation to *Beyond Good and Evil* 2–3
    good–evil/good–bad 43–45, 66–68, 237–239
    Greek myth and religion 18–19, 52–53, 104,
        198
Greek poetry 191–196
Griffen, Jasper 53n.12
Guess, Raymond 29n.5
guilt 85, 151
    and debt 92–93

Habermas, Jürgen 29n.6, 250
Halliwell, Stephen 193n.12, 193n.13, 230n.18
hatred 267
health 148
Hesiod 56
Hobbes, Thomas 244, 246n.3
Homer, heroic values in 50–61, 71–73
Honig, Bonnie 76n.2, 250n.6
Hunt, Lester H. 218n.9

immoralism 233–235
individualism 78–79
individuality in Nietzsche 211
institutions 258–259
interpretation 133–134, 156
    and the Third Essay 113

Japanese legal system 263n.19
justice
    and inequality 254
    and mercy 93–94
    and power 93–96

Kant, Immanuel 82, 82n.5, 120, 128, 163,
    207–208
    Nietzsche's challenge to his moral
        philosophy 213–216

language 134
law
  adversarial vs. inquisitorial systems
    262–264
  agonistic conception of 96, 262–264
  genealogy of 95–96
  and power 96
  Leiter, Brian 208n.4
liberalism, Nietzsche's critique of 245–250
life
  and meaning 16–18
  and philosophy 26–27
life-affirmation 17–18, 122, 200–201
  distinct from life-enhancement 140–143,
    200
  and the tragic 108–110
life-denial 143
Locke, John 252n.12
Loraux, Nicole 272n.22
love 266
Luban, David 263n.18

MacIntyre, Alasdair 218n.8, 223n.14
Madison, James 264
Magnus, Bernd 199n.17, 201n.19
master morality, *see* morality
master–slave distinction 38n.2
  ambiguity of 67–68, 100–101, 175–176
  blended in creative will to power 141–142
May, Simon 143n.16
memory and forgetting 69–75, 83–84,
    272–273
metaphysics 8, 156
mimēsis 184, 193, 193n.12, 228
Mitchell, Joshua 246n.2
moral philosophy
  Kantian 206–208
  modern 208
  Nietzsche's challenge to 208–209
moral relativism 240–241
morality
  of custom 74–75
  and domestication 48–50
  herd 234–237, 239
  and history 38, 78, 96–98, 99–100
  Judeo-Christian 64–66
  and language 38–39
  master and slave 42–49
  and tragedy 21, 186–191, 195–196, 198–199,
    216–217
  and universality 214–215
  the value/disvalue of 30, 34, 217

naturalism 9–10, 16, 160–163, 165, 209n.4
  and morality 234–235
nature 146, 161–162
  and art 177–179
  and culture 13–14, 173–175, 258
Nazism 249n.4
Nehamas, Alexander 133n.8, 225n.15
Neiman, Susan 197n.15
Nietzsche
  biography 21–24
  as political thinker 257–260
  nihilism 11–12, 32–33, 105–110
  suicidal 143, 170
  noble type 70–73
  Nussbaum, Martha C. 33n.8, 192n.10,
    227n.16

Odysseus 59–61, 185, 195
Oedipus 186–190, 228
Owen, David 76n.2, 81n.4, 220n.12, 250n.6,
    257n.13

perfection 238
perfectionism 219
perspectivism 15–16, 128–129, 130–131, 134,
    137–139, 157
  agonistic 139, 140, 239–240
  and moral commitment 239–242
  and moral judgment 201–203
  and objectivity 129
  and the self-reference problem 135–137
pessimism 30–32, 89–91, 121
philosophers of the future 111–112
philosophy
  Nietzsche's conception of 3–4, 15–16
  and tragic art 117–119, 179
phusis 178n.2
physiology 149–150
Pippin, Robert B. 267n.20
pity/compassion 33–34, 219, 267
Plato 20, 51, 160n.17, 227
  and Greek poetry 191–196
Plotinus 232
Poellner, Peter 130n.7
political philosophy
  modern 244–245
  Nietzsche's challenge to 245–250, 257–259
Pratt, Louise H. 184n.6
presumption of innocence 263
Prier, Raymond A. 193n.12
priest type 39–42, 102–103, 125–127, 140
promising 69, 73–75

property rights 252n.12
psychology 15
punishment 85–87, 99–100

Redfield, J. M. 53n.13
Rée, Paul 28, 35
reflection 85
Reginster, Bernard 17n.9
resentment/*ressentiment* and revenge 41–42, 45, 62–66, 267
respect, agonistic 255, 256–257
responsibility, *see* free will
Richardson, John 12n.4
Ridley, Aaron 39n.3, 105n.8
Risse, Mathias 105n.8

Sallis, John 9n.2
Schacht, Richard 6n.4, 32n.7, 234n.20
Schneewind, J. P. 205n.2
Schopenhauer, Arthur 30, 119–122
  Nietzsche's relation to 31–34
Schrift, Alan D. 3n.2, 130n.7, 135n.11, 250n.9
science, *see also* ascetic ideal 153–164
second nature 225–226
Segal, Charles 186n.7
selfhood
  in modern liberalism 80–82, 248
  in Nietzsche 78–81, 248, 260
selflessness 38
self-sufficiency 81–82, 232–233, 242
separation of powers 264
sickness 143–145, 146
Siemens, H. W. 14n.7
skepticism 137
  moral 205
slave morality, *see* morality
slave type, as creative 45–47
Slote, Michael 218n.9
Small, Robin 37n.1
Smith, Richard A. 200n.18
social contract theory 244–245
Socrates 20
Soll, Ivan 17n.10, 127n.5
Solomon, Robert C. 218n.9

sovereign individual 75–83, 83n.6, 125n.4, 213, 245, 260
Strong, Tracy B. 225n.15, 258n.14
subjectivism 134
suffering and meaning 90–91, 169–170
Swanton, Christine 218n.9

Tertullian 64
theodicy 197
time and human experience 144–145
tragedy and the tragic 18–21, 50–52, 108–110, 117–119, 131, 145, 168, 171, 177–179
truth, *see also* perspectivism and ascetic ideal
  in Nietzsche's philosophy 130–139
  tragic 182–183

Übermensch 178n.1
Ure, Michael 33n.8
utilitarianism 206
  Nietzsche's challenge to 212–213

values
  in Nietzsche 233–234
  and overcoming 236
van Tongeren, Paul 14n.7
Vernant, Jean-Pierre 53n.11, 258n.15
virtue, in Nietzsche 218–221
virtue ethics, *see also* Aristotle 217–220
  and politics 243

Wagner, Richard 22, 24, 115–117
Warren, Mark 76n.2, 250n.6
White, Alan 218n.9
White, Richard 76n.2
Wilcox, Richard 113n.1
will to power 12–13, 97–98, 142, 242, 260
  and action 242
  active and reactive 44–45
  and politics 249
Will to Power, The 180n.4
Williams, Bernard 62n.21, 208n.4
Woodhouse, A. S. P. 246n.2

Zarathustra 108, 200

For EU product safety concerns, contact us at Calle de José Abascal, 56–1°,
28003 Madrid, Spain or eugpsr@cambridge.org.

www.ingramcontent.com/pod-product-compliance
Ingram Content Group UK Ltd.
Pitfield, Milton Keynes, MK11 3LW, UK
UKHW020323140625
459647UK00018B/1983